*Jean-Jacques Rousseau
and the 'well-ordered society'*

For Nadia

Jean-Jacques Rousseau and the 'well-ordered society'

Maurizio Viroli

Assistant Professor of Politics, Princeton University

Translated by Derek Hanson

CAMBRIDGE
UNIVERSITY PRESS

Published by the Press Syndicate of the University of Cambridge
The Pitt Building, Trumpington Street, Cambridge CB2 1RP
40 West 20th Street, New York, NY 10011-4211, USA
10 Stamford Road, Oakleigh, Victoria 3166, Australia

First published 1988
Reprinted 1992

Printed in Great Britain by Woolnough Bookbinding Ltd.
Irthlingborough, Northants.

British Library cataloguing in publication data
Viroli, Maurizio
Jean-Jacques Rousseau and the 'well-
ordered society'.
1. Sociology
I. Title
301'.092'4   HM24

Library of Congress cataloguing in publication data
Viroli, Maurizio
Jean-Jacques Rousseau and the 'well-ordered society'/Maurizio
Viroli: translated by Derek Hanson.
p.   cm.
Revision of the author's thesis (doctoral—European University
Institute, Florence)
Bibliography.
ISBN 0 521 33342 3
1. Rousseau, Jean-Jacques, 1712-1778—Contributions in political
science.   I. Title.
JC179.R9V57   1988
320.1'01—dc19   87-30937

ISBN 0 521 333423

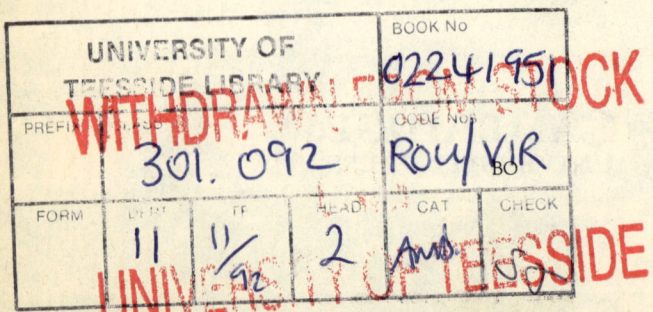

Contents

What is called union in a body politic is a very equivocal thing. The true kind is a union of harmony, whereby all the parts, however opposed they may appear, co-operate for the general good of society – as dissonances in music co-operate in producing overall concord. In a State where we seem to see nothing but commotion there can be union – that is, a harmony resulting in happiness, which alone is true peace. It is as with the parts of the universe, eternally linked together by the action of some and the reaction of others. But in the concord of Asiatic despotism – that is, of all government which is not moderate – there is always real dissension. The worker, the soldier, the lawyer, the magistrate, the noble are joined only inasmuch as some oppress the others without resistance. And, if we see any union there, it is not citizens who are united but dead bodies buried one next to the other.

Montesquieu, *Considérations sur les causes de la grandeur des Romains et de leur décadence*, translated by D. Lowenthal, New York, 1965, pp. 93–4.

Preface

An earlier version of this book was presented as a doctoral thesis at the European University Institute in Florence. I should like to record, first of all, a very great debt of gratitude to Werner Maihofer, President of the Institute, who supervised my thesis throughout its development and patiently assisted me at every stage of its composition. I also learned much from discussions with Maurice Cranston and Athanasios Moulakis.

My greatest single debt, however, is to Quentin Skinner, who read several drafts of this work while it was still in manuscript and compelled me to a greater understanding of Rousseau's place within the tradition of both classical and modern republicanism. The final version of this work was composed while I was in Cambridge as a Research Fellow of Clare Hall. I would like to thank the President and the Fellows of the College for their generosity in having appointed me to their number. The intellectual atmosphere of the College has provided an ideal environment for the completion of this work.

I would also like to express my very sincerest thanks to Norberto Bobbio for having agreed to be one of my examiners and for his comments on my thesis, which were of great help to me when I came to make the final revisions. My thanks are also due to Salvatore Veca for his invaluable observations on the theoretical problems which I encountered during my research. I would also like to mention my friends of the Political Philosophy Seminar in the Feltrinelli Foundation, who will immediately recognize in these pages an echo of the many discussions we have had.

Finally, I record my thanks to Mme Colette Kleemann, who not only corrected my French (in itself an unenviable task) but also succeeded in improving the shape of my text.

It goes without saying that I alone bear the responsibility for whatever faults this work may contain. But, if what I have written is of any interest, the merit must go to those who guided my research with such skill and enthusiasm.

Note on the text

The terms *amour de soi* and *amour-propre* have been translated as 'self-love' and 'egotism', respectively.

For quotations, already published translations have sometimes been used. Where this is the case, details are given in the notes.

Humanity in general is referred to throughout this book as 'man', 'men', 'mankind' for the sake of convenience only, and with the sincere wish that this will give no offence.

1

Introduction

Almost everything in Rousseau is the subject of debate. But one of the points which does, probably, command universal agreement is that Rousseau set out to propound a theory of a just political order, or, to use a phrase which reflects his intention, the doctrine of the 'well-ordered society'.

Every political society establishes its own political order, but it is only a political order which satisfies certain moral criteria which may correctly be described as a *just* one. It was precisely because he hoped to define these criteria that Rousseau undertook his study of political systems. For him, order is not, in itself, a primary value; it is the just political order which is the ground of value since it is the necessary condition for the primary values of liberty, virtue and happiness. It is Hobbes, not Rousseau, who can correctly be described as the philosopher of an unqualified political order, and the political philosophy of the *Social contract* may legitimately be interpreted as the search for a theoretical alternative to the order propounded in *Leviathan*.

The phrase 'well-ordered society', which we find at the beginning of the first version of the *Social contract*, suggests a society ordered in such a way that men find it in their interest to treat their fellows with justice and consideration – that is to say, to live in harmony. Men have not created the society in which they live as a whole. Social relations are the product of the chance concatenation of several different circumstances. Nevertheless, it is perfectly reasonable to try to define the nature of the political constitution which men would want to establish, if they were in a position to do so. Rousseau's political doctrine is based on the idea that neither chance nor will can alone legitimize political institutions. For a political institution to be

1

defined as just it must be possible to think of it as being capable of commanding the free consent of men.

The men that the doctrine of the well-ordered society has in view are men 'as they are'. They are individuals motivated solely by self-interest and the pursuit of their own good, who are ambitious and dominated by egotism. It is this pride which drives them to seek worldly position and preferment. As a result each man is in conflict with his fellows, and their mutual relations are in a state of discord. Moreover, in societies where the most highly valued positions and most elevated ranks are occupied by the least deserving, there is a disequilibrium in social relations. Finally, those who are enslaved by their own passions, in particular, ambition, live in disorder. A just political order should provide the answer to the problem of disorder in all its aspects. For Rousseau, a society is *well* ordered when men's passions are tempered by law and custom, and where harmony and restraint take the place of a generalized conflict. A just order exists where the highest places are occupied by the most virtuous and not the strongest or the most cunning, and where, finally, everyone can control his/her passions and act with moderation, an ability which is one of the main prerequisites of true happiness.

The antithesis between order and disorder is the major antithesis around which the work of reconstructing the political philosophy of Rousseau may proceed, and it forms the basis of the present study. The first part of the present work seeks to show the interrelations between the different conceptions of order; the second section analyses the idea of disorder, and in the final part there is an attempt to reconstruct the doctrine of a just political order.

The analysis of the interrelations of the different forms of order (moral, natural and political order) leads to one of the most frequently discussed questions in the long history of Rousseau studies: namely, nature and the artificial. The antithesis between 'natural man', who is essentially good and 'artificial man' corrupted and made wretched by social institutions, is one of the central themes in the discussions which followed the publication of the two *Discourses*. This aspect of Rousseau's thought found its most acute expositor in Kant,[1] and in our own time has been taken up again by Cassirer.[2]

---

[1] Kant, *Mutmasslicher Anfang der Menschengeschichte*, in *Immanuel Kants Werke*, Hildesheim, 1973, vol. 4, pp. 325–42 (transl. L.W. Beck and R.E. Anchor, *On History*, Indianapolis and New York, 1963, pp.53–68).

[2] E. Cassirer, 'L'Unité dans l'oeuvre de Rousseau', in *Bulletin de la Société française de philologie*, 1932, reprinted in *Pensée de Rousseau*, Paris, 1984, pp.41–63.

In this context, we have tried to show that Rousseau's political doctrine is based on the idea of a dual form of the artificial, rather than on the antithesis between nature and the artificial. The first form of the artificial (the 'first stages of art') is to be found in the 'arts' and in corrupt political institutions; the other form of the artificial (perfected art) is the art of politics, the sublime art whose masters are the great lawgivers, and which has as its goal the founding of a harmonious community.

The relationship between nature and the artificial has often been discussed by writers on Rousseau from the point of view of the relation between the natural and the political orders. For example, Rousseau's contemporaries evaluated his political doctrine on the assumption that the order of nature was the model of true order.[3]

More recently, Durkheim argued for the analogy between the social world and the state of nature. His interpretation represents a particularly significant example of a 'naturalistic' reading of Rousseau's political thought and it therefore merits close attention. For Rousseau, he writes, the natural state 'consists of a kind of peaceful anarchy in which the individual members, quite independent of one another, are linked by no social bonds and rely entirely on the 'power of nature'. In the social, continues Durkheim, 'individuals are external to one another, and their interpersonal relations are minimized, but they rely on a different kind of power additional to the forces of nature, which has, nevertheless, the same universality and the same necessity as the latter, namely, the general will'.[4]

In contrast with this view, the present study emphasizes that, as conceived by Rousseau, political and natural order are by no means the same. Firstly, the members of a well-ordered society are united by very close bonds and form a community. This is quite different from the state of isolation which characterizes the situation of men in the natural state. Moreover, the laws which govern the actions of citizens in society are very different from those which operate in the natural state. In the first instance, it is the citizens themselves who are the authors of the laws; in the second, man receives laws from nature or, more properly, from God, which laws he cannot contravene. Finally, the fundamental principle of natural order is that the 'totality' should

---

[3] See, for example, F. d'Escherny, *De l'égalité*, Basle, 1796.
[4] E. Durkheim, 'Le "Contrat social" de Rousseau', *Revue de métaphysique et de morale*, 25 (1918), p. 159; see also, R.D. Masters, *The political philosophy of Rousseau*, Princeton, 1968, p.424.

be preserved, while the prime aim of political order is to ensure the freedom and security of the individual. Durkheim is right when he says that collective life has few points of contact with the natural order, but he is mistaken in thinking that Rousseau sought to ground social being in nature. Quite the contrary, on several occasions he draws attention to the completely artificial nature of political institutions.

The analysis of Rousseau's use of the concept of disorder leads to a consideration of the question of inequality. For Rousseau, inequality represents a problem for political theory when it takes the form of moral inequality, that is, an inequality in the status individuals enjoy in the eyes of the community. From this point of view, the problem of inequality is closely linked with the question of personal identity. Personal identity is a product of the opinions that others have of us and is thus a result of the comparison between individuals. Consequently, in the case of men living alone in their natural state, one cannot speak of personal identity. But as soon as men begin to compare themselves with others, and the opinion of others assumes importance, each of them seeks preferment, to achieve superiority over their peers, or, better still, to convince others of their superiority. For Rousseau, inequality is not an abstract problem; it has repercussions on the very way that people live and influences the way people think of themselves. Moral inequality becomes concrete and visible, so to speak, through the eyes of others and in the way they treat us. The kind of inequality that causes offence is, according to Rousseau, an unjust inequality founded on caprice and chance, not the kind of inequality which can be justified by merit and virtue. Thus society, the network of enduring relations between men, is the necessary condition for the creation of individual identity, but, at the same time, life in society spontaneously gives rise to different forms of moral inequality and is the source of the desire for preferment.

Central to Rousseau's theory of inequality is an analogy between the process at work when, in economics, the price of an object is fixed in the market-place, and the process whereby the social worth of each individual is assessed. Each person living in society, amongst his fellows, is accorded a certain level of esteem, in much the same way as a price is placed upon objects. Just as the price of an object is fixed by the purchaser and not by the owner of the goods, so the esteem accorded any given individual comes to him from others. Here Rousseau is influenced by the moralists of the period and the major modern political theorists, Pufendorf and Hobbes. Stated thus, the problem of inequality amongst mankind may be rephrased in terms of the criteria by which men are awarded degrees of honour and esteem. So that society may be well ordered it is necessary for certain qualities (virtue, humanity, courage, moderation) to be more highly esteemed than others (riches, birth, power).

A just political community is characterized by the way in which the worth of individuals is assessed and how its status hierarchy is established. The equality which reason sees as necessary for a just political constitution is not arithmetical, ascribing the same thing to everyone, but is geometric or proportional. If the body politic is to be sound, it is necessary for public honour and esteem to be commensurate with the degree of individual merit and the nature of the services rendered to the community (in other words, with virtue) 'vera nobilitas virtus (sola) est'. In Rousseau we come across the old classical idea of just proportion,[5] which, especially in the writings of Cicero and Sallust, had become one of the central concepts of republican political theory. We also find another problem that was familiar to republican writers: how is it possible to make equal degrees of liberty 'aequa libertas' compatible with a hierarchy with its different degrees of honour and worth, 'dignitas et honores'?

Moreover, inequality is a problem for political theory when it takes the form of social inequality. Sharp differences in the distribution of wealth are, in effect, incompatible with a political constitution which claims to provide equality before the law. On the other hand, critics had often focussed on the question of private property. Voltaire's commentary on the famous passage which opens the second part of the *Discourse on inequality* is the most significant example of a tradition of interpretation which sees Rousseau as the adversary of the institution of private property:

What! he who has planted, sowed and enclosed his land has no right to the fruit of his labour? What! that unjust man, that thief, should be considered as the benefactor of the human race! There you have the philosophy of a rogue who would like the rich to be robbed by the poor.[6]

This view has found its supporters in our own time, as well, and Rousseau has been cast in the role of the predecessor of Marx.[7]

[5] See Plato, *The Statesman*, 307e–308; *Laws*, 690–1, see also, Aristotle, *Politics*, 1301b–1302a.
[6] G.R. Havens, *Voltaire's marginalia on the pages of Rousseau*, New York, 1966, p.15.
[7] See, for example, R. Dahrendorf, *Essays on the theory of society*, London, 1968, pp.158–9.

However, this interpretation does not seem convincing. Rousseau never considered that the abolition of private property would provide a solution to the problem of inequality. Private property is a sacred right grounded in the social contract. Thus, any attempt to confiscate private property would be unlawful. Instead, when dealing with the forms of social inequality, Rousseau insists that it is necessary for the state to attend to the problem of justice in the distribution of wealth in order to limit, in a way reminiscent of the theories of Aristotle,[8] the most extreme forms of inequality. Rousseau does not abandon the fundamental principle of the doctrine of natural law which sees the state as a guarantor of the rights to property. But, at the same time, he notes that, in order to preserve its legitimacy, the state should take steps to moderate social inequality.

As with the theory of inequality, the doctrine of the social contract is one of the ideas which has attracted the greatest amount of criticism from political theorists and commentators. In my view the weightiest criticism of the social contract is not to be found amongst those writing within the empiricist or utilitarian traditions,[9] but in Hegel, and at this point it would be helpful to pause and consider certain passages in the *Principles of the philosophy of right*, without, of course, making any claim to exhaustive analysis of such a difficult and important problem as the relation of Rousseau to Hegel.

Hegel discusses the doctrine of the contract as if it were a normative theory which seeks to define the rights of the state in relation to the rights and interests of the citizens. According to the doctrines of natural law, the rights of princes and of the state are to be thought of as arising from a contract. They are grounded in a common will which springs from the agreement of the totality of individual wills. The consequence of these doctrines is the principle that the *raison d'être* of the state consists in the protection of the lives and property of its citizens.

According to Hegel, the error here lies in the transposition of an institution of private law, such as a contract, into a sphere of a quite

---

[8] Aristotle, *Politics*, 1295b 25; see R. Derathé, 'La Place et l'importance de la notion d'égalité dans la doctrine politique de J.-J. Rousseau', in R.A. Leigh, ed., *Rousseau after two hundred years*, Cambridge, 1982, pp.55–63.

[9] See, for example, D. Hume, *On the original contract*, in E. Barker, ed., *Social contract. Essays by Locke, Hume and Rousseau*, Oxford, 1971; J. Bentham, *A fragment on government and an introduction to the principles of morals and legislation*, Oxford, 1948, pp.49–56.

different and higher nature.[10] Nevertheless, Hegel also commends Rousseau for having seen that the fundamental principle of the state is the will.

Unfortunately, however, as Fichte did later, he takes the will only in a determinate form as the individual will, and he regards the universal will not as the absolutely rational element in the will, but only as a 'general' will which proceeds out of this individual will as out of a conscious will. The result is that he reduces the union of individuals in the state to a contract and therefore to something based on their arbitrary wills, their opinion, and their capriciously given express consent.[11]

For Rousseau, the state is not 'Reason in and for itself', as Hegel would have it, but derives its rationality from the fact that it is a necessary condition for the safeguarding of liberty, of goods and of individual persons: which means that the state is rational so long as it fulfils these functions. For this reason Rousseau's doctrine must bear a grave responsibility for having destroyed 'the divine existing in itself and for itself, its absolute authority and its majesty'.[12]

For Hegel, doctrines which find a basis for liberty in the 'acquiescence of the individual' will bring the state to ruin, as was proved by the example of the Polish diet where no decision could be taken without each individual giving his consent. Even more dangerous was the idea that 'it is only the people who are in possession of Reason and Wisdom and know the true'. According to Hegel, the advocates of the principle that no law is valid unless it has the unanimous consent of all citizens fail to understand that their doctrines must necessarily lead to the dissolution of the political constitution:

If one takes the principle of individual liberty as the sole foundation of political liberty, namely, each individual must give his consent before any decision can be taken by, or on behalf of the State, then there will be, in effect, no Constitution.[13]

The practical consequences of Rousseau's ideas on liberty (and this point is emphasized both in the *Philosophy of right* and in the chapter 'Absolute Liberty and Terror' in the *Phenomenology*) were seen in the

[10] G.W.F. Hegel, *Grundlinien der Philosophie des Rechts*, 1821, s.75 (transl. by T.M. Knox, *Hegel's philosophy of right*) Oxford, 1942; on the relation between Rousseau and Hegel see S. Avineri, *Hegel's theory of the modern state*, Cambridge, 1972, in particular pp.40, 60, 183–4.   [11] Ibid., s.258 (transl. ibid., p.157).   [12] Ibid.
[13] G.W.F. Hegel, *Vorlesungen über die Philosophie der Geschichte*, 1848; (transl. by J. Sibree, *The philosophy of history*, New York, 1956).

excesses of the French Revolution.[14] But Hegel did not place himself in a position of theoretical opposition to Rousseau. He sought, rather, to take up the intellectual challenge that Rousseau had issued: how is it possible to live in a political community and at the same time be a free individual; but he is equally convinced that to elaborate a political theory of the state and modern liberty it is necessary to use very different theoretical tools from those furnished by the idea of the social contract.[15]

It is interesting to note that Benjamin Constant also criticized Rousseau for not having understood the true importance of the constitution, albeit for reasons very different from those of Hegel. While Hegel blames Rousseau for having, by his theories, opened the way to the dissolution of the constitution, understood as 'the organization of the state and the process of its organic life', Constant charges the author of the *Social contract* with failing to understand the necessity of limiting the sovereign power in the constitution. Both Hegel and Constant focus on the theory of the social contract and the sovereignty of the people, but the former is primarily concerned with preserving the unity of the State and the latter with safeguarding individual liberty against arbitrary interference from the sovereign power.

For Constant, Rousseau's error lay not in the fact that he had seen the will of individual citizens as the source of authority for the state, but that this theory condemned individuals to total subservience to the state.[16] Constant goes on to allege that, through participating in

[14] *Grundlinien der Philosophie des Rechts*, s.258; (transl. by Knox, 1942); *Phaenomenologie des Geistes*, in *Werke*, Frankfurt am Main, 1969, vol.3, pp.431–40.

[15] On this subject Hegel's comments in the *Vorlesungen über die Philosophie der Geschichte*, *(Werke*, vol.20, pp.306–8), on the concept of freedom in Rousseau, are important. See also Z.A. Pelczynski, *Political community and individual freedom in Hegel's philosophy of state*, in Z.A. Pelczynski, ed., *The state and civil society. Studies in Hegel's political philosophy*, Cambridge, 1984, pp.60–2; W. Maihofer, *Hegels Prinzip des modernen Staates* (1969), in I. Fetscher, ed., *Hegel in der Sicht der Neueren Forschung*, Darmstadt, 1973, pp.352–86; J. d'Hont, ed., *Hegel et le siècle des lumières*, Paris, 1974.

[16] B. Constant, *Principes de politique*, in *Oeuvres de Benjamin Constant*, ed. A. Roulin, Paris, 1957, pp.1071–2; during the nineteenth and twentieth centuries Constant's interpretation has been developed by several authors: for example, E. Faguet, *Dix-huitième siècle*, Paris, 1890; L. Duguit, *Souveraineté et liberté*, Paris, 1922. See on this subject R. Derathé, 'Les Réfutations du "Contrat Social" en France dans la première moitié du dix-neuvième siècle', in S. Harvey *et al.*, *Reappraisals of Rousseau*, Manchester, 1980, pp.90–110. This tradition of interpretation is also present in German literature; see, for example, G. Jellinek, *Die rechtliche Natur der Staatenverträge*, Vienna, 1880, pp.11–12. Jellinek's ideas reappear also in Cassirer, *Das Problem Jean-Jacques Rousseau*, Darmstadt, 1970, p.14. A more moderate position somewhere between the extremes of an individualistic Rousseau and a 'Staatabsolutist' Rousseau

the social contract, individuals confer absolute power on the sovereign, and the only difference between Rousseau and Hobbes is that Rousseau sees the sovereignty of the people as something absolute, while Hobbes advocates absolute government by one individual alone.[17]

The relations between Rousseau and Hegel, on the one hand, and Rousseau and Constant, on the other, deserve to be studied in greater detail, a project which would make a useful contribution to the analysis of the political thought of the nineteenth century. But on this issue the present work will merely note that neither Hegel's nor Constant's interpretation can really be said to do justice to Rousseau's thinking. In fact, according to Rousseau, the institution and preservation of the legitimate political constitution are the principle means by which not only the unity of the state is preserved, but also the liberty of its citizens. The sovereign authority of the state is not grounded in the whims of individuals, but in the general will, which is, or should be, a rational will which finds its expression in universal laws. If the whims of individuals (or factions) take over from the general will, sovereign authority is no longer legitimate, which means that the unity of the body politic has been sacrificed, as well as liberty. The political doctrine of Rousseau is based on the principle of the sovereignty of law, and thus of the rational will, not on the sovereignty of the individual will as such, as Hegel alleged.

The situation is much the same with regard to the criticism levelled by Constant. Constant fails to convince us that there is a similarity between Rousseau and Hobbes, viewed as advocates of absolute power (whether the absolute power of the people, or the absolute power of the prince). In fact, the point at which Rousseau diverges from Hobbes most notably is when the latter argues that the sovereign is above civil law. Rousseau states unambiguously that if the sovereign is above civil law he is a despot. Even when the people themselves exercise their sovereignty, they are governed by the fun-

is defended from a position within a neo-Kantian perspective, by R. Stammler, *Theorie des Anarchismus*, Berlin, 1894, p.14. With regard to Italian literature at the beginning of the twentieth century, see G. del Vecchio, *Su la teoria del contratto sociale*, Bologna, 1906; G. Solari, *La fondazione storica e filosofica dello stato moderno*, Naples, 1934; R. Mondolfo, *Rousseau e la coscienza moderna*, Florence, 1954 (republication of a work first published in 1912). For a complete bibliography of studies on Rousseau in Italy, see D. Felice, 'Jean-Jacques Rousseau in Italia: bibliografia (1850–1982)', in *Studi settecenteschi*, 3–4 (1982–3), pp.319–98.

[17] B. Constant, *Principes de politique*, in *Oeuvres*, edited by A. Roulin, La Pléiade, Paris, 1957, p.1107.

damental constitutional laws of the republic. Constant's recognition of the fact that all political power must be limited and subordinate to the constitution is justly made, but this requirement had already been noted by Rousseau, who never advocated absolute democracy.

In my view, the best interpretation of the social contract is provided not by Hegel or Constant but by Kant. In Kant's analysis this doctrine becomes 'merely an idea of Reason'[18] which has as its goal the elucidation of the fundamental rules of a political constitution which is 'entirely legitimate', that is to say, 'a Republic'. He embraces both the spirit and the letter of Rousseau's conception – the letter, because he defines the legitimate political constitution in terms of a 'republic' (in contrast, as one finds in Rousseau, with despotism). He has grasped the spirit of Rousseau's thought by seeing the social contract as the only device by which theory may provide a ground of legitimacy for the political constitution.

Moreover, when Kant observes that the original contract is 'a union of every individual and private will', he does not seem to accept that this implies the destruction of the 'absolute majesty' of the state. This means that the ground on which the legitimacy of the state rests is defined (from the normative point of view) in terms of individual interests. Instead of interpreting the doctrine of the social contract as an attempt to justify a despotic state which deprives individuals of their liberty and their rights, Kant sees it as providing the ground for a political constitution which guarantees liberty.

The act by which the people constitutes a state for itself, or more precisely, the mere idea of such an act (which alone enables us to consider it valid in terms of right), is the *original contract*. By this contract, all members of the people (*omnes et singuli*) give up their external freedom in order to receive it back at once as members of a commonwealth, i.e. of the people regarded as a state (*universi*). And we cannot say that men within a state have sacrificed a *part* of their inborn external freedom for a specific purpose; they have in fact completely abandoned their wild and lawless freedom, in order to find again their entire and undiminished freedom in a state of lawful dependence (i.e. in a state of right), for this dependence is created by their own legislative will.[19]

This text from Kant would not have convinced Constant. The latter would have admitted that the social contract underwrites liberty, but

---

[18] I. Kant, *Über den Gemeinspruch: Das mag in der Theorie richtig sein, taugt aber nicht für die Praxis* (1793), in *Immanuel Kants Werke*, Hildesheim, 1973, vol.6, pp.380–1 (transl. H. Reiss, ed., *Kant's political writings*, Cambridge, 1970, pp.79–80).

[19] I. Kant, *Metaphysische Anfangsgründe der Rechtslehre*, in *Die Metaphysik der Sitten* (1797), in *Immanuel Kants Werke*, Hildesheim, 1973, vol.7, p.122, s.47 (transl. H. Reiss, ed., *Kant's political writings*, p.140).

he would have added that the liberty of which Kant speaks – in this following Rousseau – is precisely that type of liberty which he defines as the 'liberty of the ancients' and which Isaiah Berlin has, more recently, termed 'positive liberty'.[20]

For Constant, as for Berlin, freedom understood as autonomy, that is to say obedience to a self-imposed law, is not enough to guarantee the most important liberty of all, which is that of the moderns and which he describes as negative liberty. But is it true that the political doctrine of Rousseau concerned itself only with positive liberty?

The third section of this work will attempt to show that Rousseau's understanding of freedom cannot be defined in terms either of negative or of positive liberty. According to Rousseau, there is but one form of liberty: republican liberty. This is the liberty which individuals enjoy under the law and by virtue of a just political constitution which frees them from a narrow dependence on the individual will of others. It is 'positive' because it involves obedience to laws which have been sanctioned by individual men; it is 'negative' because the sovereignty of the law protects each and every one from the wrongs, the affronts and the wilful infringements of their rights perpetrated by others, whether they be private individuals or magistrates. Freedom founded on the sovereignty of the general will and on the strength of the law is the greatest good which individuals can enjoy in a well-ordered society. But, should the just order of the republic be undermined and degenerate into despotism (or fall under the sway of a foreign power) it will immediately disappear.

The analysis of the concept of liberty makes it possible to demonstrate Rousseau's intellectual debt to the political theorists of republicanism. Rousseau's indebtedness extends not only to Machiavelli, but also to Greek and Latin authors. His 'well-ordered society' in which the individual may live in freedom and security has a marked affinity with the 'repubblica ordinata bene' of the *Discorsi sopra la prima deca di Tito Livio*.

Both Rousseau and Machiavelli express themselves in the language of republicanism. Yet, although the well-ordered republic is portrayed by both writers in more or less the same terms, the points of view they adopt are quite different. For Machiavelli the problem is not to justify the existence of the republic, but to work out how it can actually be brought into being, while Rousseau, whose point of depar-

---

[20] I. Berlin, *Two concepts of liberty*, in *Four essays on liberty*, London, 1969.

ture is the premise of individualism which he shares with the school of natural law, is primarily concerned with providing a theoretical justification for the republic, and he pays little attention to the practical question of how it can be brought into existence.

Machiavelli and Rousseau both write from within the tradition of modern republicanism and both embrace the classical idea of politics, that is to say, the art of establishing and maintaining in being a 'respublica'. Nevertheless, the brands of republicanism that they espouse are not at all the same, and the difference in the tone of their writing on the subject of the republic reveals a significant shift within the language of republicanism and casts light on the problems faced by republican politics.

The influence of republican political authors is ultimately as important as that exercised on Rousseau by the philosophers within the natural law tradition – an intellectual debt analysed so brilliantly by Derathé in his book, *Rousseau et la science politique de son temps*. By contrast, the republicanism of Jean-Jacques Rousseau has not yet been studied in sufficient depth.[21] The roots of Rousseau's republicanism may be traced back to his childhood reading and the cultural environment of Geneva.[22] The memory of the Genevan republic and the reading of classical writers come together to form the ideal of the happy and peaceful community in which individual liberties are protected

[21] This gap is only in part made good by the studies of D. Leduc Fayette, *J.-J. Rousseau et le mythe de l'antiquité*, Paris, 1974; G. Pintard, *Jean-Jacques entre Socrate et Caton*, Paris, 1972; R.A. Leigh, 'Jean-Jacques Rousseau and the myth of antiquity in the eighteenth century', in R.R. Bolgar (ed.), *Classical influences on western thought 1650–1870*, Cambridge, 1979, pp.155–68; M. Launay, *Jean-Jacques Rousseau écrivain politique*, Cannes, 1971. By contrast, works dealing with the influence of Machiavelli on Rousseau are very poor: Y. Levy, 'Machiavel et Rousseau', *Le Contrat social*, VI, 1962, pp.169–74; Cucchi P., 'Rousseau lecteur de Machiavel', in M. Launay (ed.), *Jean-Jacques Rousseau et son temps*, Paris 1969, pp.17–35; P.M. Vernes, 'Nicolas Machiavel chez Jean-Jacques Rousseau: des leçons aux rois aux leçons aux peuples', in *Actes du colloque franco-italien de philosophie*, Paris, 1977, pp.77–89; A. McKenzie, 'Rousseau's debate with Machiavelli in the "Social Contract" ', *Journal of the history of ideas*, 43 (1982), pp.209–28. Therefore the words of E. Garin written in 1971 still ring true today: 'Indeed, in spite of such a wealth of works, a definitive work on the great writers who influenced Rousseau from the classics to such writers as Machiavelli and Montaigne is yet to be written.' Introduzione a Jean-Jacques Rousseau, *Scritti politici*, Bari, 1971, p.61. A study of the sources of Rousseau's republicanism should not overlook the influence of Montesquieu; see on this subject Leigh, 'Rousseau and the myth of antiquity', p.160.

[22] M. Launay, 'Les Hésitations de l'esprit républicain dans les premiers textes de Rousseau (1728–1748)', in *L'Esprit républicain*, Colloque d'Orléans, 4–5 Sept. 1970, J. Viard (ed.), Paris 1972, pp.133–41; see also by the same author, *Jean-Jacques Rousseau écrivain politique*, ch. 1 and 2; on the relations between the republicanism of Rousseau and Geneva it is useful to consult J.S. Spink, *Jean-Jacques Rousseau et Genève*, Paris, 1934, in particular ch. 3 'Rousseau et les bourgeois'.

by the laws which the people have forged for themselves, and which is preserved by the virtue of magistrates and citizens.

While the political doctrine of republicanism is based on ideas of virtue and community, the political doctrine of natural law is based on the notion of self-interest and holds the role of the state to be the protection of private interests. The former tradition sees love of one's country and identification with the community as providing the essential conditions for the maintenance of a just political order and of liberty. The latter, however, speaks the language of self-interest and rational calculation. Each of these bodies of thought exerted an influence on Rousseau's political theory. But is it possible to be at one and the same time a republican and a 'contractualist'?

The final part of this study will address itself to this fundamental question. The model of the social contract and the ideas borrowed from the republican tradition have been used to confront different and relatively unconnected problems. Rousseau employs the first set of ideas when he seeks to provide a rational justification for legitimate political authority, while the republican tradition tends rather to be a source of ideas relevant to the preservation of a just political order. But when Rousseau is dealing with the question of the existence, or even the mere possibility of a political community, and, above all, when he confronts the problem of how to develop civil virtues, the language of rational choice is replaced by another language based on the notions of common identity and belonging. This does not mean that the preservation of a just political order is not in the interest of the citizens. If they were able to calculate where their long-term interest lay, they would probably lead a moral life. But can one really believe that the citizens would be sufficiently wise and far-sighted to foresee the uncertain and long-term effects of their behaviour? Can one expect them to become moral citizens by calculating their interest in a rational manner? According to Rousseau the answer to these questions is no. Men do not act according to the dictates of rational calculation, and it would be even more of a forlorn hope to expect them to shape their actions according to a rational understanding of what constitutes the public interest. When men act they are driven by passion. Thus it is conceivable that the individual may become a good citizen, not through self-interest, but out of love for the community. Of prime importance, therefore, for political theory are the institutions and social processes which encourage individuals to feel themselves to be members of a community and to identify with it. Rousseau elaborates the theory of the social contract in a most cogent way and uses it to prove the rational nature of the political constitution based on the rule of law and the sovereignty of the people. But at the same time he reveals that this approach faces insurmountable difficulties.

The present work is written in the conviction that it is necessary to revise the image of Rousseau as a disciple of the school of natural law in order to see his political doctrine as one of the last stages in the long history of 'republicanism'. An accurate assessment of the true historical import of Rousseau's writings cannot be made if they are not placed in the context of the discovery and diffusion of the classical republican writers which occurred with the rise of humanism at the Renaissance and which the spread of Machiavelli's ideas reinforced. There is still much scope for further research in this direction; the present work seeks merely to make some small contribution to this larger task.

2

Images of order between nature and the artificial

The whole of Nature is my witness. It is not in contradiction with itself; I see in nature an admirable physical order always consistent with itself. The moral order should be the same. Yet my life's experience has been the apparent breakdown of this order, and so it will begin after my death.[1]

In this letter to Moultou, Rousseau introduces us directly to the problem of order, one of the most important themes in his thought. In his autobiographical writings, towards the end of his life, Rousseau emphasizes the principles which inspired his thinking about morality and politics.

There is a natural order which comes from God and to this there corresponds a moral order, which also comes from God.[2] In contrast, relations between men are corrupt both in the realm of natural and moral order. Men's lives unfold amidst the turmoil of disordered relationships, which prevent any one of them from living in harmony with his true moral nature and enjoying a state of union with his fellows.

The only hope for man who has sought in vain for love, friendship and fatherland,[3] lies now in the world beyond, to which everything

---

[1] Rousseau to Moultou, 14 February 1769, in *Correspondance complète de Jean-Jacques Rousseau*, ed. R.A. Leigh, Oxford, 1980, vol.37, p.57.
[2] *Les Rêveries du promeneur solitaire, Oeuvres complètes*, ed. B. Gagnebin and M. Raymond, 4 vols., Bibliothèque de la Pléiade, Paris, 1959–69 (henceforth abbreviated as *OC*), vol.1, pp.1018–10.   [3] *Rousseau juge de Jean-Jacques, OC*, vol.1, pp.954 and 979.

must 'finally return'. In the metaphysical order, justice will at last be sovereign and virtue will have its reward.[4]

But this is, in a manner of speaking, to start at the end. Henceforth, Rousseau is, or at least he feels himself to be, a man who has withdrawn from society, which for him now appears to be no more than empty appearance and injustice. This is the man who appended to his work, *Rousseau juge de Jean-Jacques*, 'A Document entrusted to Providence', since, rightly or wrongly, he believed himself to be a stranger amongst men, 'alone, without succour, without anyone to defend him on the face of the earth, insulted, mocked, reviled, betrayed by a whole generation, for fifteen years he had suffered cruelties worse than death, sufferings such as no man before him had experienced and yet he had never understood the reason for all this.'[5]

While Rousseau in his final writings placed all his trust in a metaphysical order, for several years previously the problem of good government had seemed to him a subject worthy of close study. The purpose of such a study was to clarify what the fundamental characteristics of a well-ordered society should be.[6]

This is not the place to trace the stages of the personal and intellectual history[7] which led Jean-Jacques to arrive at the gloomy conclusions of his final years. It is more to the point here to note that the necessity of order is one of the guiding themes of Rousseau's meditation.[8] As is shown by recent lexicographical studies of his language,[9] the word 'order' and its synonyms are among the terms which recur most frequently in his writings. Yet there are several images of order: moral, cosmic, social and political.[10] Moreover, each of these ways of

[4] Ibid., p.827.   [5] Ibid., p.978.   [6] *De l'état de nature, OC*, vol.3, pp.479–80.
[7] On the relation between Rousseau's ideas and his life, see J. Starobinsky, *Jean-Jacques Rousseau. La transparence et l'obstacle*, Paris, 1971; R. Grimsley, *Jean-Jacques Rousseau. A study in self-awareness*, Cardiff, 1969, in particular pp.152–330.
[8] P. Burgelin, *La Philosophie de l'existence de Jean-Jacques Rousseau*, Paris, 1952, pp.411–12; see also M. Launay, *Le Vocabulaire politique de Jean-Jacques Rousseau*, Geneva and Paris, 1977, p.154; L. Bréhier, 'Lectures malebranchistes de Jean-Jacques Rousseau', *Revue internationale de philosophie*, 1 (1938), pp.98–120; P. Burgelin, *La Philosophie de l'existence de Jean-Jacques Rousseau*, Paris, 1952, pp.411–15; R. Polin, *La Politique de la solitude*, Paris, 1971, pp.64–71; B. Baczko, *Rousseau. Solitude et communauté*, Paris, 1974, pp.168–204; A. Robinet, 'Lexicographie philosophique de "l'ordre de la nature" dans la "Profession de foi du vicaire savoyard"', *Revue internationale de philosophie*, 32 (1978), pp.238–59.   [9] See Launay, *Le Vocabulaire politique*, pp.151–3.
[10] 'Apart from a few clearly a-political examples', writes Launay, 'it is difficult to make any hard and fast distinction between the political, moral, social and philosophical uses of the word "order", and taken together the various ways of using the term would provide material for an analysis which would provide insight into Rousseau's originality of thought and style' (*Le Vocabulaire politique*, p.154).

conceptualizing order often has several dimensions. For example, as the following chapters will demonstrate, the concept of natural order sometimes connotes harmony, and at others finds its expression in the concept of an adequate hierarchy of all living beings.

A complete analysis of all the uses of the word 'order' is beyond the scope of this study. Instead, emphasis will be placed on just one of its aspects: political order. As far as the other types of order are concerned, we will attempt to clarify only those aspects which are most closely linked to the problem of political order. It is not possible to analyse the theory of political order in Rousseau's work independently of his conception of natural order and his doctrine of moral order. The task of this first section is to reconstruct their interrelationship.

The knowledge and love of order

Rousseau differs from the two other great theorists of the social contract, Hobbes and Locke, in that he has no real philosophy of nature and still less a systematic philosophy of knowledge. But this is not to say that Rousseau does not have his own way of understanding the natural order and his own opinions about human knowledge. Moreover, we can say that his ideas about human knowledge and the way he views nature exercise a great influence on his approach to political philosophy.

With regard to the metaphysical questions of the philosophy of nature and philosophy of knowledge, Rousseau adopts a position which makes his thought unique in the context of eighteenth-century philosophy.[11] Unlike those who considered human reason capable of finding an answer to the important questions concerning the nature of the universe, he draws attention to the limits of the human intellect. The famous sections from the *Profession de foi du vicaire savoyard* are most illuminating from this point of view,

We do not have the measure of this immense machine, we are incapable of calculating the many interconnections involved: we know nothing either of its first laws nor of its final cause; we are ignorant about ourselves; we comprehend neither our own nature, nor the inner dynamic of our lives; we are not even sure whether man's being is simple or complex: impenetrable mystery surrounds us on all sides; it is beyond the boundaries of the empirical

---

[11] See E. Cassirer, *Das Problem Jean-Jacques Rousseau*, Darmstadt, 1970; see also *Die Philosophie der Aufklärung*, Tubingen, 1932, by the same author.

realm; we believe ourselves to be endowed with an intelligence which can go to the heart of these mysteries and yet all we have is imagination.[12]

In his opinion philosophical investigation into the great questions about the fundamental nature of the universe is not able to free men from the doubts which torment their souls. Instead of reason, for Rousseau it is feeling, the inner light, which can give men the answers to the questions which they are in search of. As for all the other problems, we must simply admit our ignorance and our limitations. Rousseau is not really interested in elaborating a metaphysical theory of the universe of the kind capable of being presented with all the rigour of mathematical certainty.

He does not see it as his task to prove the truth of ideas about the 'immense machine of the Universe' or about human knowledge. He simply declares that he will accept notions consonant with feeling. He writes:

Having within me the love of truth as my only philosophy, and as my only method an easy and straightforward rule which makes it unnecessary for me to have recourse to the vain subtlety of argument, I follow this rule as I examine those items of knowledge which interest me, determined to admit as evident all those things which, in the sincerity of my heart, I am forced to acknowledge as such, and as true all those which seem to have a necessary link with the former, and to have an agnostic attitude to everything else, neither accepting nor rejecting these things, and not goading myself to unravel those mysteries when a solution would bring no positive good anyway.[13]

The last part of this passage shows very clearly that Rousseau views nature and human knowledge through the eyes of a moral philosopher rather than through those of the metaphysician. If, therefore, he entertains a certain idea of nature, it is for the importance that it has in connection with political and moral philosophy. This is equally true for human knowledge. It is not necessary to look for a complete or methodological consistency between the conception of nature and knowledge, on the one hand, and political and moral philosophy on the other. It would seem more rewarding to attempt to show that the answers Rousseau gives to political and moral problems are affected by his understanding of nature and conception of knowledge.

In his notes on *De l'esprit* by Helvétius, Rousseau comments on the gap between his idea of human knowledge and that of the philosophers

[12] *Profession de foi du vicaire savoyard*, *OC*, vol.4, p.568.
[13] *Profession de foi du vicaire savoyard*, *OC*, vol.4, p.570.

of sensationalism. When Helvétius, an example of this school, had written:

It makes no difference whether I say 'I judge' or 'I feel' that, of two objects, one which I call 'arm' affects me differently from the other one which I call 'foot'; or that the colour which I refer to as 'red' affects me differently from that other colour which I term 'yellow' . . .

Rousseau comments as follows:

. . . here we have a very subtle sophism which requires careful attention. It is one thing to feel a difference between an arm and a foot, and another to measure this difference. In the first case the mind is responding in a purely passive way but in the second it is active.[14]

A few pages later, disputing the claim that it is not possible to suppose that there is a faculty of judgement distinct from the faculty of feeling, he adds: 'Not so: it is, in fact, very easy to conceive of two quite different mental operations performed by two different faculties.' His disagreement with Helvétius is centred very precisely on the issue of the faculty of judgement, or, put more specifically, the problem of the autonomy of judgement with regard to sense impressions. The two possible operations are, first, that judgements are determined by impressions and, secondly, that man defines the relations between things in an active way – an activity for which he both is, and must be, held responsible.

Empirical knowledge, which is entirely dependent on sense impressions, is limited to the knowledge of isolated objects, 'just as they are in nature'. Strictly speaking, such knowledge is not knowledge at all, since it is void of suggestion of relation or order between objects. As long as one remains on the level of empirical knowledge, the problem of error does not arise. Error is possible only when human understanding makes judgements on the relation between sensations and when it makes comparisons.

As for sense impressions, they are merely something sensed and thus are neither true nor false. With regard to knowledge, and equally with regard to ethics and politics, man is not just a natural and passive being, he is also active: the ideas of relation and order are not merely imposed upon him, he constructs them himself.

[14] *Notes sur 'De l'esprit' d'Helvétius*, *OC*, vol.4, pp.1122–3. On these problems see also H. Gouhier, *Les Méditations métaphysiques de Jean-Jacques Rousseau*, Paris, 1970, in particular chs. 1 and 2.

It does not matter what you call that faculty of mind which brings sensations together and compares them – whether it is called attention, meditation, reflection, or whatever; it is still true that it exists in me and not in the things themselves, that it is I alone who am the source of this power, though for this to happen it is necessary for objects to impress themselves upon my senses. Though I am not free to choose whether I will receive sense impressions or not, I do exercise control over how closely I examine these impressions. I am, therefore, not only a passive receptacle of sensations, but also an active and intelligent being, and, whatever philosophers may say, I will not allow myself to be deterred from taking pride in having this capacity for thought.[15]

Rousseau's idea of human knowledge is thus a form of dualism: it is based on the notion that the act of cognition has two components, one active or artificial, and the other passive or natural. Equally, his moral doctrine is also dualist.

The very existence of the moral problem depends on the ability to intuit the ideas of connection and relation. Connections and relations are established, or discovered, by men, thanks to their faculty of judgement and the ability to make comparisons. The active nature of man, which finds its expression in the ability to understand and define order, is one of the prerequisites for Rousseau's ethics.

The moral problem, as such, does not arise for *natural man*. It becomes real only for artificial or civilized man. Artificial man becomes aware of the problem of morality in that he can make comparisons and see the relations that exist between himself and his fellows, and in so far as he has learned how to judge the appropriateness or inappropriateness of an action. The moral problem presupposes the ability to understand what order is.

In his *Lettre à Monseigneur de Beaumont*, Rousseau makes very clear the nature of the relationship between knowledge and morality as it exists within the framework of a dualistic anthropology:

Man is not a simple being, but is composed of two substances. Even if this is something which is not readily acceptable to everyone, you and I are in agreement on this point, and I have tried to convince the others of this fact. This granted, egotism is not an unmixed simple passion: it comprises two principles, namely, the intellectual self and the self of sensation; the well-being of these is not the same.

The appetite of the senses tends towards the well-being of the body, and the love of order towards that of the mind. This love of order, when it has developed and become active, bears the name of conscience, but conscience is not able to develop and become active without man's reason. It is only

¹⁵ *Profession de foi du vicaire savoyard*, OC, vol.4, p.573.

through reason that he is capable of comprehending order and it is only then that his conscience induces him to love it. The conscience of the man who has never made comparisons and fails to see the connection between things is therefore worthless.[16]

The knowledge of order and love of order converge in the definition of one of the most important concepts of Rousseau's moral and political theory, namely the concept of virtue. Virtue is always defined, as it is in St Augustine, as 'the love of order',[17] but this love presupposes that it is possible to intuit moral relations and the order which emerges from this.

The necessary precondition, if this mode of cognition is to develop, is that man should emerge from his purely natural condition, in which he knows no other life than the inner life of feeling. Moral life presupposes that man has gone beyond the condition of isolation which, according to Rousseau, is his lot in the natural state. Men take their first tentative steps beyond the limitations of the natural state only when they become aware of each other's existence. This is the moment when they enter the sphere of the moral life, which was totally beyond their experience when they lived in isolation.

When, by means of a process whose stages I have delineated, men start to notice their fellows, they also start to see their relationships and the inter-connections between objects, to grasp the notions of rightness, justice and order; the splendours of the moral world are first revealed to them and conscience becomes active. Now they possess values, and if they retain their vices it is because their interests are in conflict and their ambition has awoken as their inner light spreads.[18]

Although Rousseau states that the moral problem comes into existence at the same time that knowledge develops, he nevertheless notes that there is a difference between knowledge and moral feeling. Man's moral life has its source and origin in his conscience, not in reason.[19] Knowledge of relationships and of the moral order is not innate. It is based on the active principle of judgement. On the other hand, because man knows what is good, it does not automatically follow that he will come to love it. While the knowledge of good and of order springs from reason, the love of what is good originates in conscience.

[16] *Lettre à Monseigneur de Beaumont*, *OC*, vol.4, p.936.
[17] St Augustine, *The City of God*, ed. D. Knowles, London, 1972, Bk 15, ch.22.
[18] *Lettre à Monseigneur de Beaumont*, *OC*, vol.4, pp.936–7. In this connection it is still useful to consult the work of R. Derathé, *Le Rationalisme de Jean-Jacques Rousseau*, Paris, 1948, in particular the chapter 'La Raison et la conscience', pp.74–138.
[19] *Profession de foi du vicaire savoyard*, *OC*, vol.4, p.599.

For social man the latter is an inborn feeling, while the former, a faculty, is not innate.

La Profession de foi du vicaire savoyard is quite explicit on the matter:

For this, all that is necessary is to get you to make a distinction between our acquired ideas and our natural feelings; for we feel before we know; and to pursue these things which are for our good and avoid harm is not something we learn, but is part of our nature, so too are the love of good and the hatred of evil as natural as our love of ourselves. The acts of our conscience are not judgements but feelings. Though all our ideas come to us from outside, the feelings whereby we evaluate them are within us and it is through them alone that we know whether there is harmony or disharmony between us and the things we must seek or avoid.[20]

There is, therefore, a complex relationship between the natural and the artificial dimensions as far as both knowledge and morality are concerned. So long as a man is not capable of making comparisons and judgements on the interconnection between things and between cause and effect, he will not be capable of leading a moral life either. But the activity of conscience without which moral judgement is impossible proceeds from feelings and the conscience itself is an inborn feeling. Rousseau's ethic assumes that there is an artificial condition (the activity of making comparisons which is in the domain of reason) and a natural feeling (conscience). The influence of this natural feeling may direct man towards virtue. But conscience may also be stifled by passion and prejudice. Man is then drawn towards evil. Whatever the moral choice, it is the idea of order and the understanding of what the different outcomes of various actions may be (which may be termed 'the intuiting of moral relations') which constitutes the basis of Rousseau's ethic.

Virtue is the 'love of order', but vice is also 'love of order', understood in a different sense. Moral order is not a result of social conventions. It is independent of the moral judgement of individuals since it has been established by God. In consequence, whether a disposition is thought of as virtuous or corrupt depends on the attitude adopted toward the moral order which comes from God:

While there is feeling and intelligence, there also is a moral order. The difference is that good orders itself in relation to the whole and evil orders the whole in relation to itself. The latter makes itself the centre of everything; the former measures the radius and places itself at the circumference. Thus, it is

[20] Ibid.

ordered in relation to the common centre, which is God, and in relation to all the other concentric circles formed by the other creatures.[21]

Rousseau's idea of moral order suggests it is related to the image of natural order – in particular, the system of planetary bodies which revolve around the sun. Good and evil, virtue and vice are defined by the position that the individual occupies in relation to the whole. If knowledge of moral order depends on reason, human moral conduct in relation to order is guided by conscience when it is virtuous, and by passion and prejudice when it is corrupt.[22]

Thus, Rousseau's ethic and theory of knowledge presuppose an objective moral order and the existence of objective truth. Each of these is laid down by God. Though human knowledge is in part the work of man, it comes into contact with an independent reality which is intrinsically rational in that it is a product of the divine intelligence. Truth and rational knowledge are not, in Rousseau's view, human conventions. They consist, rather, in the recognition of an order and a reality which already exist in things. In a similar way Rousseau's ethic, while adopting wholeheartedly the idea of free moral choice, does not for this reason argue for any reshaping of the moral order through human artifice, for it does not owe its existence to human conventions, but to God, and men cannot and should not change it. Rousseau's philosophy is therefore based on a metaphysic which is quite different, with regard to ethics and epistemology, from that of the other classical thinker within the contractualist tradition, Hobbes. As has been stated elsewhere,[23] the political philosophy of the author of *Leviathan* exists within the ambit of a general theoretical framework which, in the sphere of ethics and the theory of knowledge, is indisputably a form of conventionalism.

The ensuing chapters will attempt to show how Rousseau comes to formulate a contractualist theory of political order, having started from a very different metaphysical position from that of Hobbes. By adopting this approach, what is specific in Rousseau's understanding

[21] Ibid., p.602.
[22] 'Ever at strife in my natural feelings, which spoke of the common weal and my reason, which spoke of self, I should have drifted through life in perpetual uncertainty, hating evil, loving good, and ever at war with myself, if my heart had not received further light, if that truth which determined my opinions had not also settled my conduct, and set me at peace with myself' (Ibid., p.602; transl. by B. Foxley, Everyman 1974, p.255).
[23] See T. Magri, *Saggio su Th. Hobbes. Gli elementi della politica*, Milan, 1982, in particular pp.13–38.

of the social contract will become apparent. The next chapter, which deals with the general concepts of natural order and artificial disorder, provides a basis for the discussion which follows.

Natural order and artificial disorder

At the beginning of the eighteenth century, Shaftesbury, a philosopher with whom Rousseau was familiar, wrote a eulogy of nature which may be regarded as a representative example of one of the intellectual trends of the period. In the dialogue *The moralists, a philosophical rhapsody*, the 'friend of man' presents a eulogy of the order and harmony of nature which exists in opposition to all the creations of human art which in comparison with nature are inferior and less perfect.

O glorious *Nature*! supremely fair, and sovereignly good! All-loving and all lovely, all divine! . . . whose every single work affords an ampler scene, and is a nobler spectacle, than all which ever art presented! O mighty Nature! wise, substitute of *Providence*! Empowered creatress! . . . thee I invoke, and thee alone adore . . . I sing of Nature's order in created beings, and celebrate the beauties which resolve in thee, the source and principle of all beauty and perfection.[24]

Nature, the creating of God, is the epitome of harmony, and the gardens of princes cannot be compared with the beauty of natural landscapes. The contemplation of the harmony of nature leads man in the path of virtue, defined, exactly as it is by Rousseau, as 'love of order':

This too is certain, that admiration and love of order, harmony and proportion in whatever kind, is naturally improving to the temper, advantageous to social affection, and highly assistant to virtue; which is it-self no other than the love of order and beauty in society. In the meanest subjects of the world, the appearance of order gains upon the mind, and draws the affection towards it.[25]

[24] A. Shaftesbury, 'The moralists' in *Characteristics of man, manners, opinions, times*, Basle, 1790, vol.2, p.286.
[25] A. Shaftesbury, 'An inquiry concerning virtue and merit', in *Characteristics*, pp.60–1; a French translation of this work had been printed in Amsterdam, 1745, under the title *Philosophie morale*. The passage corresponding to the one quoted here reads as follows: 'La vertu qui n'est elle-même qu'un amour de l'ordre, des proportions et de l'harmonie dans les moeurs et dans les actions. . .', pp.128–30.

To be filled with awe in the face of an order of such justice and beauty is to experience a powerful impetus in the direction of the moral life. The hearts of men cannot but be touched by the beauty of the divine order and this draws them on to experience the most elevated emotions.

While, for Shaftesbury, nature embodies perfection and the products of human art are considered as being, by definition, of lesser worth, at roughly the same period there occurred a re-evaluation of art in relation to nature. Human art is no longer thought of as merely 'imitatio naturae', or as an appendage to nature ('additamentum'). Human art completely transforms nature, creating new entities which are not necessarily inferior to, or less perfect than, the works of nature.[26] The products of human art have their own value – and sometimes they may even be considered as superior. This is true of the body politic, a clear example of an artificial creation, as Hobbes explains at the beginning of *Leviathan*, using an image that was to become classic.

Nature, the Art whereby God hath made and governs the world, is by the art of man, as in many other things, so in this also imitated, that it can make an artificial animal. For seeing life is but a motion of limbs, the beginning whereof is in some principal part within; why may we not say, that all *automata* ... have an artificial life? ... Art goes yet further, imitating the rational and most excellent work of nature, *man*. For by art is created that great LEVIATHAN called a COMMONWEALTH, or STATE, in Latin CIVITAS, which is but an artificial man; though of greater stature and strength than the natural, for whose protection and defence it was intended.[27]

To a certain extent, Hobbes and Shaftesbury may be considered as figures representative of the two major traditions of modern political philosophy: the 'naturalistic' and the 'artificial'.[28]

Shaftesbury outlines a naturalistic solution to the problem of social order; this is based on the wisdom of nature which has ordered things in such a way that virtuous action contributes directly to the well-being of society. His representation, constructed around the idea that man is, by nature, a social animal, is in harmony with his understanding of the natural order. Hobbes, on the other hand, insists on the need

---

[26] See P. Rossi, *I filosofi e le macchine (1400–1700)*, Milan, 1971, pp.139–47.
[27] T. Hobbes, *Leviathan, in The English works of Thomas Hobbes*, ed. W. Molesworth, London, 1966, vol.3, p.ix.
[28] See on this question M. Bovero, 'Politica e artificio. Sulla logica del modello giusnaturalistico', *Materiali filosofici*, 6 (1981), pp.71–95.

for an artificial solution to the problem of order. In his view, a natural solution is neither possible nor desirable.

In contrast, there are aspects of Rousseau's work which may be situated within the natural tradition, while others clearly belong to the artificial tradition of political philosophy. For the author of the *Social contract*, nature is a system which receives the impress of an external will. Natural bodies move in accordance with certain laws, which provide evidence for the activity of a superior intelligence. Nature evinces order and harmony because it is the product of an intelligent and beneficent will. Each part of the whole is assigned its own place. The universe is seen as a whole whose order is dependent on an external intelligence. In one of his first works, *Les Institutions de chimie*, Rousseau expresses his conception of the 'Machine of Nature' very clearly.[29] Each part of the universe has its own proper function and possesses a 'relative perfection', which fills all those who become aware of it with admiration. But, were it possible, still more awesome would be the contemplation of 'the overall harmony and the workings of the whole machine'.[30]

The order of nature has, as its active principle, an intelligent and beneficent being and is sustained by 'general laws' established by a divine will. As will be shown in due course, the natural order – in this mirrored faithfully by the political order – has its existence in and is sustained by the will of the lawgiver and a system of law.[31]

For Rousseau, the universe is most fittingly epitomized by the analogy of a large and perfectly regulated clock:

I perceive the order of the world, though I have no knowledge of its purpose, because it is only necessary for me to compare the parts one with another, to observe carefully their smooth functioning in all their multiple interconnections. I know not why the universe exists; but I cannot fail to see how it is being gradually changed: I cannot fail to note how the beings which people this world respond to each other's needs in a deeply personal way. I am like a man who one can imagine seeing for the first time a watch with its back taken off and who cannot help admiring the intricacy of its works though he has no idea what the machine is for, and he has not seen the face. I do not know, he would say, what the purpose of it all is; but I see that each part is made for the others; I admire the craftsmanship manifest in the detail of the work, and I am

---

[29] *Institutions de chimie*, published and annotated by M. Gauhier, *Annales de la Société Jean-Jacques Rousseau*, 12 (1918–19) and 13 (1920–1). M. Gauhier suggests that the *Institutions de chimie* was most probably written in 1747.
[30] Ibid., vol.12, p.45.   [31] Ibid., vol.12, p.46.

quite sure that all these cogs work together in such harmony to realize some common purpose which is beyond my understanding.[32]

These analogies of clock and clockmaker occur frequently in the intellectual context of the period, and it is clear that Rousseau absorbed the influence of this way of thinking from the way he views nature and also from his political philosophy.

For 'Rousseau the musician',[33] 'order' means the mutual harmony of parts, concord, an absence of conflict, obedience to universal laws. Yet, his writings on music show that it is not harmony in the sense of a 'sequence of chords which obeys the laws of modulation'[34] which is most important for him. He thinks of melody as something which exists in contradistinction to 'gothic' harmony, since it is capable of expressing human passions. There is not the slightest connection between the chords of a harmonic system and the passions. In contrast, melody 'does not only imitate, it also speaks and its inarticulate, but eloquent, thrilling and impassioned language has a hundred times more emotion than mere words'.[35] Order, bereft of any powerful feeling, is not the order that commends itself to Rousseau.

In a well-regulated system, each being may be thought of as the centre which is common to all the others, in relation to which they have a given order, so that in their mutual relations they are, at one and the

---

[32] *Profession de foi du vicaire savoyard*, *OC*, vol.4, p.578. Besides the imagery of machine and mechanic, Rousseau also uses as a symbol of order the imagery of palace and architect. In the *Jugement sur la polysnodie* he makes an analogy between the 'politician' and the 'skilful architect' which is a good example of Rousseau's imagery of order: 'Now, the perfection of an entity as complex as the body politic does not depend only on the perfection of each part, just as in planning a palace it is not enough to arrange each room to best effect, but it is also necessary to take into account the overall pattern, the most appropriate ways of interrelating the parts, the most suitable order, facility of communication, the perfection of the whole and the most regular symmetry. These general goals are so important that the skilful architect, for the sake of overall unity, sacrifices a thousand charming details, which he might have retained in a less perfect, more complicated arrangement. In the same way politics is not simply concerned with the economy, defence or trade, but unites all these sectors behind a common purpose and by giving each of them due weight general projects can be worked out, infinitely varied in their scope, depending on the ideas and opinions of those who first formulated them, or possibly with an eye to which scheme will be the least complicated in practice, and as a result it is often difficult to decide which of these plans is best' (*OC*, vol.3, p.641).

[33] See M. Raymond, *Les écrits autobiographiques*, in *OC*, vol.1, p.11.

[34] *Dictionnaire de musique*, in *Oeuvres de J.-J. Rousseau*, 20 vols., Paris 1827, vol.14, p.342, see also *Dissertation sur la musique moderne*, vol.13, pp.121–41.

[35] *Essai sur l'origine des langues*, in *Oeuvres de J.-J. Rousseau*, Paris, 1827, vol.13, p.203.

same time, both means and ends for each other.[36] According to Rousseau, the human race has the best position in the general order of things. Man is in a position to make use of natural objects and tame animals for his own well-being. He has no right to complain to God about the position he occupies as a species. But neither should he imagine that the whole universe has been created merely for him as an individual. This is the mistake the evil man makes.[37] The order and harmony of nature does not extend to relations between individuals. While it is true that the divine intelligence has devised an admirable system of order for all natural creatures, mankind itself is free of such constraints.

In the *Lettre à Voltaire*, Rousseau explains that human affairs do not form part of the great order of the universe and that they are not subordinate to divine providence.

Thus, whatever the course nature takes, Providence is always justified in the eyes of the Pious, and at fault as far as the philosopher is concerned. Maybe, from the point of view of the order imposed upon human affairs, it is neither right nor wrong, because everything depends on the common law, and there is no exception made. We may believe that individual events here below have no significance in the eyes of the Ruler of the Universe, that his providence is merely universal, that he is content with preserving the different races and species, and with presiding over the whole, without concerning himself with the way that each individual spends his short life.[38]

It is for men themselves to seek to establish order in their relationships. In this quest they may take the harmony of the 'great clock' as their model, but they are not governed, in the way they treat each other, by the dictates of a supreme will, which ensures that each is in his right place, as is the case with the machine, where the parts do not have the power to decide the position they should occupy. For mankind order is a problem, the solution to which is not to be found in either nature or providence. For all these reasons relations between men do not exhibit the harmony that one finds in nature.

[36] *Profession de foi du vicaire savoyard*, *OC*, vol.4, p.580. Useful on this point is A. Robinet, 'Lexicographie philosophique de "l'ordre de la nature" dans la "Profession de foi du vicaire savoyard"', *Revue internationale de philosophie*, 32 (1978), pp.238–59; see also the chapter 'Ordre et justice' in R. Polin's book, *La Politique de la solitude*, Paris, 1971, in particular, pp.75–81. He writes that Rousseau's conception of justice is dependent on a 'metaphysics of order'. See also B. Baczko, *Rousseau. Solitude et communauté*, Paris, 1974, especially the chapter 'L'Ordre et le mal', pp.168–204. The problem of order in connection with theodicy was dealt with in an earlier work by P. Burgelin, *La Philosophie de l'existence de Jean-Jacques Rousseau*, Paris, 1952, pp.411–25 ('L'Ordre').   [37] *Lettres morales*, *OC*, vol.4, p.1100.
[38] *Lettre de J.-J. Rousseau à Monsieur de Voltaire*, *OC*, vol.4, p.1069.

But when, seeking to understand my place as a member of the human race, I consider the multiplicity of ranks within society, and the men who occupy them, how then do I see myself? What a spectacle! Where is the order that I had observed? The canvas of nature presented only harmony and regular proportions to my gaze, but where I turn to look at the human race I see nothing but confusion and disorder! Harmony reigns in the lower creation, but the order of men is in chaos! The animals live contentedly, it is only their king who is wretched! Oh Wisdom, where are thy laws? Beneficent Creator, what has become of Thy power? I see evil on the face of the earth![39]

Man cannot find happiness in disorder; rather, it is when there is order that he is able to enjoy true happiness. To live in a state of disorder means to lead a life of misery.

Rousseau had found these ideas on the connection between order and happiness set out in the *Entretiens sur les sciences* by Le Père Lamy, a book which he read over and over again and which greatly influenced him.[40] Lamy held the view that the love of order was 'natural' and that it is 'order which lies at the heart of the Beauty of the Universe'. He had also stated that for man life 'without being subject to laws determining the time of all their actions' was an evil. Order, according to Lamy, is so necessary that to distance oneself from it is to court disaster, for to those in a state of disorder the punishment meted out will consist of the affliction caused by that same state of disorder.[41] By contrast, 'peace and joy are the fruits of order, even as grumbling,

[39] *Profession de foi du vicaire savoyard*, *OC*, vol.4, p.583; It is interesting to note that even Rousseau's contemporaries interpreted his political doctrine on the basis of an opposition between natural order and social disorder. For example, the anonymous author of the pamphlet *De l'égalité* (F. d'Escherny), wrote: 'Civil society, in all times, and in all places, under whichever form of government that we may observe, only presents us with a spectacle of division, injustice, disorder and vice. Can what we behold be natural? Is there anything more contrary to the ideas that we associate with nature, to the ideas through which we grasp and conceive it? Universal nature everywhere presents us with an image of order and regularity; that is its most striking and impressive characteristic. Above our heads worlds too many to count roll, circle, cross each other's paths and move in concert: our globe is no more than a point in the universe; harmony reigns in the Whole, but there is discord on the civilized earth. Thus civil society is quite different from general nature but conforms to the particular nature of man.' *De l'égalité*, Basle, 1796, pp.24–5.

[40] *Les Confessions*, *OC*, vol.1, p.232.

[41] B. Lamy, *Entretiens sur les sciences. 'Première lettre de Théodore à Eugène'*, Lyon, 1706, pp.374–9. In his turn Rousseau writes in *Emile*: 'What then is human wisdom? Where is the path of true happiness? The mere limitation of our desires is not enough, for if they were less than our powers, part of our faculties would be idle; and we should not enjoy our whole being; neither is the mere extension of our powers enough, for if our desire were also increased we should only be the more miserable. True happiness consists in decreasing the difference between our desires and our powers, in establishing a perfect equilibrium between the power and the will' (*OC*, vol.4, p.304; transl. Foxley, 1974, p.44.)

quarrels and bitterness are the result of the confusion which separates men from one another. Would any rational person decide to enter a mad-house or, having imprudently done so, choose to remain there?'[42]

According to Lamy, relations between men seem to be in a state of disorder in comparison with a certain idea of order which takes the universe as its model. While natural order is seen as something positive in the moral sphere, social order has a negative connotation. Order is always associated with virtue and justice, but disorder is linked with injustice and wickedness.[43] For Rousseau, the problem of order may be reduced to the question of justice amongst men. This point will be discussed again later, but for the moment it is necessary to attempt to analyse in greater detail what is distinctive about social order and show in what sense artificial disorder is, in Rousseau's theory, opposed to natural order.

The concept of social disorder is defined by Rousseau in a negative way, that is to say, as a negation of natural order.

Oh, if an order reigned in human affairs similar to that which reigns in nature, how touching and how good the sight that would transform the face of the earth. But instead, wretched and uncivilized mankind takes pleasure in disfiguring it with their crimes and their misdeeds; in their perversion they even gain enjoyment from the torments they inflict upon each other. Treacherous and cunning even when outwardly affectionate, they treat friends and enemies alike with the same spite, and transform the heavenly spectacle of this world into the very likeness of hell.[44]

Thus, disorder signifies a complex of relationships between individuals in which each is in conflict with the others and each one seeks to improve his lot at the expense of his fellow beings. Disorder occurs when every individual believes himself to be the centre around

[42] B. Lamy, ibid., p.380; amongst the many sources which Rousseau may have used for his idea of order, one should not overlook Malebranche. On the influence of Malebranche on Rousseau see L. Bréhier, 'Lectures malebranchistes de Jean-Jacques Rousseau, *Revue internationale de philosophie*, 1 (1938) pp.98–120; see also, A. Postigliola, 'De Malebranche à Rousseau: les apories de la volonté générale et la revanche du "raisonneur violent"', *Annales de la Société Jean-Jacques Rousseau*, 39 (1972–7), pp.123–38.

[43] The relation between order and justice is almost a commonplace of political philosophy. N. Bobbio has recently written that 'From Plato onwards justice is the virtue which presides over the constitution of a totality composed of parts and as such allows the parts to co-exist, which keeps them from falling apart and returning to the primordial chaos: and thus to constitute an order', 'Sulla nozione di giustizia', *Teoria politica* 1, (1985), p.17.

[44] *Traité élémentaire de sphère*, in *Oeuvres et correspondance inédites de J.-J. Rousseau*, published by M.G. Streckeisen-Moultou, Paris, 1861, p.212.

which everything else should revolve, and it is not surprising that the same philosopher who wrote the most inspired and sincere eulogy on the order of nature should be so forthright in his condemnation of social disorder.

We may admire human society as much as we please; it will be none the less true that it necessarily leads men to hate each other in proportion as their interests clash, and to do one another apparent services, while they are really doing every imaginable mischief. What can be thought of a relation, in which the interest of every individual dictates rules directly opposite to those the public reason dictates to the community in general – in which every man finds his profit in the misfortunes of his neighbour?[45]

When Rousseau speaks of the condition of man in society his language is far removed from that of Shaftesbury and is more reminiscent of those pages in which Hobbes provides his famous description of nature as being in a state of warfare. In the *Second discourse* he speaks of 'society coming into existence' and being 'replaced by the most horrible state of warfare'.

Disorder amongst men is the inevitable outcome of the individual's determination to order his conduct in a way which runs contrary to the general interest. But conduct which violates the general order is often the most profitable line of action and it is not true that the person who seeks the public good can at the same time also satisfy his own private interests. The *Discourse on inequality* is quite clear on this point:

It will perhaps be said that society is so formed that every man gains by serving the rest. That would be all very well, if he did not gain still more by injuring them. There is no legitimate profit so great, that it cannot be greatly exceeded by what may be made illegitimately; we always gain more by hurting our neighbours than by doing them good. Nothing is required but to know how to act with impunity; and to this end the powerful employ all their strength, and the weak all their cunning.[46]

From the individual's point of view a state of disorder may accord more closely with his own selfish interest than its opposite, and the evil man often seems to be behaving more logically than the just man. This makes the problem of order in society a much more difficult one. But the interest of Rousseau's investigations into the problem of

---

[45] *Discours sur l'origine et les fondements de l'inégalité parmi les hommes*, OC, vol.3, p.202 (transl. by G.D.H. Cole, 'A discourse on the origin of inequality', *Great books of the western world*, Univ. of Chicago, 38 (1952), p.363).
[46] Ibid., p.203 (transl. ibid., p.364).

political order lies precisely in the fact that he faced the issue in all its complexity.

In Rousseau's theory social disorder is not only something which stands over against the harmony of the universe, it is also defined in relation to the notion – this time a hypothetical one – that there is such a thing as a natural human condition: the natural state. In order to illuminate the extent to which social disorder is either natural or artificial, it is necessary to take into account some of the implications of Rousseau's concept of the 'state of nature'.

The human condition in its natural state is one of isolation. Properly speaking, one cannot rightly speak of relations between men. They have no relationships because they do not need them. They are not in a position of mutual dependence as far as their fundamental needs go. Living in isolation, they have no means of comparing themselves with others or of establishing bonds of mutual esteem, nor do they have any reason to do so.

It is obvious that the idea that there is something which may be described as the natural state is the product of theoretical reasoning, arrived at by imagining what the human condition might be like if there were no such thing as society or political authority. If there were no political authority, men would be independent; if there were no social bonds, men would exist in isolation. It is precisely the qualities of independence and isolation which are the essential characteristics of the natural state. From these two primary qualities flow all the others. These also are defined in opposition to those qualities characteristic of men who live in society. Thus, 'primitive' man is concerned only with the question of survival and self-preservation, while 'civilized man' can think of nothing else but how to attain superiority over others and ensure that his uniqueness is recognized. Civilized man is in permanent conflict with his fellows: primitive man is unaware of them. The former is dominated by egotism: the latter by simple self-love.

It is this self-love which provides the motive force behind primitive man's desire for self-preservation. The urge to survive as a simple living being is completely natural and is in harmony with the natural order. Men whose only concern is their personal survival and yet who feel for others in their suffering are not alien to the order of nature. In the natural state the survival of any given individual represents no threat to the safety of all the rest. Each one is self-sufficient. Even though primitive man has few possessions, his needs are simple, revolving as they do round the basic question of survival. For men in the natural state the satisfaction of their individual needs does not prevent others satisfying their own needs[47]. Thus, they do not see their fellows as obstacles to their own happiness, even though each of them may be seeking the same goal. Abject poverty does not sow the seeds of dissension: the misfortune of one individual does not profit his neighbour.

Savage man, when he has dined, is at peace with all nature, and the friend of all his fellow-creatures. If a dispute arises about a meal, he rarely comes to blows, without having first compared the difficulty of conquering his antagonist with the trouble of finding subsistence elsewhere: and, as pride does not come in, it all ends in a few blows; the victor eats, and the vanquished seeks provision somewhere else, and all is at peace.[48]

In the natural state men form part of the natural order and are in harmony with it. Nevertheless, it is necessary to take into account that there is a clear difference on the conceptual level between the concept of the natural order and that of the natural state.

The former is an order in which each part is co-ordinated with all the others, to their mutual benefit; thus harmony and co-operation are the rule. The latter represents men in isolation, with no form of co-operation for their mutual benefit. While this is not a state of generalized conflict, it would be incorrect to describe it as harmonious since there is no real harmony or co-operation. Moreover, the natural order is the result of the activity of a moral will. The condition of men in the natural state, on the other hand, cannot really be described in this way. Men follow their natural inclinations, which means putting the desire for self-love first. They have no moral responsibility for their actions, for, living in the natural state, they do no more than follow their instinct and so moral distinctions are not applicable to their behaviour.

It appears, at first view, that men in a state of nature, having no moral relations or determinate obligations one with another, could not be either good or bad, virtuous or vicious; unless we take these terms in a physical sense, and call, in an individual, those qualities vices which may be injurious to his preservation, and those virtues which contribute to it; in which case he would have to be accounted most virtuous, who put least check on the pure impulses of nature.[49]

[47] See I. Fetscher, *Rousseaus politische philosophie zur Geschichte des demokratischen Freiheitsbegriffs*, Neuwied am Rhein and Berlin, 1968, ch.2.

[48] *Discours sur l'inégalité*, *OC*, vol.3, p.203 (transl. by G.D.H. Cole, 1952, p.364). See on this point R. Polin, *La Politique de la solitude*, Paris, 1971, p.81.

[49] *Discours sur l'inégalité*, *OC*, vol.3, p.152 (transl. ibid., p.343).

A man feeling pity for someone else who is suffering may seem to be behaving virtuously, but similar behaviour may also be found amongst primitives and in the animal kingdom.

It is true that in the natural state there are no conflicts, but that has nothing to do with men being virtuous. It is rather a case of the wisdom of providence at work, which creates an equilibrium between needs and their fulfilment and this equilibrium prevents conflict.

It appears that Providence most wisely determined that the faculties which he potentially possessed, should develop themselves only as occasion offered to exercise them, in order that they might not be superfluous or perplexing to him, by appearing before their time, nor slow and useless when the need for them arose.[50]

Rousseau thinks that the natural state cannot, properly speaking, be classed as a form of order, nor as its opposite. The fact that it cannot be talked of in these terms is a concomitant of its neutrality in the moral sphere.

If one tries to fit the term 'natural state' into one or other of the mutually exclusive categories 'natural order'–'social disorder', then it must be placed under natural order, in spite of the fact that, in Rousseau's version of ideal history, social disorder comes after the natural state and is a result of the way in which this state has been transformed. What is being argued here is that Rousseau does not consider that there is any fundamental contradiction between the concepts of social disorder and of the natural state – rather, the real opposition occurs, on the level of theory, between the concept of the natural order and social disorder in the human world.

In fact, the concepts of the natural state and of social disorder are only partially comparable, because the former has no moral connotations and exhibits no stable structure of interpersonal relations which might justify the use of the term 'order'. By contrast, a comparison may be made between natural order and social disorder. For the former, as for the latter, there are one or more moral agents: in the case of the natural order, this is God; in the case of social disorder, these agents are men (understood as the social whole). Moreover, in both the natural order and in social disorder there are permanent relations formed between the parties concerned.

Now, a more detailed examination of the two concepts as used by Rousseau reveals that they are mutually opposed. While in the natural order each part is ideally placed in relation to the whole, in the

[50] Ibid.

state of social disorder each individual subordinates the whole to himself. In the first instance, each part is, in relation to the others, both end and means; in the latter, each individual desires others to be no more than a means to the fulfilment of the ends that he proposes. In the natural order, individuals are ready to help each other: in society they use others to secure advantage for themselves. The natural order was brought into being by the act of a moral will – that of the Creator:

The goodness of God is the love of order; for it is through this order that he is able to preserve in being from moment to moment all created things and unite the parts with the Whole.[51]

Social disorder, on the other hand, emanates from wills which are diametrically opposed to virtue, that is to say, to the love of order. From the theoretical point of view, therefore, social disorder is defined as the negation of the order which exists in nature. But from the point of view of a hypothetical history of humanity, social disorder appears as the corruption of the natural state.

Before examining Rousseau's solution to the problem of social disorder, it will be useful to pause for a moment to consider this concept in greater depth in order to determine whether it would be thought of as natural or artificial. The answer to this question is not as obvious as might appear at first sight. To grasp the essence of Rousseau's thought it is necessary to distinguish between his hypothetical reconstruction of the process at work in the formation of civil society and the moral judgement he pronounces on the condition of men in that same state.

Rousseau describes this process as a natural one in that it occurs without specific purpose or conscious plan. This does not, however, signify that man's situation in society, with all the disorder which appertains to it, is anything other than an artificial one – a fact which guarantees the possibility that it can be changed by human agency. It follows that men themselves are morally responsible for disorder.

The famous pages in the *Discourse on inequality* in which Rousseau provides an account of the transition from the natural to the social state, have justly been described as an example of the natural history of society, comparable, from this point of view, with Adam Smith's the *Wealth of nations* and Ferguson's *An essay on the history of civil society*. In his work, *Social change and history*, Nisbet has drawn attention to this aspect of the *Discourse on inequality*:

[51] *Profession de foi du vicaire savoyard*, *OC*, vol.4, p.593.

He gives us in its answer [to the question whether it is possible to separate man's responsibility for his advancement from the primitive state from the contribution made by circumstance and general progress] no simple-minded, stark contrast between a happy state of nature and a corrupt civilization, as the misrepresentations of Rousseau so often have it, but instead a remarkable panorama of the evolution of mankind as this might be reconstructed from the data of comparative psychology and ethnography and, to a lesser extent, of the ancient classical historians. Granted that the underlying motive of the *Discourse* was polemical, even revolutionary . . . we still are forced to recognize the work for what it is: the natural history of human society.[52]

Even the slightest of causes can have an astonishing effect, says Rousseau, when they act unrelentingly. Thus, the creation of civil society is a process determined by chance combinations of causes of this kind, and not by the activity of a conscious will. The fact that this process is a natural one is a consequence of the kind of causes which helped to shape it.

The process which brought civil society into existence is entirely fortuitous and natural, but the civil state is an *artificial* condition. First, because nature bears no responsibility whatsoever for the wretched condition of men in society: it is 'the infatuation of man, which, to gratify his silly pride and vain self-admiration, induces him eagerly to pursue all the miseries he is capable of feeling, though beneficent nature had kindly placed them out of his way'.[53]

Moreover, the civil state is an artificial one, for its birth is accompanied by the invention of the arts of mankind, especially agriculture and metallurgy. Finally, in the civil state, man is dominated by egotism, which, as Rousseau defines it, is a faculty opposed to the natural one of self-love.

Egoism is a purely relative and factitious feeling which arises in the state of society, leads each individual to make more of himself than of any other, causes all the mutual damage men inflict one on another, and is the real source of the 'sense of honour'.[54]

It is not nature which has ordained that men should put their own selfish interest before the good of their neighbour. The social state is thus the point at which the natural history of humanity begins; but the conduct of men is not natural and so they must bear the responsi-

---

[52] R.A. Nisbet, *Social change and history*, Oxford, 1969, p.145. On the idea of natural history see G. Gusdorf, *Dieu, la nature, l'homme au siècle des lumières*, Paris 1972, in particular the chapter 'L'Histoire naturelle dans la culture des lumières'; A.O. Lovejoy, 'The supposed primitivism of Rousseau's "Discourse on inequality"', in *Essays on the history of ideas*, Westport, Conn., 1978, pp.14–37.

[53] *Discours sur l'inégalité*, *OC*, vol.3, p.202 (transl. by G.D.H. Cole, 1952, p.363).

[54] Ibid., p.219 (transl. ibid., p.344, n.1).

bility for the disorder promoted by such conduct. The problem posed by Rousseau's political philosophy is not the question of how to impose order upon the disorder of nature. On the contrary, it is a matter of creating order from artificial disorder. As will be seen shortly, Rousseau's solution to this question is also an artificial solution.

The 'well-ordered society'

For Rousseau, it will be possible for order to reign in human society only if a new form of the artificial is developed to offset the ill effects of the old. Human arts have changed the natural condition of man and favoured social disorder; a new artifice is therefore necessary to create a society which, this time, will be 'well-ordered'. In this connection there is an important passage which comes from a fragment to which Vaughan has appended the title: *Du droit naturel et de la société générale*, while in Derathé's edition, the title is *De l'état de nature*. The same argument is found also in the *Geneva manuscript* and this is not contradicted by the definitive version of the work.

Yet although there is no natural and general society among men, although they become unhappy and wicked in becoming sociable, although the laws of justice and equality mean nothing to those who live at one and the same time in the liberty of the state of nature and subject to the needs of the social state, yet we should not think that there is neither virtue nor happiness for us and that heaven has abandoned us without remedy to depravity. We should rather try to extract from the evil itself the remedy which can cure it. If possible, we must make up for the lack of the general association by creating new associations. Let our violent interlocutor himself to be the judge of our success. Let us show him that the art of living together can, as it develops, repair the evils which, in its initial stages, it caused to human nature.[55]

This passage comes at the beginning of the first version of the *Social contract* and was written, even from the point of view of chronological order, at the beginning of the discussion on the problem of 'Political institutions'. It introduces two interrelated concepts which play an important part in Rousseau's theory: these are 'the origins of art' ('art commencé') and 'art perfected' ('art perfectionné').

The first term implies a form of society in which disorder reigns.

---

[55] *Manuscrit de Genève, OC,* vol.3, p.288; (transl. Cole, *J.-J. Rousseau, The 'Social contract' and 'Discourses'*, London, 1973, pp.161–2). *De l'état de nature, OC,* vol. 3, p. 479. The perfected art which is to establish a just political order, writes Victor Goldschmidt, is a specific art: the art of politics. It is precisely this art which comes to the relief of nature. See *Anthropologie et politique. Les principes du système de Rousseau*, Paris, 1974, pp.570–1.

The second suggests something very different – a 'well-ordered society'. The first artifice is unconscious: the corruption of the natural state now fallen into disorder is an involuntary effect of the evolution of human emotions and crafts (in particular, agriculture and metallurgy) and commerce. By contrast, the second artifice is completely rational and consciously willed: a just political order cannot be achieved by chance; it can be established only by taking conscious thought and men must have attained a sufficient degree of rationality to be able to appreciate its worth and be capable of bringing it into being.

Since, in the examples so far encountered, order in Rousseau has always referred to natural order, one might imagine that the idea of the 'well-ordered society' has been arrived at by transposing the model of natural order onto the complex of social relations. In my opinion Rousseau does, without question, employ the image of natural order as a model to define the general characteristics of the 'well-ordered society'. This is hardly surprising since natural order was the only image of order which he was able to employ, apart from the literary evidence supplied by the ancient republics, which Rousseau always regarded as the true examples of a just political order.[56] Nevertheless, there are important differences between the ideas of natural and social order. It is true that to describe political society Rousseau uses natural analogies, such as the body.[57] Moreover, the political order founded on the sovereignty of law requires, from the juridical point of view, that each individual should be defined as a part of a whole on which he is dependent for his 'life and his very being', just as the well-being of the parts of an organism depends on the health and well-being of the whole body.[58]

However, the fundamental principle of the natural order should

---

[56] See R.A. Leigh, 'Jean-Jacques Rousseau and the myth of antiquity in the eighteenth century', R.R. Bolgar (ed.), *Classical influences on western thought*, Cambridge, 1979, pp.155–68.

[57] *Economie politique*, *OC*, vol.3, p.244, J.E. Schlanger points out that for Rousseau the analogy between the political body and the living body is 'merely external and accidental'. He adds that 'it does not provide sufficient evidence to link Rousseau to the current of political organicism', *Les Métaphores de l'organisme*, Paris, 1971, p.135; see also J. Ehrard, *L'Idée de nature en France dans la première moitié du XVIII siècle*, 2 vols., Paris, 1963; R.J. Howells, 'The metaphysic of nature: basic values and their application in the social philosophy of Rousseau', *Studies on Voltaire and the eighteenth century*, 60 (1968), pp.109–200; P. Benichou, 'Réflexions sur l'idée de nature chez Jean-Jacques Rousseau, *Annales de la Société Jean-Jacques Rousseau*, 39 (1972–7), pp.25–45.

[58] *Manuscrit de Genève*, *OC*, vol.3, p.313; *Contrat social*, *OC*, vol.3, p.381.

not be confused with that other one which should guarantee order amongst men. The governing principle of natural order is the preservation of the whole. When Rousseau speaks of divine providence he stresses that it is concerned with the maintenance of the universe and not individual beings. If the same criterion is applied to the body politic, it follows that the principle of a 'well-ordered society' is the continuous existence of the totality. This means that individuals do not exist as separate entities. The individual may also be sacrificed for the preservation and the good of the greater whole. In the chapter of the *Geneva manuscript* on the respective rights of sovereign and citizen, there is a passage which offers firm evidence in support of this interpretation. It will be quoted here as it appears in the first version of the *Social contract*. The same passage also occurs in the definitive version in a shorter form (Bk 2, ch. 4).

If the State is a moral person whose life is in the union of its members, and if the most important of its cares is the care for its own preservation, it must have a universal and compelling force, in order to move and dispose each part as may be most advantageous to the whole.[59]

The body politic should be able to exercise the same kind of absolute control over its subordinate parts as in the physical realm the individual is able to do with regard to his or her own limbs. Nevertheless, the analogy between the natural body and the body politic should not be taken too far. The parts of a watch, like the parts of a man's body, have no individual existence apart from the whole. It is impossible to think of them except as parts of that whole. By definition they have existence only as parts of a whole. Rousseau is well aware that the situation of individuals with regard to the body politic is different.[60] 'But', he adds, immediately after the passage quoted above,

besides the public person, we have to consider the private persons composing it, whose life and liberty are naturally independent of it. We are bound then to

---

[59] *Manuscrit de Genève, OC*, vol. 3, p. 305.
[60] 'The difference between the works of man and of nature is clear from what is implied by each of these. However much citizens may refer to themselves as members of the state, they can never be united with it in the same way as are the true members of the body; there is no getting away from the fact that each of them has a separate existence because of which he is quite capable of sustaining his being without help from anyone else.' *L'Etat de guerre, Pol. Writ.*, 1, p. 298. On the so-called organicism of Rousseau see R. Derathé, *Rousseau et la science politique de son temps*, Paris, 1970, in particular Appendix 4: 'The organic view of society in Rousseau and in his predecessors', pp. 410–13.

distinguish clearly between the respective rights of the citizens and the Sovereign. This is an issue which needs to be discussed further.[61]

This passage makes it clear that the argument that, for Rousseau, the well-ordered society is founded on the principle that individuals should be considered merely in so far as they contribute to the preservation of the totality should not be accepted too readily.

The problem of the preservation of the body politic is not dealt with independently of the question of the legitimacy of the body politic itself. The preservation of the body politic is not a goal which overrides the requirement that political authority should be legitimate. Legitimate political authority is instituted to ensure the security and liberty of each and every one. If the sovereign authority seems to sacrifice an individual to the public good, it is acting illegitimately, as will be shown in the third part of this work.

In *On political economy*, Rousseau explains very clearly that the well-being of the least individual is as important as the good of the state. Not only does the individual exist for the state; the state, providing it is legitimate, also exists for the individual. Neither individual nor state can be said to exist in isolation:

In fact, does not the undertaking entered into by the whole body of the nation bind it to provide for the security of the least of its members with as much care as for that of all the rest? Is the welfare of the single citizen any less the common cause than that of the whole State? It may be said that it is good that one should perish for all; I am ready to admire such a saying when it comes from the lips of a virtuous and worthy patriot, voluntarily and dutifully sacrificing himself for the good of his country; but if we are to understand by it that it is lawful for the government to sacrifice an innocent man for the good of the multitude, I look upon it as one of the most execrable rules tyranny ever invented, the greatest falsehood that can be advanced, the most dangerous admission that can be made, and a direct contradiction of the fundamental laws of society.[62]

The concept of the 'well-ordered society' requires not only that each individual should be orientated in the best possible way towards the totality, but that the totality should be similarly orientated towards the individual. If the first condition is fulfilled but not the second, the body politic may have order, but it will not be legitimate. In this case it will be a tyranny. On the other hand, there will be dis-

[61] *Manuscrit de Genève, OC*, vol.3, p.306.
[62] *Economie politique, OC*, vol.3, pp.256-7 (transl. by G.D.H. Cole, 'A discourse on political economy', *Great books of the western world*, Univ. of Chicago, 38 (1952), p. 374).

order even if the totality is ordered if it is only for the benefit of a few individuals. In fact, it is the evil man, as we have seen, who wishes to be at the centre of things and demands that everything should revolve around him. The fact that there is a two-way relationship between the individual and the totality marks the difference between social and natural order. Natural order involves the interconnection of things; social order involves the web of human relationships. Objects may be considered as having a purely relative existence. But men cannot be thought of in this way, either in relation to other men, or in relation to the state. In his *Lettre à Voltaire*, Rousseau emphasizes the difference between the order which reigns in nature and the moral order within which beings endowed with sensitivity and intelligence have their existence.

If we are to understand these things properly, it seems that objects in the physical world should be viewed as having a relative existence while in the moral sphere everything is absolute: so that the greatest conception I can form of Providence is that each material entity is arranged in the best possible way in relation to the whole and each intelligent and feeling being most appropriately in relation to himself; or, to express the same idea differently, it is better for the person who is aware that he exists to be than not to be.[63]

Rousseau's depiction of a well-ordered society was shaped by the conviction that the existence and happiness of intelligent beings has moral value in itself, quite independent of its relation to anything else. As will be shown in the third part of this study, it would be more precise to compare political order not with the order of things, but with the moral order. The artifice of the body politic represents a radical alternative to the 'natural' inclinations of mankind. The more perfect the body politic, the more it will succeed in crushing the natural forces of the individual. Although the word 'natural' has a positive connotation in other contexts, it always has a negative one when used of the body politic. Now the coupling perfection–nature is replaced by perfection–artifice. The natural desires of civilized man are a threat to the well-being of the body politic. Their effect is always to induce the individual to think of himself as if he were the absolute. In the context of the body politic, the word 'natural' becomes a synonym for 'individual'. The natural conduct of man is deemed virtuous only in the context of the family and community life. But this same mode of conduct becomes corrupt and blameworthy when it appears in the

[63] *Lettre de Rousseau à Monsieur de Voltaire*, *OC*, vol.4, p.1070.

sphere of public institutions and the wider society. If the head of the family is to be a good father then he need do nothing more than obey his natural inclinations and ensure that they are not corrupted. But if a magistrate follows his natural inclinations, he will be a bad magistrate.

The antithesis between 'natural' and 'artificial' corresponds, to a certain extent, to the one between 'public' and 'private' or the general and particular. The strongest and most dynamic impulse is, in harmony with the natural order, the will of the individual focussed on his own personal interest. The impulse to pursue the common good is weaker and less active, precisely because it is artificial. But the maintenance of a just social order demands that this state of affairs should be reversed and the general will should become more active.

The chapter in the *Social contract* on the 'principle on which the various forms of government are based' is a remarkable document on the relation between the natural and the individual with regard to political order.

In a perfect act of legislation, the individual or particular will should be at zero; the corporate will belonging to the government should occupy a very subordinate position; and, consequently, the general or sovereign will should always predominate and should be the sole guide of all the rest.

According to the natural order, on the other hand, these different wills become more active in proportion as they are concentrated. Thus, the general will is always the weakest, the corporate will second, and the individual will strongest of all: so that, in the government each member is first of all himself, then a magistrate, and then a citizen – in an order exactly the reverse of what the social system requires.[64]

What is good and perfect in the political order is to be found, so to speak, on the side of the artificial, not on that of nature. The more perfect the political institution, the more successful it has been in weaning man away from nature and depriving him of his independent existence. For Rousseau, therefore, a just political order is in total opposition to the 'natural' relations between men, meaning by this relations arising from conduct governed by the individual will. As the primacy of the individual will over the general will is something which conforms to the natural order and is contrary to what is required by a just political order, it follows that the fundamental theoretical relation is for Rousseau not that between artificial disorder and political

[64] *Contrat social, OC*, vol.3, p.401, (transl. by G.D.H. Cole, 'The social contract', *Great books*, Univ. of Chicago, 38 (1952), p.409).

(artificial) order, but that between natural order and political (artificial) order.

I would argue that both pairs of concepts are equally valid and reflect Rousseau's thought accurately. If understood correctly there is no contradiction here. Consider the first pair: artificial disorder – political (artificial) order. The keywords are the nouns: order and disorder. The concept of disorder denotes a specific relationship between the whole and the parts of which it is comprised, one in which each part sees the whole as existing merely to satisfy its own particular needs and views the other parts as so many obstacles. On the other hand, the concept of order denotes a whole in which each part is arranged in the most favourable manner possible in relation to the whole and where the whole is also perfectly arranged for the benefit of each part. The adjective 'artificial' applied to the two nouns in question indicates that neither of these can be described as states which fulfil nature's designs. Social disorder – men seeking their own selfish ends at the expense of others – is not something which originates in nature. At the same time, if men were to create a well-ordered society, it would be they themselves who should be commended, not nature. In the one instance, they are creators, in the other, worthy of blame. Social disorder is, as has been emphasized, the outcome of the natural history of society. The fact that man finds himself in this wretched condition is due to a fortuitous concurrence of quite separate causes. But if he does not choose to liberate himself he must bear the responsibility if no change for the better occurs. Nature has not made man in such a way that pursuit of his natural desires will of necessity bring him into conflict with the interests of others; but neither can these same natural inclinations provide the dynamic required for the creation of a 'well-ordered society'.

As far as the second pair of terms, natural order – political (artificial) order are concerned, the qualifier 'natural' has a different meaning: it now means 'independent'. It refers to the conduct of individuals who see themselves as a perfect and isolated whole, while men, once political society has developed, are no longer so. According to Rousseau's theory, they have submitted themselves to the political yoke in accepting the supremacy of the general will. They are, therefore, no longer those same isolated and independent individuals that they were in the natural state. When man places his own 'self' at the centre of existence, this is, as has already been stated, quite natural. The point is that each individual is no longer just a 'self'; he also forms part of a 'communal self' and it is no longer feasible for him to behave, now that legitimate authority has been established, as if he were still independent. With the creation of political society, writes Rousseau, 'everywhere nature has disappeared; everywhere human arts have taken its place', with the important exception of the relations between states.

It is now possible to suggest some conclusions with regard to the two pairs of concepts (a) artificial disorder – political (artificial) order; (b) natural order – political (artificial) order.

If, as has been said, these pairs do not contradict each other, the first terms must to a certain extent be interchangeable – and in fact they are. If we take political order and natural order together, attention is drawn to the way mankind passes from the natural state to the enjoyment of civil liberty and subjection to the sovereign authority whose cornerstone is the social contract.

If, on the other hand, we link political order and 'artificial' disorder then emphasis is laid on the fact that political (artificial) order is an alternative to the wretched condition of mankind now emerged from the isolation of the natural condition as far as basic needs are concerned (mutual dependence), but which has failed to model its institutions on the basis of an equitable social contract (even though there may be general agreements on rights and accords entered into by the citizens as described in the *Second discourse*). The two paired concepts (a) and (b) can therefore be brought together into a single equation with three terms: natural order (condition) – artificial disorder – well-ordered society. This equation corresponds term for term with the following: natural state – civil society – political society.

The organizing principle is the concept of order (and its antithesis, disorder). The word 'condition' has been added to the first term of the equation (natural order) because in the context of relations between men in the natural state the word 'order', in Rousseau's sense of the term, is inappropriate.

This schema does not, of course, pretend to be exhaustive. In the *Discourse on inequality*, for example, Rousseau speaks of emergent society ('société naissante').[65] This condition of humanity may not be equated with the natural state for several reasons. In the first place, men no longer live in a state of isolation. They are not subject to law,

[65] *Discours sur l'inégalité*, *OC*, vol.3, pp.169–76.

but they have the same nature. Moreover, long-term social relationships bring rivalries unknown to men in their natural state. In
'emergent society' men have already reached the point at which they
are capable of making comparisons; they formulate the concepts of
value and beauty which engender in them the ability to make judgements of relative merit. Their quest for the respect and esteem of
their fellows ushers them into a world of conflict and rivalry. Finally,
natural compassion, a sentiment which more than any other characterizes man in his natural state, has already begun to be weakened.
But on the other hand 'emergent society' is not the same thing as
artificial disorder. Firstly, the arts of mankind are still in a primitive
state: neither agriculture nor metallurgy exist at this stage. Moreover,
egotism – the passion which rules the lives of civilized men – has not
yet come to dominate their hearts. In consequence, conflict is not yet
widespread, as in the case of civil society proper. Therefore, this 'half-
way stage' (Rousseau speaks of the 'juste milieu') may be said to
exhibit certain of the traits of civil society, that is to say artificial disorder, but it is really neither one thing nor the other. In terms of the
schema outlined above, 'emergent society' may be placed in an intermediary position between natural order and artificial disorder.

The equation with its three terms set out above may also be represented as follows in order to clarify the metaphysical framework of
Rousseau's political theory:

   a) natural order – beginnings of art – perfected art,
   b) natural order – artificial disorder – well-ordered society,
   c) natural state – civil society – political society.

The terms in the first set may be distinguished according to whether
they belong to the category of art or nature. The fact that a situation
or a complex of relations is defined by Rousseau as 'natural' or 'artificial',
in the first place has to do with whether it is possible to single out one
or more individuals who are in a position of responsibility. The
fundamental categories which form a division within the second set of
terms are organized around the formal concepts of 'order' and 'disorder'. This set conveys information about the kind of relations which
characterize the various states. The third set, which would require a
more detailed commentary, is mainly based on the concepts of
independence (absence of political obligation) and isolation (mutual
independence). The second set offers two 'real' terms and one 'ideal',

in that the natural order and human disorder are empirical realities while a well-ordered society is an ideal.

From these conditions it is evident that the problem Rousseau faces is not, as with Hobbes,[66] the question of how the transition from natural disorder to political order is to be effected, but rather how a state of artificial disorder brought about by 'emergent art' may be transformed into political order. A well-ordered society is seen as a possible goal of 'perfected art'. At this point it is necessary to explain why human order cannot, in Rousseau's view, be understood as a prolongation of natural order and then to make clear why political artifice is necessary.

The necessity of artifice

For Rousseau a well-ordered society cannot come into being through a natural process whereby men, relying only on their natural impulses and the laws of nature, may attain a political order. His investigation is carried out in a context which is far closer to the artificial than to the naturalistic model.[67] However, unlike Hobbes, he does not pose the problem of social order in terms of a transformation of natural disorder into a peaceful society. For Rousseau a well-regulated society should take the place of artificial disorder. The basic theoretical relation, as has already been noted, is that between rudimentary art ('art

[66] M. Cranston has suggested that one can find in Hobbes a model which has three elements. The image of the machine, he writes, 'is presented in three forms': (1) the whole universe, a natural machine; (2) man: machine both natural and artificial, by nature a self-centred animal, by culture a moral being; (3) the state, the city or the political society: a completely artificial machine. ('Violence et force chez Thomas Hobbes', *Cadmos*, 12 (1980), p.61.) It is possible to note here similarities and differences with Rousseau's model. The similarity is clearly seen in the third element, that is to say, the idea of the state as an artificial product. The differences are centred on the first two terms and more precisely the nature and origin of disorder. For Hobbes disorder appears with man. It is man who has disturbed the order of the mechanical universe. This is natural man. For Rousseau, the root of disorder is just as clear: man was created as a free agent; his will and his actions are not governed by mechanical laws of nature. He can, therefore, bring into being either harmonious relations, or the most horrible disorder. This explanation could not be derived from Hobbes's system. Finally, for Rousseau, it is not natural man who has upset the order of nature. He has his niche in the order of nature. It is artificial man who is the author of disorder. The idea of 'natural' disorder is foreign to Rousseau. For Hobbes, by contrast, the self-centred disorder is caused by natural man, the self-centred animal. The disorder which follows is thus a natural disorder.

[67] See S. Veca, 'Politica', in *Enciclopedia*, Einaudi, Turin, 1980, vol.10, pp.855–79; M. Bovero, 'Politica e artificio. Sulla logica del modello giusnaturalistico', in *Materiali filosofici*, 6 (1981), pp.71–95.

commencé') and perfected art ('art perfectionné'). For Hobbes, on the other hand, the artificial is indivisible and the fundamental relationship is the one between nature and the artificial.

Now that the main lines have been drawn, the next task will be to elaborate on the necessarily artificial nature of political order. For Rousseau, man is naturally endowed with certain instincts which exist for his self-preservation. These are self-love, fear of pain, aversion to the thought of death, desire for one's own well-being.[68] Man's potential as a social being is entrusted to the moral system formed by the double relationship of man to himself and his fellows. In both these relationships, the infallible arbiter is conscience. Conscience is a faculty which should instruct men in the difference between good and evil. It is an inborn and natural feeling (in the sense that it comes from God), which always counsels man to pursue the good.[69] Having rejected the view that man has been led to found political societies to satisfy his natural need, Rousseau seems to ground the human tendency to come together to form societies on a moral feeling, the conscience. But it is precisely the fact that it is a natural feeling which makes it very weak. It speaks to man with the voice of nature, a voice to which man is no longer responsive once he has left the natural state behind. The very fact that it is described as 'natural' makes any natural sociability impossible. It is true that conscience, being a natural feeling, speaks the same language to all men and never errs. But for precisely this reason it is ineffectual. The men to whom it should speak, and who would, in fact, benefit greatly from it, have already gone beyond the natural state. On the other hand, when they were in the natural state they were not in such great need of it since the natural state is a (hypothetical) pre-moral condition as well as being pre-social, and in such circumstances it is not clear what role a moral feeling such as the conscience could play.

Even though Rousseau does not dispute that conscience exists and has an important part to play as a moral guide for the individual, it nevertheless has not sufficient weight to act as the basis of social order. If this feeling ruled supreme amongst men, the problem of how to create a well-ordered society would not even arise: men, directed by their conscience, would act towards each other in a perfectly just way. The result would be a wholly peaceful and harmonious society.

[68] *Discours sur l'inégalité*, OC, vol.3, p.165.
[69] *Discours sur les sciences et les arts*, OC, vol.3, p.30.

In other ways the situation would then be very much like the one described by Hobbes with regard to social animals. In the former case, as in the latter, a well-ordered community comes into existence as a result of individuals obeying a natural voice, although in the first instance it is instinct and in the second a moral feeling. In the case of social animals, as also in the hypothetical case of men who follow the dictates of their conscience, there would not be a need for any government or law, since there would be, to use Hobbes's terminology, 'peace without subjection'.[70] The assertion that it is not possible for conscience to provide an adequate ground for a just order amongst men is in Rousseau followed by another consideration.

Relations between nature and the animal kingdom are very different from those between nature and mankind. Amongst the animals, nature commands and they never fail to obey. Amongst men, nature also commands but in most cases its voice is unheard.[71] Man, like the animals, is endowed by nature with all the instincts for survival. He is unique, however, in that, as a free agent, he is responsible for taking the necessary measures to ensure his survival. By contrast, the animals have a built-in mechanism, like some ingenious machine, to act to ensure their own survival without finding it necessary to form social groupings. Animals cannot, even though it would be an advantage for them to do so, act otherwise than nature intends. Men are capable of going against nature, even though in doing so they harm themselves.

Thus a pigeon would be starved to death by the side of a dish of the choicest meats, and a cat on a heap of fruit or grain; though it is certain that either might find nourishment in the foods which it thus rejects with disdain, did it think of trying them. Hence it is that dissolute men run into excesses which

---

[70] *Leviathan*, Bk 2, ch.17.

[71] On this problem the present interpretation differs from the conclusions reached in R. Polin *La Politique de la solitude*, Paris, 1971, p.91. He writes that 'all the citizens of the State of the Contract finally enter the "moral order", an order elaborated in accordance with reason which, guided by conscience, has rediscovered an order in harmony with nature' (p.91). In the first place, the order established by the contract is different from natural order for reasons which have to do with the kind of relations existing between the parts, and the regulatory principle. For the order of nature the question of the parts which comprise the system giving their consent to the rules which govern the functioning of the totality does not arise. By contrast, this problem does exist, and is a very real one, in the political order. It is therefore, not really true to say that the order established by the contract is a rediscovery of the order of nature. In the second place conscience does not have a role to play in establishing political order. The contract is necessary because conscience does not influence man's behaviour and it is also possible because men consider it to be in their interest.

bring on fevers and death; because the mind depraves the senses, and the will continues to speak when nature is silent.[72]

Man's relationship with nature, and more specifically the relationship between man's will and the voice of nature, is such that, even if nature had made man a sociable creature, it would not follow that he would be truly sociable. Although Rousseau states that man has in any case been created with the intention that he should become sociable, one should not therefore conclude that nature and the divine architect have made man in such a way that life in society and the institution of the state represent his true end.

Even though the voice of nature incites man towards sociability, he is quite capable of ignoring this and acting in a contrary way. Whether the voice of nature speaks as conscience ('the divine instinct') or whether it speaks as the voice of self-preservation, the will may be unaffected.

It is now necessary to demonstrate to what extent, for Rousseau, there are one or more voices of nature urging man to form a social union with his fellows and to create the institution of the state. In this respect it will be helpful to refer to his critique of Hobbes's theory of man's natural inclination towards evil. In his refutation of this argument Rousseau appeals to the natural feeling of pity, which he defines as, 'by so much more universal and useful to mankind, as it comes before any kind of reflection; and at the same time so natural, that the very brutes themselves sometimes give evident proofs of it'.[73] This feeling involves identifying oneself with a fellow human-being who is suffering. Pity and the ability to show compassion are the joint sources of the social virtues of generosity, mercy and humaneness. This is no more than the application of the one quality, pity, to different categories of people: first to the weak, secondly, to the guilty and, thirdly, to humanity in general. It is the same with other less general feelings such as kindness and friendship which are nothing more than pity steadily applied to the same object. To seek and desire someone's happiness is the same as to desire that he will not suffer. This desire is rooted in the identification of the self with one's fellow being. For Rousseau the natural feeling of pity counterbalances egotism. Sometimes the quest for personal gain at the expense of others may be tempered with the grief we feel at seeing others suffer. Before egotism

---

[72] *Discours sur l'inégalité, OC*, vol.3, p.141 (transl. G.D.H. Cole, 1952, p.337).
[73] Ibid., p.154 (transl. ibid., p.344).

had developed, natural pity acted as a restraint on the ardour with which men pursued their own well-being; if the drive for self-preservation did not take the form of general conflict this was thanks to the moderating influence of natural pity. In the natural state, the feeling of pity acted to regulate social life in the same way as customs and laws. No one ignored its promptings. Natural pity thus contributes in a very important way to the natural condition of man being such that each individual may attain his own personal goals without preventing his fellows from attaining theirs.

This condition of peaceful independence does not mean that the 'sublime maxim of rational justice', which enjoins that 'you should do to others, as you would that they should do to you' has been realized. Rather, pity is the inspiration of that other less elevated but more useful maxim of 'natural goodness': 'do good to yourself with as little evil as possible to others'.[74]

Nature has thus endowed men with a feeling which makes them suited to life in society, without that same society necessarily being an arena for conflict.[75] But the designs of nature have not been realized. The voice of pity makes itself heard in the natural state, but as egotism develops, its prompting becomes progressively weaker. If pity teaches man compassion for his suffering fellow beings, reason, which has now developed more fully, teaches him to turn in on himself and to distance himself from his brothers. Instead of the maxim 'do good to yourself with as little harm to others as possible', now, when faced with the sight of someone suffering, men hold to another maxim: 'Perish, if you wish. I am all right.'

In 'civilized man' there is no more than a faint echo of natural pity. The idea that man is naturally disposed to be sympathetic to others is one of the fundamental arguments that Rousseau marshals against Hobbes's position. But the fact that man is so inclined is not in itself sufficient to guarantee the transition from the natural order to a well-ordered society. Although Rousseau modifies Hobbes's model, he still has to face the problem of the 'somewhat more' which is a prerequisite of order amongst men.

Rousseau is far from adopting a naturalist perspective. There is little evidence that he ever held the view that nature, lacking as it did the means of bringing people together in political communities, should

[74] Ibid., p.156 (transl. ibid., p.345).
[75] See on this subject R. Derathé, *Rousseau et la science politique de son temps*, Paris, 1950, pp.142–51.

nevertheless have implanted in them the desire for social unity. If nature has created man to live in society, why has it not also endowed him with language, the most important tool for life in society?

But be the origin of language and society what they may, it may be at least inferred, from the little care which nature has taken to unite mankind by mutual wants, and to facilitate the use of speech, that she has contributed little to make them sociable, and has put little of her own into all they have done to create such bonds of union.[76]

Nature has not created man with the kind of needs that can be satisfied only with the help of others. Even if it is possible to imagine that individuals may have similar needs it is not easy to see why or for what natural purpose anyone should seek to meet the needs of anyone else. Moreover, it is impossible to enter into a contract or make an agreement without using language, but this is precisely what nature has failed to provide. Nature has prepared the way for man to live in a state of self-reliance, in conditions of peace and with the means to satisfy his physical needs, but without having prepared him for life in society. The evidence for this is that nature is responsible, according to Rousseau, for the fact that man remained so long in his natural state. The *Discourse on inequality* is quite clear on this point:

I know it is incessantly repeated that man would in such a state have been the most miserable of creatures; and indeed, if it be true, as I think I have proved, that he must have lived many ages, before he could have either desire or an opportunity of emerging from it, this would only be an accusation against nature, and not against the being which she had thus unhappily constituted.[77]

Thus it seems that one is faced with one of the following alternatives: either nature has not taken any great pains to prepare man for the task of creating a 'just society'; or nature has provided man with all the faculties and feelings required for life in society, so that nothing is lacking in this respect, but man has stifled these feelings and faculties. Whether one adopts the first or the second view, the conclusion is the same, namely that, without having recourse to some power other than nature, men can only hope to live in isolation from one another or in disorder. This is true in all cases whether one understands by 'nature' natural needs, or natural feelings (the urge for self-preservation and pity), or yet again the 'voice of nature', that is to say conscience. For Rousseau, since nature is not able to induce men to create a just political

---

[76] *Discours sur l'inégalité*, *OC*, vol.3, p.151 (transl. G.D.H. Cole, 1952, p.342).
[77] Ibid., pp.151–2 (transl. ibid., p.342).

order, a just society can be achieved only by means of political artifice. A just society is neither the continuation nor the restoration of natural order. It is founded on an authority which is required to establish and maintain order often against the natural inclinations of men. When it is a question of establishing and preserving a just order amongst men, nature gives place to a very specific art: the art of politics.

3

Disorder and inequality

Order as 'degree' and the place of man in the system of beings

To understand more fully Rousseau's theory of political order, it is first necessary to make a careful analysis of what he means by disorder. This analysis will make it possible to see the problem of inequality in a fresh light. In this connection it will be helpful to focus once more on the idea of order. For Rousseau 'order' does not only mean harmony and the mutual support of all the parts for the common good and the preservation of the system to which they belong. The term 'order' also connotes 'degree', 'place', 'rank', and lastly the allocation of each part of the whole, whether it be a person or some other sentient being, to a position which is right and fitting. It is precisely in the light of this conception of order that the theory of inequality reveals its various dimensions and its theoretical richness. *La Nouvelle Héloise* provides a particularly clear example of the relation between 'order' and 'place'. The relevant text is the one where Mme de Wolmar, in the middle of a discussion on the education of children, remarks: 'Everything happens for the best in the system of the universe. Everyone has his proper place in the ideal order of things; the important thing is to find that place and avoid upsetting that order.'[1]

---

[1] *La Nouvelle Héloise*, OC, vol.2, p.563.

There is a passage in the *Profession de foi du vicaire savoyard*[2] where Rousseau uses the terms 'place' and 'rank' to depict the disorder which rules in human affairs.[3] The two texts give a very similar impression: order is defined as the allocation of each part of the whole to its proper rank and place. Seen in this way, order implies a series of ranks and stations, some more elevated than others. It is not only that each part has a different role to play, but that there are also different degrees of merit and worth. Now, the form of inequality which, for Rousseau, represents a real moral and political problem is the inequality in the degree of dignity and esteem which each individual is able to command in his dealings with others. The basis of this form of inequality is mutual appraisal and it always finds its expression in relative concepts. Thus Rousseau's theory of inequality is closely linked with his portrayal of order as hierarchical. The idea that order consists in everything being in its 'right place' did not, of course, originate with Rousseau. The idea of order has a long history, and as an example one could take Cicero's famous definition from the first book of *De officiis* where he explicitly takes the Greeks as his authority:

Next we must go on to discuss the correct order and timing of our actions. Both these elements are included in that branch of knowledge which the Greeks called *eutaxia*. The word has two equivalents in Latin: one is *modestia* (moderation from the root modus, the mean); the other is *ordinis conservatio* (the preservation of due order). I shall use the word 'modestia', but the sense of the latter – according to the definition of the Stoics, who explain it as the knowledge of how to put all our actions and words in their appropriate place. Thus it will be clear that ordering and correct placing are two terms identical in meaning; for the Stoics also define due order as a setting out of things in the positions most suited and fitted for them.[4]

The *Lexicon totius latinitatis* is clearly linked to Cicero's definition when it states that order is 'dispositio unius rei post aliam suo quamque loco collocando'.[5]

The idea of order as the allocation of everything to its right place was taken up again by St Augustine in the context of his definition of 'peace'. In the *City of God* (Bk 19, ch. 13), he states that it is impossible

---

[2] In the *Rêveries*, Rousseau states that the 'Profession de foi' represents the result of his 'anguished investigations'. See *OC*, vol.1, p.1018.   [3] *OC*, vol.4, p.583.
[4] Cicero, *De officiis*, Bk 1, 142; (Eng. transl. by J. Higginbotham, *Cicero on Moral Obligation*, London, 1967); from a letter (1736) to M. Barillot, librarian at Geneva, we learn that Rousseau had ordered Cicero's *Opera omnia*; see *Correspondance complète de Jean-Jacques Rousseau*, ed. R.A. Leigh, Geneva and London, 1965–85, vol.1., pp.37–42.   [5] *Lexicon totius latinitatis*, ed. Aegidio Forcellini, Bononia, 1965.

to find and preserve peace without order. Thus, 'the peace of men is orderly harmony. The peace of the home is the orderly harmony of command and obedience on the part of those who live together. The peace of the city is the orderly harmony of command and obedience on the part of the citizens.' To bring a just order into being – and this alone can ensure peace – it is necessary to allocate things to their proper place, taking into account those respects in which they are equal or unequal: 'Ordo est parium dispariumque rerum sua cuique loca tribuens dispositio.'

In the sixteenth century, those who wrote on the subject took the image of order as 'suum locum' and transformed it into a series of gradations, an appropriate hierarchy which comprehended all the creatures in existence. In the natural universe, as in society, the absence of, or overturning of, positions, brings chaos and disorder. The order and well-being of the universe – and thus also of society – require that degree and rank should be respected and that no part of the whole should abandon the place assigned to it. In this context, the speech of Ulysses in Shakespeare's *Troilus and Cressida* provides an example:

> The heavens themselves, the planets and this center
> observe degree priority and place
> Insisture, course, proportion, season, form
> Office and custom, in all line of order;
> And therefore is the glorious planet Sol
> In noble eminence enthron'd and spher'd
> Amidst the others whose med'cinable eye
> Corrects the ill aspects of planets evil
> And posts like the commandement of a king,
> Sans check, to good and bad. But when the planets
> In evil mixture to disorder wander,
> What plagues and what portents, what mutiny
> . . . O, when degree is shak'd
> Which is the ladder to all high designs,
> The enterprise is sick . . .
> Take but degree away, untune that string,
> And, hark, what discord follows. Each thing meets
> In mere oppugnancy.[6]

The idea that social order is a small part of the larger cosmic order developed in the seventeenth century into 'Cosmic Toryism', to use

---

[6] Shakespeare, *Troilus and Cressida*, Act 1, sc.3, 11. 91–104 (ed. H.N. Hillebrand, Philadelphia and London, pp.53–4).

Willey's definition.[7] According to this view each man is forced to accept his place in society since social order requires – and in this it is an exact parallel of what happens in the universe – that differences of rank should be respected and preserved just as they are. If it were not so the body politic, like the universe, would fall into chaos.

The idea that there are varying degrees of inequality amongst men does not always lead to cosmic conservatism. For example, Pufendorf, in the chapter of his *Law of nature and of peoples* entitled 'On the obli-gation laid upon all men to regard each other as equal by nature', notes that nature has endowed men with bodily and mental gifts to an infinitely varied degree.[8] But this natural inequality should not be transformed into a moral inequality. For Pufendorf, the fact that men occupy different ranks because of their various natural qualities does not excuse the existence of moral inequalities. The problem to which political right should address itself is consequently that of defining a principle capable of introducing a 'well-ordered harmony' into the infinite variety of degrees of merit. For Pufendorf this principle con-sists in the idea of equality before the law. This, however, does not mean that the order which reigns in the universe and in society does not involve different degrees of merit, a system of ranking and the existence of differences between individuals.

In the eighteenth century the idea of order as degree formed an essential part of the theory of the Great Chain of Being.[9] Rousseau was well acquainted with this theory but he did not share the 'con-tinuum' view espoused by Leibniz.[10] According to this interpretation the continuity and plenitude of the universe are such that it would be impossible to intercalate other classes of being between those already existing. To be consistent with the principle of continuity one must assume that the entire series of natural beings forms no more than one single chain and that the various classes are so closely interlinked that it becomes almost impossible to distinguish clearly, by the senses or by the imagination, the point where one begins and the other ends. The borderline between the species is therefore very imprecise.[11]

[7] B. Willey, *Eighteenth century background. Studies on the idea of nature in the thought of the period*, London, 1946, ch.3.

[8] Pufendorf, *Le Droit de la nature et des gens*, transl. by J. Barbeyrac, Amsterdam, H. Schelte and J. Kuyper, 1712, vol.1, Bk. 3, ch.2, s.2, p.310.

[9] As Lovejoy noted, the theory of the 'Great Chain of Being' was as influential in the Enlightenment as the theory of evolution was to be in European culture at the end of the nineteenth century; see A.O. Lovejoy, *The Great Chain of Being*, Harvard, 1978, 14th edn, p.184.   [10] Ibid., p.145.

[11] *Profession de foi du vicaire savoyard*, *OC*, vol.4, p.580.

For Rousseau, by contrast, the divine wisdom has not only established universal order by creating an ideal niche for each species to inhabit, but has also taken care to preserve this harmony. Consequently, the differences between the species have been clearly demarcated:

Even the act of procreation, producing living bodies of determinate form, is shrouded in mystery for the human mind; the insurmountable barrier that nature has placed between the various species, so that they remain distinct from each other, is a clear indication of its intentions. Not satisfied with merely establishing order, it also took firm measures to prevent anything upsetting that order.[12]

If political order were to be seen in the same light, the conclusion would be that inequality amongst men, which arises from the fact that they come from different ranks in society, is necessary for the preservation of the body politic. Moreover, these differences in social standing should be made manifest and men should not try to leave the place to which fate or their industrious life has assigned them in order to occupy a more elevated position, for to do so would be to undermine the order of things. Rousseau never actually went on to draw these conclusions from his conception of natural order. Nevertheless, he states several times that in certain instances it is better for men to accept the place where they are rather than to seek to escape from it.[13]

The cosmic dimension and the relation between the species has an important part to play in the theory of inequality. If we analyse the transition from the natural state to civil society, it is to be noted that the disorder which characterizes the latter comes about when men seek to attain a more elevated position and are no longer content with the place they already have. Thus, disorder springs from pride and the desire to be more highly esteemed and honoured than others. This kind of pride, which should not be confused with a just sense of one's

---

[12] Ibid., 'In spite of all the care taken by Montaigne and Pope to ennoble instinct, there nevertheless always remained a big gap between it and Reason . . . Yet, we do not know of any being to fill the gap between the animals and ourselves.' Rousseau to François Joseph de Conzié, Comte des Charmettes, 17 January 1742, *Correspondance complète de Jean-Jacques Rousseau*, ed. R.A. Leigh, 43 vols., Geneva and Oxford, 1965–85, vol.4, letter no. 43, pp.132–3.

[13] 'Oh, man!', says Rousseau in *Emile*, 'Live your own life and you will no longer be wretched. Keep to your appointed place in the order of nature and nothing can tear you from it . . .' *Emile*, *OC*, vol.4, p.308 (transl. B. Foxley, Everyman, 1910), p.47. Rousseau also adds, in a later part of his description of the Olympic Games of Pythagoras's time, that it is better to watch men contending for honours than to participate in the contest yourself, Ibid., p.525.

own worth as a man, is the source of disorder. The idea that pride is the principal cause of disorder has a long history which can be traced back at least as far as the church Fathers. In the eighteenth century this idea had been taken up again by Pope, one of the most ardent defenders of the idea of the Great Chain of Being.

In the *Essay on man* he states that pride is a 'sin against the laws of order', that is to say, against the hierarchical principle. Because of this vice men seek to elevate themselves to places more lofty than those which nature has in view for them: 'Pride still is aiming at the blest abodes, men would be angels, angels would be gods.'[14]

Pride, ambition, the desire to distinguish oneself, start to take root in the hearts of men, from the moment when they begin to live in society. It is not a question of natural passions, as these arise from life in society and are therefore artificial. Nevertheless, one should note that (following the ideal order of Rousseau's reconstruction), when the feeling of pride and the idea of superiority first appear, they are connected with relations between men. These are born when man compares himself with other natural beings – especially the animals. The comparison between man and the animals does not concern man as an individual, but the human species. What is at issue here is to which of the many ranks which make up the universe as created by the Divine Wisdom it is appropriate to assign the human species.

It is at this level that the ideas of excellence, pre-eminence and superiority first make their appearance. For this reason it is useful to analyse Rousseau's theory of inequality from the perspective of order as hierarchy. Savage man, we read in the *Second discourse*, 'lived surrounded by other animals and he soon found it essential to compete with them in strength and skill'. In this struggle he learnt to 'combat the other animals, when it proved necessary', and he developed his intelligence in this struggle for survival. As soon as he began to excel almost all the animals, even those which were stronger than him, he became aware of his superiority:

Thus, the first time he looked into himself he felt the emotion of pride; and at a time when he scarce knew how to distinguish the different orders of beings

---

[14] Quoted by A.O. Lovejoy in his article '"Pride" in eighteenth-century thought', in *Essays in the history of ideas*, Baltimore, 1978, p.63. Diderot annotated the French translation of Pope's *Essay on man*. In this translation (Silhouette) the text which we have quoted is translated as follows: 'L'orgueil vise toujours aux demeures célestes: les hommes voudraient être des anges, et les anges des dieux. Si les anges qui ont aspiré à être dieux sont tombés, les hommes qui aspirent à être anges sont rebelles; et qui veut renverser les lois et l'ordre, pèche contre la cause éternelle', in Diderot, *Oeuvres complètes*, vol.1, 'le modèle anglais', Paris, 1982, pp.200–1.

by looking upon his species as of the highest order, he prepared the way for assuming pre-eminence as an individual.[15]

From the first moment when man looks at himself and compares himself with the animals he gains a feeling of superiority. For the first time he has an intimation of his own identity. This consciousness of his own great worth becomes even more acute as the talents acquired living in society with his fellows are developed:

If man lived in isolation, his situation would be little better than any of the other animals. It is through mutual social contacts with others that his incomparable mental powers have developed and the excellence of his nature is made manifest.[16]

In the order of the universe, man is subordinate only to God. On the earth he feels himself to be the king of all the other animals and made in the image of the king of the universe. The pride he feels as he contemplates his place in the hierarchy of being is no more than a first manifestation of the same passion which will later impel each individual to try and excel the others.

Rousseau was not the first to have noted the relation between 'pride of species' and individual pride. Man's superiority over the animals was the subject of a very lively discussion in the seventeenth and eighteenth centuries. The aptness of the title 'the king of the earth' was questioned by various philosophers and moralists.

For example, Pierre Charron had devoted a chapter of his principal work, *On wisdom*, to a comparison between man and the animals, from the moral point of view. His position is a fairly moderate one. He neither accepts the argument that man is superior to all other creatures and can justly call himself the master of the earth, nor the one which would have it that man is but a subordinate part of nature. In his view, men are not generally capable of understanding their true place with regard to the animals for they are almost always unjust, either towards their fellows or to God.

Those who maintain that man is a superior being argue that man has spiritual qualities no animal can pretend to. Moreover, man regards slavery and captivity as a moral affront, while animals will often seem quite ready to accept such indignities without protest. In short, the superiority of man lies in his ability to exercise the most sublime moral virtues.

Charron counters this by instancing those occasions when animals

---

[15] *Discours sur l'inégalité*, *OC*, vol.3, p.166 (transl. Cole, 1952, p.349).
[16] *De l'état de nature*, *OC*, vol.3, p.477.

exhibit a degree of gratitude, magnanimity or generosity sufficient to put many men to shame. By contrast, 'there is no animal in existence so unjust, ungrateful, lacking in feeling, treacherous and perfidious, given to lying and deception that it may be compared with man'.[17] Animals do not experience the 'unnatural and empty' passions which drive men to wrong their fellows and wage war amongst themselves: 'there is more harmony to be found amongst serpents and wild beasts than amongst men', ('Maior serpentum ferarumque concordia quam hominum'). Charron concludes that men have no grounds for claiming superiority or authority over the animal kingdom. Moreover, the life of this would-be monarch of the earth is often more pitiful than that of his 'subjects'. It is true that man has a greater quickness of mind and understanding, but to balance this 'he is subject to a thousand ills, which play no part in the experience of animals: inconstancy, irresolution, superstition, anxiety about things to come, ambition, avarice, envy, curiosity, spite, lies, a world of uncontrolled appetites, of discontent and boredom'.

Man's higher faculties and his reason of which he is so proud serve only to plague him with innumerable misfortunes and sufferings. Animals live in harmony with nature, they are contented, live at liberty, free from anxiety and show moderation in all things. By observing them the wise man could learn the value of simplicity, innocence and natural gentleness – qualities now lost to human society, stifled by man's 'artificial inventions'. Consequently, relations between man and the animals should not resemble those of a tyrant with his subjects.

These ideas are very close to Rousseau's, especially when he draws attention to the ills which the misuse of reason and the existence of artificial passions bring to men, who as a result are often more wretched than savages and animals.[18]

At the beginning of the eighteenth century, those who rejected the picture of man as master of the earth voiced their dissent in terms even more uncompromising than those employed by Charron. In particular, they emphasized man's moral degradation. In the writings of the moralists one finds many examples of just such a negative view of man as this. Boileau, with whose works Rousseau was well acquainted, devoted one of his *Satires* to a refutation of the argument put by a

[17] Pierre Charron, *De la sagesse*, in *Toutes les oeuvres de Pierre Charron*, Paris, 1635, Bk 1, ch.24, s.12; see G. Pire, 'J.-J. Rousseau lecteur de Pierre Charron', in the *Revue de littérature comparée*, 42 (1962), p.484ff.
[18] See *Discours sur l'inégalité*, *OC*, vol.3, pp.202–8 (note 9).

'Doctor of the Sorbonne', that man deserved the highest place on earth.[19] For Boileau, the link between individual pride and the pride of species is very clear: the one who boasts the title of ruler of the earth is driven by his pride to seek the honours which would elevate him above his fellows.

Bernard de Mandeville, in his famous *Fable of the bees*, was another who noted that the idea that man by nature excelled all the animals was no more than a piece of flattery concocted by philosophers. By heaping praise on the all-embracing human spirit, and asserting the superiority of man's rational soul, they caused the feeling of pride and the desire for honour to grow ever stronger within the heart of man.[20]

Many other examples in this vein could be provided but let us now consider Rousseau's position. In several of his writings Rousseau proclaims the supremacy of man over all other creatures. Indeed, he alone is capable of grasping the totality in a unified way and of bringing into a common focus the public world of collectivities and the private world of individuals. Since man is the only creature capable of relating everything else to himself, it is not absurd to imagine that everything is made for him.

Rousseau zealously defends the view that man is king of the universe and he rejects any philosophy that refuses to contemplate the uniqueness of man's place in the universe:

So, it is true that man is the ruler of the earth, his dwelling place, for, not only does he tame all the animals, not only does he employ the earth's raw materials for his industry, but he is the one creature on earth who can do this and, through the power of thought, he even takes possession of the stars, although he is unable to approach them ... What? I have the power to observe and understand the animal kingdom in all its complexity, I have a feeling for order, beauty, virtue, I can contemplate the universe and thus think the thoughts of the one who controls all things, I not only have the capacity to love the good, but also to do it, and I compare myself with the animals![21]

---

[19] 'Of all the animals who rise in the air, who walk on the earth, or swim in the sea, from Paris to Peru, from Japan to Rome, the most foolish of all, in my opinion, is man.' Boileau adds in the same Satire that man believes himself to be the ruler of the earth but is really under the yoke of his passions: 'Ambition, Love, Avarice or Hatred have his spirit in chains like a convict.' As he cannot govern himself he has even less reason to proclaim his superiority over all the other species. Nicolas Boileau-Despréaux, Satire 8, in *Satires*, Paris, 1952.

[20] Bernard de Mandeville, *The fable of the bees or private vices, publik benefits*, London, 1714, especially p.151.   [21] *Profession de foi du vicaire savoyard*, *OC*, vol.4, p.582.

The position of the human species in the universe is, without dispute, the highest and man can hardly fail to be satisfied with the place he holds in the order of things. However, man should not permit this awareness of his elevated rank to make him arrogant. Indeed, none of the merit for his noble faculties is due to him, for it is God who has created him thus and, instead of succumbing to pride, he should, rather, render homage to his Maker's goodness and power. The fact that Rousseau acknowledges the excellence of the human species in comparison with all other creatures does not mean that he is willing to condone overweening pride. On the contrary, the only lesson that man should derive from contemplating his rank in the universe is the need for humility. Rousseau accepts the idea of the pre-eminence of the human species but does not find that sufficient justification for man being proud of himself as a species. By contrast, he sees a place for individual pride. If this distinction is not kept in mind, the ideas of the *Profession de foi du vicaire savoyard* quoted above will seem quite contradictory to those of the *Lettres morales*. Whereas in the former he had defended the proposition that man is master of the earth, this viewpoint is clearly rejected in the latter:

Let us be reticent concerning the virtues of our species but let us take a proper pride in ourselves as individuals. Let us not say in the foolishness of our pride that man is ruler of the earth, that sun, stars, firmament, air, earth and sea are made for his pleasure, that crops grow in order that he may be fed, that the animals' only reason for living is so that he can devour them; according to this logic, each one of us, having as we do within us this fierce thirst for happiness, excellence and perfection, might argue that the rest of mankind has been created for us and us alone, and that the purpose of all created things is fulfilled in ourselves.[22]

The conclusion arrived at in this extract suggests a comparison with the *Discourse on inequality*: man who, as a member of his species, considers himself to be the master of the world would also, as an individual, like to have pride of place over his fellows. The question of the place of humanity in the order of things should not, therefore, be a source of human pride.

Man may legitimately feel proud because he possesses the most sublime inner feeling – his conscience – providing that he learns to listen to its voice. This feeling is the 'true title of nobility which nature has engraved in the heart of man'. It is through his conscience that man has learnt to distinguish between justice and injustice, to love virtue

---

[22] *Lettres morales, OC*, vol.4, p.1100.

and scorn vice. This 'divine instinct' which is common to all men, is the reason why they are made in the image of God. It is to conscience alone that they owe their moral liberty and their superiority over the animal kingdom:

If it were not for thee [Conscience], I could find within me no other force capable of raising me above the level of the beasts, except, perhaps, that I enjoy the doubtful privilege of wandering endlessly from error to error, the eyes of my understanding being darkened and my Reason confused and uncertain.[23]

It is not by virtue of the rank he occupies in the system of things nor through his intellectual powers that man can be said to excel other creatures. He owes his dignity to his virtue and his virtue alone. The pride he feels as a member of his species, which is based on the possession of skills of different sorts, is the germ of the desire to receive distinction and be elevated above his fellows. On the other hand, the pride of the individual, which is rooted in virtue and conscience, leads the individual to live in peace and harmony with others. It is the first kind of pride only which is the source of disorder; the second is the principle of order and justice amongst men.

Thus Rousseau finds it possible to argue that man occupies an exalted position in the hierarchy of beings while refusing to countenance the pride of species, which is nothing other than vain ambition in another guise. The concept of order as hierarchy has made possible the reconstruction of a very important but often neglected aspect of Rousseau's theory of inequality. The following pages attempt to draw out the implications of this theory for individual relations. This entails the focussing of attention away from the cosmic dimension, which is the context for the relationship between man and the rest of creation. The theory now focusses, not on the relationships of human beings as a species with other species of the animal kingdom, but of individuals with each other. The object of study is now society; not the Great Chain of Being. What is at issue is not the identity of man in general, but his identity as an individual. However, even if the dimension of the problem has changed, there are remarkable similarities between the cosmic level, which was the first object of analysis, and the social level. In each case the central issue has to do with order conceived as a hierarchy. It will be helpful if the theory of inequality is seen in this light.

[23] Ibid., p.1111.

Natural inequalities and artificial inequalities

The fact that there is an almost infinite variety of differences between man was a commonplace for most of the writers in the seventeenth and eighteenth centuries who devoted themselves to a study of human nature. On the level of theory, Rousseau's analysis of the problem of inequality has much in common with those writers. The point at which he resembles them most is in the distinction – and this is fundamental for Rousseau – between natural and artificial inequality. In order to place Rousseau's thought in the intellectual context of the period and to shed light not only on his intellectual debts but also on those aspects of his thought which are truly original, some consideration will now be given to certain writers who most apparently exercised an influence on him.

The idea that the members of the human race vary so much amongst themselves that it is impossible to find two individuals of equal merit was almost a commonplace amongst the moralists of the period. Moreover, it was considered essential, if one was to arrive at a true understanding of man, first to analyse the qualities which made men different from one another. The categories which are relevant to any consideration of the kinds of inequalities which mark men off from one another, are rooted, for the majority of writers, in the concepts of essence and accident, or in the somewhat similar concepts of nature and the artificial. The qualities thought of as essential (or natural) are those which are unalterable and are beyond the scope of the human will. Those differences which are deemed to be accidental (or artificial) are based on qualities which are dependent on human activity.

A systematic classification of differences based on the categories of the 'essential' and the 'accidental' is to be found in Charron, in the chapter of *On wisdom* entitled 'On the differences between men in general'. The main differences between men, he writes, may be subdivided in the following manner:

First natural, and essential, and universally true of all men's minds and bodies. The second, natural and mainly essential, which is not acquired, involves the power and range of the intellect. The third, which is accidental, refers to the state, condition and duty, and has to do with superiority and inferiority. The fourth is accidental and refers to the profession and condition of life. The fifth and final one is connected with the blessings bestowed either by nature or by fortune.[24]

[24] Charron, *De la sagesse*, Bk 1, ch.41.

The typology is further developed and each class is then divided into more specific groups. The same method is applied to the differences, this time accidental, of degree, of social standing and public responsibilities. If comparison is made of the subdivisions into which Charron divides each of the main 'types' of inequality, it is possible to see this as a general anthropology of the ways in which men differ. Nevertheless, he does not proceed to an analysis of the causes of inequality (notably accidental inequalities) and he does not consider in any depth, as Rousseau will later do, the links between the various forms of inequality.

Although there is this difference of approach, it should be noted that the division between the qualities of mind or of body, on the one hand, and the differences of rank and social status on the other will be taken over more or less completely by Rousseau. While the qualities of body or of mind are described as natural, the inequalities of rank and social status are said to be accidental or artificial. They are artificial because subject to change. But what is even more important is that these inequalities give rise to 'natural envy' and are a source of 'conflict and slandering or ceaseless complaining'. By contrast, the 'natural' differences produce neither envy nor disputes.

More detailed remarks could be made here on the inequalities comprehended by the terms 'greatness' and 'smallness' and those others which are connected with prestige, fame and wealth which, for Charron, are inequalities arising from, at the same time, chance and natural causes. But for the moment the argument can best be taken further by turning to another writer in whom one finds (although from a point of view very different from that of Charron) a distinction between natural and artificial inequalities. This writer is Hobbes.

In the first book of *De cive*, which deals with the condition of man in his natural state, we find the famous assertion that all men are by nature equal and that the inequality which one observes amongst them has been introduced by the civil laws, that is to say, by artifice:

They are equals, who can do equal things one against the other but they who can do the greatest things, namely, kill, can do equal things. All men therefore among themselves are by nature equals; the inequality we can now discern hath its spring from the civil law.[25]

For Hobbes, differing degrees of talent or different natural gifts of body or mind take second place (which does not mean that they are

[25] Thomas Hobbes, *Philosophical rudiments concerning government and society*, ch.1, s.3; *The English works of Thomas Hobbes*, vol.2, ed. W. Molesworth, London, 1966.

not important) in comparison with an equal capacity that all men have
to harm their neighbour. *Leviathan* is more explicit on this subject
than *De cive*:

And as to the faculties of the mind setting aside the arts grounded upon
words, and especially that skill of proceeding upon general, and infallible
rules, called science . . . I find yet a greater equality amongst men than that of
strength. For prudence is but experience; which equal time equally bestows
on all men, in those things they equally apply themselves unto.[26]

What, then, is really important is the ability men have to harm and
to wreak havoc in the lives of others, destroying their goods and
depriving them of their liberty. To behave in accordance with the
principles of natural equality means, for Hobbes, nothing more nor
less than acting in a prudent fashion. The man who acts prudently is
the one who 'rightly values his powers'. By contrast, he who considers
himself superior to other men and overestimates his strength acts in a
way which is quite opposed to natural equality. Such a man believes
that he has a right to demand more honour and respect than other
men and to act as he pleases.[27]

Hobbes's argument that men are born equal and that inequality is a
product of civil law was flatly opposed by Pufendorf. It will be useful
to look at these criticisms more closely, since Rousseau appropriates
several of the arguments for himself. Pufendorf reverses Hobbes's
scheme of things: men are unequal by birth as far as the qualities of
body or mind are concerned; the task of bringing about equality
depends for its successful accomplishment on the artifice of law.

Pufendorf's case against Hobbes is developed in a chapter of the
Law of nature and of peoples, the title of which, 'The obligation laid upon
all men to regard themselves as equal by birth', seems to repeat word
for word the following extract of *De cive*: 'That men by birth are all
equal'. In reality, however, the two propositions are very different:

---

[26] Thomas Hobbes, *Leviathan or the Matter, form and power of a commonwealth ecclesiastical
and civil*, in *The English works of Thomas Hobbes*, vol.3, Part 1, ch.13.
[27] Barbeyrac who, with Cumberland, is one of the astutest of Hobbes's critics, has provided us with a very accurate interpretation of this concept of natural equality.
Hobbes, he says, was concerned only with the equality of natural powers, inasmuch
as this equality, which can be described as *purely physical*, causes men to fear each
other; he notes that all the consequences of this may be reduced to a maxim of
Prudence, which is that one should restrain oneself from rashly insulting others,
because, since they are as strong as we are, they can return the same to us with
interest. See the commentary to Samuel le Baron de Pufendorf, *Le Droit de la nature et
des gens*, translated from Latin by Jean Barbeyrac, Amsterdam, H. Schelte and J.
Kuyper, 1712, vol.1, Bk 3, ch.2, s.2, note n.3 of the translator.

Pufendorf's is normative while Hobbes's is descriptive, and this difference encapsulates the divergence between the two doctrines.

Pufendorf rejects the contention that inequality defined as prudence arises as a consequence of men judging their abilities too highly. It is not difficult for an unbiased observer to see that some men are more intellectually gifted, more skilful and wiser than others. The mental faculties are naturally different and experience is not enough to make up for this. Pufendorf writes that

One constantly finds that certain individuals are better able to grasp the consequences of a given principle, put into practice more successfully what they have learnt from observation and judge more intelligently points of similarity or difference obtaining in specific cases. How is it that often when two men have been involved in the same activity for the same period of time, one demonstrates outstanding ability, while the other stays as stupid as he was born, however long he stays at the task?[28]

For Pufendorf, the antithesis between the equality which characterizes man's natural ability and the inequality introduced by civil laws, which is the picture painted by Hobbes, is too simple. Civil laws do not make men stronger or cleverer; they only make superficial changes to his condition and have a bearing on his social status and the honours he enjoys. The point of departure of political theory should be natural inequality; moreover, the creation of a well-regulated *respublica* requires that the infinite variety of degrees of merit to which nature has assigned different men should be harmonized in a systematic way. The only principle which, in Pufendorf's view, is able to bring into being a just order from the many natural inequalities is 'equality under the law', or 'moral equality'. Once this principle is respected, even the inequalities which spring from the fact that some have been more lavishly endowed by nature in body or mind, or have more possessions and wealth than others, will cease to promote dissension amongst men, as happens when these differences are also a source of moral inequality.

One can see in embryo in these arguments of Pufendorf's Rousseau's famous principle that natural inequalities should not be allowed to develop into moral or legal inequalities. It is also very clear that the distinction between natural and moral inequalities which forms the basis of Rousseau's doctrine also corresponds to the distinction made by Pufendorf. For each of them it is nature and the natural

---

[28] Pufendorf, *Le Droit de la nature et des gens*, 1712, Bk 3, ch.2, s.2.

history of society which produces and reproduces differences amongst men, and it is the task of law, or more precisely, political science, to bring about equality. On this point Rousseau distances himself from Hobbes and is close to the viewpoint of the natural-law theorists. The passage in the *Discourse on inequality* in which he explains the differences between 'natural or physical' and moral and political equality is illuminating on this subject.

I conceive that there are two kinds of inequality among the human species; one, which I call natural or physical, because it is established by nature, and consists in a difference of age, health, bodily strength, and the qualities of the mind or of the soul: and another, which may be called moral or political inequality, because it depends on a kind of convention, and is established, or at least authorised by the consent of men. This latter consists of the different privileges, which some men enjoy to the prejudice of others; such as that of being more rich, more honoured, more powerful or even in a position to exact obedience.[29]

The uniqueness and originality of Rousseau's theory, in comparison with Pufendorf's, lies in the fact that he is not content merely to describe inequalities, as was the case with Charron and most of the other modern moralists. Neither is his a doctrine which is simply prescriptive in that it sets out to distinguish between just and unjust forms of inequality. Rousseau manages to compound each of these viewpoints in a single vision. In particular, he sets himself the task of explaining why these *differences* are transformed into forms of *moral inequality*. That is to say he attempts to show how it is that these differences become important for individuals. This aspect of Rousseau's theory can be seen as an analysis of the conditions which make it possible for individuals to form their own personal identity. In fact, awareness of oneself as an individual develops through the activity of comparing oneself with others, which gives rise to ideas of inequality. In this respect the first problem to be faced is what is the exact meaning of this 'convention' or 'agreement' which is the basis of moral and political inequality.

Difference and inequality

Real equality is only conceivable, for Rousseau, in the natural state, when people do not depend on one another:

[29] *Discours sur l'origine de l'inégalité*, *OC*, vol.3, p.131 (transl. Cole, 1952, p.333).

Since it is impossible in this state of Nature that the difference between man and man should be great enough to make one dependent on another, there is in fact in this state of Nature an actual and indestructible equality.[30]

There are differences between men in the natural state, but not inequality: men have different mental and, more particularly, bodily gifts; there are differing degrees of strengths, beauty and skill. Nature has not been even-handed in distributing its gifts. It is true that the 'natural' differences which are evident amongst men are in reality much less natural than one might suppose: 'It is in fact easy to see that many of the differences which distinguish men are merely the effects of habit and the different methods of life men adopt in society.'[31]

This statement, which seems to go against Pufendorf's view, does not mean that natural differences do not exist at all. On the contrary, these differences exist in the natural state and persist even in the civil state. But these differences have no importance for men who live in the natural state. In this state, which is for Rousseau a theoretical reconstruction,[32] it is imagined that men are living in solitude and without any enduring social ties. True equality can exist only when society has not yet developed. In this state those who are most favoured by nature are unable to gain thereby. The fact that they excel in natural gifts is of no special help to them. Let us imagine, writes Rousseau, one man who is stronger than another; what can the stronger do to the other? He can, of course, take possession of the fruit that his weaker brother has gathered, the game he has killed, and deprive him of the cave which provided him with shelter; but, he concludes, 'how would he ever be able to exact obedience, and what ties of dependence could there be among men without possessions?'[33] To reduce someone to a state of servitude, even though he may be weaker, would carry with it the risk of exposing oneself to a number of difficulties which would outweigh the advantages that could be gained. Beauty itself, which in the civil state is one of the most important determinants of superiority or inferiority, is of no importance. Since love is but a natural impulse to be satisfied with no matter whom, beauty and the other qualities do not count. For the male 'any woman will do' and the selection of a mate does not involve comparison.

[30] *Emile, OC*, vol.4, p.524 (transl. Foxley, 1974, p.197).
[31] *Discours sur l'inégalité, OC*, vol.3, p.160 (transl. Cole, 1952, p.347).
[32] Ibid., pp.132–3.   [33] Ibid., p.161 (transl. Cole, 1952, p.347).

Contrary to what Pufendorf believes, man does not, by nature, have any feelings of self-esteem. For Rousseau, natural man may well realize that another has harmed him, but he has not formed the concept of having been 'wronged'. Consequently, he is incapable of experiencing resentment, and this is equally true of other feelings, such as vanity, consideration for others, esteem and scorn.

If, like Rousseau, one imagines men who do not live in society, it will be clear that these men do not have cause to compare themselves with others. The absence of comparison is precisely the reason why natural differences are not important and remain as differences without developing into a form of inequality. Since men do not compare themselves with others, they do not form the concepts of superiority, excellence, or pre-eminence. It is possible to imagine a hypothetical case in which a man may have truly outstanding talents but is quite unaware of the fact. He would not even succumb to pride. As soon as men begin to live together, they immediately start to notice each other and make comparisons. Rousseau develops this theme in the *Discourse on inequality*, and he also touches on it in *Emile*: 'Hitherto, my Emile', he writes, 'has thought only of himself, so his first glance at his equals leads him to compare himself with them.'[34]

When man leaves behind the sphere of the purely natural, he enters a world where comparison is the norm. So long as man lives alone he lives in perfect equality, but in this state of equality he is unable to acquire an individual identity. Each man who lives in the natural state is simply *a* man.

It is possible to have a species identity which is formed by comparison with other natural creatures. When he looks at the animals and compares himself with them, natural man is led to formulate the concept of difference. But no member of the species is capable of considering himself as an individual *different from* the others, either from the point of view of morality (the ideas of good and evil not being applicable to men in isolation), or from the point of view of other endowments of mind or body. The reason they cannot see themselves as different is that they are incapable of making comparisons; this is also why savage man would not be able to recognize any of his fellows as an individual even if he were to meet him two or three times. Now it follows that a man who cannot be recognized as an individual has no

[34] *Emile, OC*, vol.4, p.523 (transl. Foxley, 1974, p.197).

individual identity. Perfect equality, therefore, has its price: it rules out the very concept of the individual.

In addition to the *Discourse on inequality*, the same argument is, as has already been stated, presented in *Emile*, in the section which discusses the way in which personality is formed. But there is also another work which puts forward the idea that individual identity is not possible without some kind of social relationship. This occurs in Rousseau's final autobiographical writings, where he reveals himself in all the concreteness of his individual existence, although one should not too readily equate what he says in the context of an investigation into the evolution of society with his thoughts about himself interacting with his contemporaries.

Jean-Jacques is not a man living in the natural state who has known nothing but solitude. He is now living alone, having once lived in society, and he is writing for posterity so that men should know what this Jean-Jacques was really like. The natural savage never had any individual identity; Jean-Jacques's intention is to assert his true identity and in so doing to counter the errors, as he calls them, of his contemporaries. On this question he states, on many occasions, that he is the only one in possession of this particular consciousness, able to say what Jean-Jacques Rousseau is really like. In the solitude of nature he can, at last, listen to the gentle voice of conscience and it is only to this voice that he feels the need to respond. Far from the disorder which reigns amongst men, far from the prejudices and the warring opinions of others, Rousseau has been able to rediscover the natural order and abandon himself to it. But here again he finds himself faced with the problem of his personal identity. For men who live in society the answer to the question 'who are you?' is easy enough: everyone can reply by saying who he is in relation to others. In the solitude of nature, completely out of contact with other men, it is difficult to find an answer to the question 'who are you?' and this is precisely the question posed by the ageing and solitary Rousseau.

Here am I, then, alone upon the earth, having no brother, or neighbour, or friend, or society but myself: the most sociable and loving of human beings has been proscribed by unanimous agreement. They have sought in the refinements of their hatred whatever torment could be most cruel to my sensitive soul, and they have violently broken all the links which attached them to me; I would fain have loved men in despite of themselves; they have been able to conceal themselves from my affection only by ceasing to be men. They are the strangers, unknown, nothing finally for me, because they have wished it. But I, detached from them and from all, what am I in myself?[35]

The tone of this passage is quite different from his more theoretical writings: the dramatic tone so appropriate to personal experience has replaced carefully constructed argument. The relation between self and other is transformed with the change from the analysis of a social system to an account of lived experience. Yet, in each case, the same basic truth is apparent, namely, that the construction of individual identity requires society. Without society there is no such thing as the individual. Rousseau does not believe that the individual exists out-side and independent of society. In spite of its illustrious paternity, the traditional charge levelled against him that he is an 'atomist' does not apply in Rousseau's case.[36] The individual only makes his appearance with the coming of society and it is only in and through society that the collectivity 'men' becomes different individuals, conscious of being different and capable of realizing themselves as such. Thus, individual identity emerges as a result of mutual comparison. But with this activity comes the desire to excel, and competition makes its entry into the world of men. So, while the price to be paid for the peace which reigns in the natural state was the non-existence of individual identity, the price of individual identity is disorder.

The summary Rousseau provides towards the end of the *Discourse on inequality* of the way inequality has developed opens with the distinc-tion between rich and poor and concludes by referring to the master–slave relationship:

If we follow the progress of inequality in these various revolutions, we shall find that the establishment of laws and of the right of property was its first term, the institution of magistracy the second, and the conversion of legitimate into arbitrary power the third and last; so that the condition of rich and poor was authorised by the first period; that of powerful and weak the second; and only by the third that of master and slave, which is the last degree of inequality, and the term at which all the rest remain when they have got so

[35] *Les Rêveries du promeneur solitaire, OC*, vol.1, p.995. J. Charvet, *The social problem in the philosophy of Rousseau*, Cambridge, 1974 (in particular the first chapter: 'Natural goodness and social corruption') explains very precisely Rousseau's argument con-cerning the link between the development of social relationships and the formation of the individual identity. According to Charvet, Rousseau considered that man in the natural state was already possessed of a personal identity, which, in my view, does not accurately represent Rousseau's thinking.

[36] This originates with Hegel; See N. Bobbio, *Studi hegeliani*, Turin, 1981; especially the chapter 'Hegel e il giusnaturalismo'.

far, till the government is either entirely dissolved by new revolutions, or brought back again to legitimacy.[37]

This text has sometimes been interpreted as suggesting that inequality amongst men is a product of the institution of private property. His famous denunciation of the inaugurator of the institution of private property also seems to support the view that Rousseau's theory of inequality revolves around the issue of private property.[38]

In his theory the transition from a state in which, although men are different, these differences count for nothing (their effect on men's lives being virtually nil) to a state of inequality is made possible through the formation of a community which makes judgements, awards its esteem, compares and thus assigns values to individual qualities, to actions and objects. No individual can be appreciated, esteemed or valued except through the agency of others. It is because society exists that there can be a hierarchy of values.

The act of ascribing a certain value to individuals, which has as its necessary consequence their incorporation into a hierarchical system, cannot take place unless there is a regular pattern of social relations and unless men are aware of their fellows. In the natural state men do not have any reason to compare themselves with others and so do not make comparative judgements about each other. For this reason differences between people are not important: people pay no attention to them and so they have no value.

As soon as men begin to compare themselves with others, other people's opinions become important. The dynamics of esteem places each individual in a different slot, according to the values placed upon him. The problem of 'placement', which does not occur in the natural state, comes to the fore as soon as men live in society. The desire to

---

[37] *Discours sur l'inégalité*, *OC*, vol.3, p.187 (transl. Cole, 1952, p.359).
[38] This is Dahrendorf's position in his study 'On the origin of inequality among men', in *Essays in the theory of society*, London, 1968, pp.158–9: 'The assumption of an original state of equality, and the explanation of the origin of inequality in terms of private property, remained unchallenged from Rousseau to Lorentz von Stein and Karl Marx.' Rousseau and Marx, adds Dahrendorf, 'are unrivalled in their radical insistence on property as the sole cause of social inequality'. From a completely different viewpoint, E. Griffin-Collard sees the theory of inequality in Rousseau in terms of the equilibrium of the body politic: see 'L'Egalité: condition pour l'harmonie sociale pour J.-J. Rousseau' in *L'Egalité*, ed. P. Foriers, C. Perelman, Brussels, 1971, pp.258–71. My interpretation of Rousseau's theory of inequality is quite different, as the reader will see, from both Dahrendorf's and that of Griffin-Collard: see also R. Derathé, *La Place et l'importance de la notion d'égalité dans la doctrine politique de J.-J. Rousseau*, in R.A. Leigh (ed.), *Rousseau after two hundred years*, Cambridge, 1982, pp.55–63.

have the esteem of one's fellows brings with it the desire to occupy the highest ranks in the hierarchy of public esteem and honour. No sooner has Emile turned his gaze on others and begun to compare himself with them than, 'this act immediately arouses in him the desire for preferment'.[39]

Rousseau studies the first manifestations of the feelings of preference and of the activity of comparison at the most rudimentary level of interpersonal relations, that is in the relationship between a man and a woman, or, more precisely, in the dynamics of love. When for the first time more systematic relations develop between human beings, love ceases to be merely physical and acquires a broader scope. The passion of love loses its vague generality and focusses on specific individuals who are preferred to others. By contrast, when human beings live in solitude and meet only occasionally, one is as good as another. The fact that one person is preferred to another comes about because comparisons are made and ideas of merit and beauty have developed for the first time. The fact that people now have preferment and the move towards individualism bring in their train other ideas and other feelings previously unknown:

The preferment you grant others is something you would also like for yourself; love must be reciprocated. To be loved you must make yourself lovable; to be the one who is loved best of all you must make yourself worthier of that love than your rival, in fact, more than any rival, at least in the eyes of your beloved. This is why people start looking at their fellow beings; this is why they compare themselves with them; hence also arise emulation, rivalry and jealousy.[40]

What is true of the microcosm of relations between the sexes is a pointer to the other passions which were to develop later in the broader sphere of society. The analysis of inequality therefore has as its point of departure the most fundamental level of human relations, long before the institution of property comes into existence and with it the birth of economic interests. In addition, Rousseau paints a picture of the primitive festival which he describes as the birthplace of comparison and preference.[41] Beauty, the harmony of movement,

---

[39] *Emile, OC*, vol.4, p.523.   [40] *Emile, OC*, vol.4, p.494.
[41] *Discours sur l'inégalité, OC*, vol.3, p.169 (transl. Cole, 1952, p.351). On Rousseau's use of the metaphor of the festival see Jean Starobinsky's note in n.4 on the page quoted above; see also by the same author *Jean-Jacques Rousseau. La transparence et l'obstacle*, Paris, 1971, pp.114–20.

individual voices, all attract the eyes of the onlookers and arouse their admiration:

Each one began to consider the rest, and to wish to be considered in turn; and thus a value came to be attached to public esteem. Whoever sang or danced best, whoever was the most handsome, the strongest, the most dexterous, or the most eloquent, came to be of most consideration; and this was the first step towards inequality, and at the same time towards vice. From these first distinctions arose on the one side vanity and contempt and on the other shame and envy; and the fermentation caused by these new leavens ended by producing combinations fatal to innocence and happiness.[42]

The historical development of inequality is marked by several stages. The account that appears in the *Second discourse* describes the imaginary history of the formation of different types of inequality and their reciprocal relations. The story is of an evolution which has all the traits of natural history. Men are drawn into the universe of comparison in a spontaneous way. Like the birth of society, the creation of inequality itself is the result of chance circumstances which actually occurred but which might equally well not have happened in the course of time.

Once society exists, it is inevitable that men will start to make comparisons between themselves and others. As soon as men were united in a single society, says Rousseau, 'they were forced to compare themselves with one another and take into account the differences which they encountered from the continual social interactions which now occurred between each man and his neighbour'.[43]

The continued use that men make of each other is the basis of comparison and esteem. The term 'use' suggests an analogy with the value accorded to material objects. Use, or more accurately utility, is the basis of the comparison between objects and especially of the price that is put on them. When, as they come together to form a society, men start to be useful to one another, they acquire value and thus it is that they begin to ascribe to one another different degrees of esteem. In this respect Rousseau's theory of inequality reveals underlying links with the philosophical thought of the period, and it is this latter which must now receive some consideration in order to acknowledge the extent of Rousseau's intellectual indebtedness, while at the same time drawing attention to the originality of his views.

[42] *Discours sur l'inégalité*, pp.169–70 (transl. Cole, 1952, p.351).
[43] Ibid., pp.188–9 (transl. ibid, p.360).

The price of things and the value of men

Amongst the sources of Rousseau's theory of inequality, the works of the moralists merit particular attention – in particular those who analysed the birth of the feeling of preference and who set out to explain the concrete mechanisms involved in the process of human evaluation.

In the work of Duclos, a writer for whom Rousseau has a high regard, there are observations which recall others which appear in the *Discourse on inequality*. Duclos, like Rousseau, notes that love is a passion based on preference:

When I speak of love I do not mean ardent, indeterminate desire, which will take anything as its nourishment, that nothing can stabilize and which is incapable of choice by virtue of its own violence: I speak of the person who directs his will towards an object to the exclusion of all others.[44]

Love, the most acute of all feelings, is an expression of a personal interest and can even be useful to the individual, if the term is used to include not only material services and benefits but also 'pleasure and everything which can affect us in an agreeable way, although it may subsequently be harmful to us in reality'. Love, friendship and esteem do, however, have one thing in common: they are all based on comparison and on an expression of preference.

The generally agreed price of things, writes Duclos, is arrived at in accordance with the public interest, which is what causes a just assessment to crystallize from the flux of general opinion. 'What', he asks, 'do we mean by esteem, if it is not a feeling which urges upon us what is useful to society'. Sentiments of love and esteem, therefore, are based on the idea of utility: in the case of love it is something useful to the individual; as for esteem, it is usefulness to society that is referred to.

Like Rousseau, Duclos often compares the sense of worth typically found in modern society with that associated with people in the past. Amongst the Lacedemonians and the Romans, for example, supreme worth called forth respect, and respect was a recognition of the superiority of someone. When respect was gained through merit and virtue, then respect and contempt were two totally contradictory terms. In our time, however, respect is something which one acquires through social status and has nothing to do with personal qualities.

[44] Duclos, *Considérations sur les moeurs de ce siècle*, 7th edn, Paris, 1780, p.281.

This means that it is possible to respect the rank while having contempt for the person. Duclos emphasizes the common ground between love, respect and esteem. In each case worth is attributed to someone and, in the case of respect, a worth which goes beyond one's own sense of self-worth. The logic which underlies the status system is very similar to the logic which operates in economics in the fixing of prices. On this point Duclos anticipates Rousseau's ideas. In the chapter of the *Considérations* on 'honour and respect', he states that 'to esteem someone means no more nor less than to value'. Judgements about the real price of objects are based on their utility as well as their rarity. On the other hand, in judging the worth of a person, the extent to which there are others like them plays no part in the judgement. The moral value of a person does not diminish just because there are several others like him. By contrast, the price of an object goes down if there is a plentiful supply. Duclos maintains that this is the only difference between human worth and the price of goods.

The idea that moral worth could be assessed on the basis of its rarity value was almost a commonplace for the moralists of the seventeenth and eighteenth centuries. Virtue, although very rare, is not, in fact, highly prized. 'If it be usual to be strongly impressed by things that are scarce, why are we so little impressed by virtue?'[45] By contrast, qualities of body and mind are valued very highly:

Men do not value very highly the affections of the heart, but idolize the gifts of body and mind. A person who, in speaking of himself, would coolly say that he is good, constant, faithful, sincere, just, and grateful, does not imagine he offends against modesty; but he would not venture to say that he is sprightly, or that he has fine teeth or a soft skin; that would be rather too much.[46]

But when men are judged from the point of view of their abilities, rarity value now becomes very important. In this instance men are viewed like objects. In addition to considering whether a man's worth was in any way comparable to the economic price of goods, the moralists strongly emphasized the desire, universally shared, to obtain the esteem and respect of one's fellows. This is why men become slaves to opinion.

Men passionately desire to have the esteem and high regard of their fellows. The fact that it is talent and general worth which attract men's attention provides a strong motive for demonstrating, and what is

[45] La Bruyère, *Les Caractères ou les moeurs de ce siècle*, Paris, 1964 (1st edn, 1688), p.117 ('Du mérite personnel') (transl. Henri van Laun, 1929, p.45).
[46] Ibid., p.308 ('De l'homme') (transl., ibid., p.301).

more, proving, that one has outstanding qualities of body and mind. The analogy between enjoying the esteem of other men and the economic value set upon goods is once more evident. If goods are to be admired and bought they must be put on display with the utmost skill; so should men be able to show themselves to advantage if they are to gain preferment.

Even if one lacks talent one should pretend to have it. As esteem is something which comes to us from outside, it does not matter much whether there is really anything there to admire or not. What counts is other men's opinion. A perverse consequence of this logic is that the more vain men are, the more they will seek to parade themselves; the more true qualities and talents they possess, the less likely they are to seek to impress.[47]

This, as will readily be apparent, is Rousseau's famous argument about the gap between reality and appearance, which he develops in the *Discourse on inequality*.[48] And it is also from the moralists of his time that he borrows his other argument, no less renowned, concerning the tyranny of opinion. Rousseau, therefore, is greatly indebted to these writers, but it would be misleading to look no further than the moralists. There is another writer who should not be overlooked, one who has also analysed the structure of the inner feeling of preference and the way it is formed (although from a point of view quite different from that of the moralists), and that is none other than Hobbes.[49]

The relevant text to consider here is the tenth chapter of *Leviathan* which is entitled 'Of power, worth, dignity, honour and worthiness'. This is where Hobbes sets out his definition of human worth – a definition which contains within it the relation between the value placed on men and the economic price of goods:

The *value*, or worth of a man, is as of all other things, his price; that is to say, so much as would be given for the use of his power: and therefore is not absolute; but a thing dependent on the need and judgement of another.[50]

Men cannot decide for themselves the level of recognition their qualities should attract. It is also others who set a price on us and decide what we are worth. What Rousseau refers to as our dependence on the opinion of others, Hobbes defines even more precisely:

[47] Ibid., p.115 ('Du mérite personnel').   [48] *Discours sur l'inégalité, OC*, vol.3, p.174.
[49] For a more general reconstruction of the sources of the *Second discourse*, it will be helpful to consult J. Morel's work, 'Recherches sur les sources du "Discours sur . . . l'inégalité parmi les hommes"', *Annales de la Société Jean-Jacques Rousseau*, 5 (1909), pp.119–98.   [50] Hobbes, *Leviathan*, Part 1, ch.10.

As in other things, so in men, not the seller, but the buyer determines the price. For let a man, as most men do, rate themselves at the highest value they can; yet their true value is no more than it is esteemed by others.

If a man rates another more highly than himself, then, following Hobbes, we should say that the former honours the latter. He ascribes superior status to him. For Hobbes there is not only the inequality established by the civil law. It is true that 'public worth' is a mark of superiority which the sovereign authority attributes to those it judges worthy of it.[51] Nevertheless, Hobbes makes explicit reference, providing several examples to prove his point, that men are by nature in the habit of ascribing degrees of merit to one another without the sovereign authority's involvement. The honours which have originated in this way are those which Hobbes refers to as 'natural'. Since to invest someone with status in this way is to recognize in them a degree of superiority we see that Hobbes allows for a form of inequality which is based on the opinion of men and not on the will of the sovereign.

If a man is held in high esteem this is entirely due to his being invested with power, or rather that others see him in this light: 'honour consists only in the opinion of power'. A man's power is, for Hobbes, the means he has at a given moment which will make it possible for him to obtain no matter what benefit some time in the future. This power may be divided into natural and instrumental power.

Natural power is the eminence of the faculties of body or mind: as extraordinary strength, form, prudence, arts, eloquence, liberality, nobility. *Instrumentals* are those powers, which acquired by these, or by fortune, are means and instruments to acquire more: as riches, reputation, friends, and the secret working of God, which men call good luck.[52]

These different forms of power confer honour on their possessor, and the qualities which ensure the enjoyment of honour are also a mark of a given individual's superiority over others.[53]

On this point Hobbes and Rousseau are totally at one. For each of them the different forms of human inequality, those which play a significant part in the private life of the individual, are those which

---

[51] See on this subject the definition of honour expounded by Mandeville in the *Fable of the bees*, p.50.   [52] Hobbes, *Leviathan*, Part 1, ch.10.

[53] In a work published a few years after the *Discours sur l'inégalité*, John Millar wrote: 'Superiority in strength, courage and other personal accomplishments is the first circumstance by which any single person is raised to be the leader of a clan, and by which he is enabled to maintain his authority'; *Observations concerning the distinction of ranks in society*, London, 1771, p.123.

have as their source the evaluation and re-evaluation that men are constantly making, the one of the other. This is the activity which sets a comparative value on qualities of body and mind, just as it does for such social advantages as wealth, rank and birth, or when it erects a status hierarchy wherein individuals find their place on the basis of these comparisons.

The resemblance between the theories of the two men is not called into question by the fact that in other respects there are many dissimilarities between the author of *Leviathan* and the author of the *Discourse on inequality*. Hobbes sees the problem of social distinction and the fact that all the men hanker after it mainly in the context of the formation and dissolution of the state. In fact, he refers to the struggle for wealth, status and the sources of power as one of the reasons for the state of warfare. Moreover, he sees ambition as one of the causes of the internal decay of the state[54] and what is ambition but the desire for status and preferment? These ideas, which after all are quite commonplace may also be found in Rousseau, but in the latter case much closer attention is paid to the effect that moral inequality has on the life of individuals. When Hobbes analyses the origins of inequality, he does so as a detached observer without introducing moral judgements into his description. This approach leads him to state that any great and difficult accomplishment, whether the act is just or unjust, brings honour to the author of the deed for the simple reason that it is a manifestation of great power. By contrast, Rousseau makes a distinction between a form of status which is built on virtuous deeds and another more specious variety which comes from the possession of power, wealth and good birth, and this is a fundamental aspect of this theory. Moreover, as will shortly be made clear, the distinction between these two forms of status corresponds exactly to the distinction between legitimate and illegitimate forms of inequality. On this point Rousseau allies himself with Pufendorf, who had subjected Hobbes's thesis to far-reaching criticism.

Pufendorf explains very clearly how esteem serves to create a convenient system of relations of superiority and inferiority amongst men and how individuals compare themselves with others and thus establish a status hierarchy. The way in which moral inequality develops is very much like the way in which prices are regulated. As

---

[54] Hobbes, *Philosophical rudiments*, ch.12, s.10.

has already been pointed out, this idea was current in the writings of the moralists; but Pufendorf elaborates it with much greater theoretical precision:

Thus we find there is a near affinity between the two most noble branches of moral quantity, esteem and price. The first is considered in persons, the second in things; because as the one is the rate of persons in common life, so the other is of things. And the chief reason why a price was set upon things was that, when they were to be exchanged or removed from one person to another, they might be better compared with one another: so the end intended by esteem is, that we may be able to form a comparison between men, by setting as it were a value upon them and in consequence to establish a becoming order and distance between them, whenever they should happen to be united; it evidently appearing that nothing was more absolutely inconsistent with the convenience of life than an universal equality.[55]

To know if two things are equal or not, one must compare, estimate and measure them, and to do this it is necessary to attribute quantities to the objects concerned. Quantity is essentially the property attributed to objects for the purpose of comparison. The price of goods and the individual's reputation are moral quantities on the basis of which it is possible to make comparisons. Price and reputation apply to goods and individuals, respectively, in so far as they enter into a system of economic or social relations.

Thus it is not possible to conceive of inequality existing amongst men outside of the social order, that is to say where the conditions which alone make reciprocal comparison possible do not apply. For Pufendorf, the differing degrees of excellence of body and mind are objective differences easily apparent to a detached observer. However, if – to take a hypothetical case – they are not subject to comparison or evaluation, they have no significance and are not transformed into inequalities of *value*.

This is the same argument as was employed by Hobbes, but Pufendorf distances himself from Hobbes when he states that there is something which cannot be estimated in terms of money, and this 'inestimable' quality is man himself in so far as he is a 'free individual'. If an individual has a price, then it implies that he can be sold, but if that were so he would no longer be free. This is what Pufendorf means

[55] Pufendorf, *Droit de la nature et des gens*, Bk 8, ch.4, s.1 ('Of the power of the sovereign, in determining the value of subjects').

when he says that liberty is a good beyond all comparison.[56] Even though there is this important difference between men and things on this question of whether their value can be assessed or not, the broad analogy still holds good. Just as the price of goods is determined by the buyer and not the seller, so esteem is something which emanates from others and not from ourselves. 'For though a man may', and here Pufendorf is at one with Hobbes, 'set what value he pleases upon himself as the seller does upon his commodities; yet as in these, it is the buyer at last who determines the price; so the value of men is no more than as others are pleased to rate it.'[57]

Pufendorf considers that prestige may be classified in two ways: there is the ordinary variety (estime simple), or natural honour, and then there is high prestige, or honour properly speaking (estime de distinction). In the natural state to have ordinary prestige is to have the good opinion of others: a man earns this by treating his fellows with the degree of civility expected of him. In civic societies ordinary prestige may be defined as having the reputation of a straightforward and honest citizen in the context of the laws and customs of the country.

Both those who live in the natural state and those in the civil state may enjoy high prestige. Whereas ordinary prestige is indicative of a relationship of equals, high prestige is evidence of a state of inequality.[58]

For Rousseau, it is unthinkable that men in the natural state should employ a system of status relations, whether of the ordinary or the prestigious kind. This difference springs from different ways of conceiving the natural state. For Rousseau it is a hypothetical condition of isolation and solitude. For Pufendorf, on the other hand, the natural state is one in which men live together. For Pufendorf it is possible, therefore, to make the kind of comparison which provides the basis for the system of high prestige, which, according to Rousseau, could not possibly exist in the natural state.

This difference should not, however, be allowed to conceal the more general theoretical affinity between the two, namely, that the

---

[56] Rousseau criticizes Pufendorf (and Grotius) because he is willing to grant the legitimacy of a bargain entered into by someone who in doing so gives up his liberty: 'Pufendorf says that just as one can transfer one's goods to someone else by means of agreements and contracts, so it is possible to hand over your liberty to someone else.' *Discours sur l'inégalité*, *OC*, vol.3, p.183; see also the *Contrat social*, Bk 1, ch.4 ('De l'esclavage').

[57] Pufendorf, *Le Droit de la nature et des gens*, Bk 8, ch.4, s.11.

[58] Ibid., ch.4, s.24; see also Hobbes, *Leviathan*, Part 1, ch.10.

relations of inequality arise from the varying degrees of esteem that each person receives from his fellows. It is only through 'public esteem' that certain personal qualities acquire value as signs of high or low status. Thus society conceived as a collectivity which evaluates is the necessary theatre, so to speak, of moral inequalities.

For this reason no personal quality ever has absolute value. Everything depends on the criteria adopted by each community for the purpose of measuring and evaluating. Pufendorf observed that in certain countries civic values are held to be the most excellent, while in others military virtue is valued more highly. Even though the criteria by which men are judged are not absolute, the members of a given community are capable of making a distinction between what is praiseworthy and what is not.[59]

Pufendorf's approach to the question of inequality which arises from communal value judgements is not a purely descriptive one. Unlike Hobbes, he is not satisfied with enumerating the qualities which attract admiration. He tackles the problem of whether social distinction has any rational basis and he lists the titles which make men worthy of honour and esteem.

Within this perspective he criticizes Hobbes's thesis that social distinction is no more than the prestige which an individual gains through his power. Hobbes does not see any difference between the prestige which unjust acts attract and that acquired through just deeds. Pufendorf argues that distinction and honour are linked with power, defining that term as the capacity to produce results. What does not have any effect on human life is not worthy of esteem. But a powerful man who channels his power to achieve evil ends does not really enjoy the esteem of those who suffer misfortune through the exercise of that power. The emotion here is fear rather than admiration. Fear, concludes Pufendorf, may find expression in flattery or be transformed into hatred, but neither of these is the same as sincere respect: 'Power alone, as it implies an ability to do harm, does not include any such excellence in it, as is naturally proper to command a sincere respect; for all respect has a mixture of love in it, but a power to do harm can certainly procure nothing but hate.'[60]

Rousseau allies himself with Pufendorf rather than Hobbes; he also confronts the moral and political problem of whether inequality is

---

[59] Pufendorf, *Le Droit de la nature et des gens*, Bk 8, ch.4, s.14.
[60] Ibid., ch.4, s.18.

legitimate or not, but he shares common ground with each of the other two in his belief that there are forms of inequality which originate in the opinion of the public at large and not in the system of inequality established by the sovereign.

For Rousseau, men first experience inequality when they find that the opinions others form of them are often totally at variance. This is where the theoretical construct of the 'natural state' proves so valuable as a heuristic device. Rousseau uses the concept of the natural state as an ideal type to enable him to speculate what might be the nature of human inequality if society did not exist. By using his reason to reconstruct the way in which society evolved from the initial state of isolation, he was able to trace the different stages of a 'rational history' (parallel and hypothetical) of inequality. Rousseau's redefinition of the concept of the natural state represents a theoretical development by means of which he revises and makes more coherent the model employed by Hobbes and Pufendorf to explain the way in which moral inequality first arose amongst men. Pufendorf and Hobbes admit the existence of natural inequalities. For Hobbes, even men in the natural state wish to be admired and to receive acclaim.[61] Likewise Pufendorf states that high prestige and basic respect for one's fellows both exist in the natural state and in civil society alike.

Rousseau agrees that relations of superiority and inferiority in the moral sphere exist only because men compare themselves with others and observe the behaviour of their fellows. But for him this is not a natural process because moral inequality is conceivable only in the social context. To take the activities of making comparison and exercising preference for one thing over another as they occur in their most rudimentary form in the least complicated aspects of social life, that is to say in love and in social festivities, even here it is clear that neither of these activities exists in the natural state. If the concept of the natural state expands to embrace the notion of isolation as well as independence, the problem of inequality appears in a different light. From this new viewpoint, what in Pufendorf was implicit is now spelt out clearly, namely, that it makes sense to talk of individuals as being unequal only within a social context. When there is no society there may be differences but not moral inequality.

On our journey through life, we each form part of one or more social groups which may value us highly or else deem us to be of little

---

[61] Hobbes, *Philosophical rudiments*, ch.1, s.2.

worth. We also soon realize that others rate us highly because we have certain qualities and look down on us if we do not. For Rousseau, the existence of society implies the existence of a social group which has its own criteria for ranking individuals according to their relative worth. What men are or what they do outside their social group is of no consequence. Such a situation would be comparable in every respect to the (imaginary) case where objects exist but there was no such thing as a market or commerce. Considered in this light, Rousseau's theory of inequality takes on its full meaning.

At the beginning of the *Discourse on inequality* Rousseau makes the famous distinction between natural inequality, which derives from nature alone, and moral or political inequality, which rests upon 'a kind of convention' and which came into being, or was at least legitimized, by 'the consent of mankind'. This assertion that moral inequality in society depends on a kind of convention and that it is legitimized by the consent of men means that this inequality exists only in so far as it is recognized by others. Its existence is entirely bound up with the assessment that 'others' make of man's worth. Each man who was in the natural state simply a man, now in society becomes an *individual*, and, in particular, a *moral* individual. This moral dimension is shaped by the relations which the individual enjoys with his fellow beings and with society in general. This is why men living in the isolation of the natural state do not have moral qualities. They cannot be classed as good or evil, since from the moral point of view they are quite indistinguishable.[62]

But when an individual lives in society it is entirely appropriate to speak of moral qualities because these have to do with the relation of each individual with his fellows and with society in general. Since in this context it is possible to attribute moral qualities to others and individuals do in fact do so, each person receives his moral identity from the hands of his fellows.

For Rousseau, moral (and indeed aesthetic) qualities do not reside in the individual (or thing) in any atomistic way, but derive from the relations between the individual (or thing) in question and the whole of which he forms a part:

When you cast a philosophical eye on the interplay of all the parts of the vast universe, you soon realise that the beauty of each of the entities which together make up the whole does not lie in the part, itself, for its sole purpose

---

[62] *Discours sur l'inégalité*, *OC*, vol.3, p.152.

is to be set side by side with all its fellows which in their entirety constitute the excellence of the machine. The same is true of the moral order. Each man's vices and virtues do not concern him alone. Their true context is society and it is what they are with regard to order in general which confirms their essential character.[63]

In his dealings with others the individual may lead a blameless life or he may get into evil ways. In either case he has a moral identity – something which was lacking in the natural state. But it is not just an individual moral identity which men receive through their experience of life in society, for not only do they achieve a kind of self-definition in moral terms – their good or evil deeds being reflected back to them in the opinions of others – but through the same means they also come to know whether they are handsome, cowardly, clever or stupid, or again if they are rich or poor, strong or weak. In the natural state nobody could possibly give a reply to the question 'who are you?' but in society the answer is straightforward enough as also is the task of describing and identifying one's fellow citizens. So it is that each member of society has the capacity to develop an awareness of his own personal identity. Nevertheless, to know who we are, we must also know what we are for others.

For Rousseau, the process of socialization means attaining self-awareness by being sensitive to the opinion of others. In fact, even such attributes as beauty and the very meaning of our lives depend on what others think. Men in society do not rely on their own feelings, even when it comes to deciding whether they are in a good mood or not, but they find it necessary to consult the opinion of 'others'. By contrast, 'primitive man' who has no regard for the 'opinion of the rest of the world, can be made happy and satisfied with himself: he lives within himself; social man lives constantly outside himself and only knows how to live in the opinion of others, so that he seems to receive the consciousness of his own existence merely from the judgement of others concerning him'.[64]

Generally speaking, Rousseau thinks that being so dependent on the views of others is not a good thing – the exception being when the views in question are held by admirable and virtuous men – but, where there is no mutual esteem, no discernment, no openness to the existence of others, men are incapable of forming an individual identity. When a social order comes into existence, so too does inequality. Social relations assume the form of a status hierarchy which replaces

[63] *Des moeurs*, *OC*, vol.3, p.554.
[64] *Discours sur l'inégalité*, *OC*, vol.3, p.193 (transl. Cole, 1952, p.362).

the perfect equality of the natural state. In society natural differences become moral inequalities, but at the same time men can now acknowledge each other as separate individuals. Their identity is constructed from the perception others have of them, but it is acquired at the price of enslavement to the tyranny of opinion. The explanation Rousseau gives for the transformation of natural differences into social inequalities also accounts for the development of individual personality. The next task must be to show how this perspective allows him to develop a theory concerning the origin of social disorder.

Inequality and conflict

The *Dictionnaire de l'Académie française* (3rd edn, 1740) states that disorder 'is the absence of order, overturning, an upsetting, a confusion of things which are not in their true state, in their right place or arranged in the way they should be'. The same *Dictionnaire* goes on to speak of the conflict or dissension which may arise amongst people who were before united: 'this family was united; a slight conflict of interest has brought disorder to it'.[65]

The definition of the *Dictionnaire de l'Académie française* gives us the essence of Rousseau's idea of disorder. It offers three definitions which correspond to the three connotations which the term 'order' has: order as hierarchy, as a system (harmony), and as moderation. When disorder is opposed to order defined as harmony or agreement, it has the sense of mutual conflict between parties which belong to the same whole. This idea is particularly relevant to the situation of men in society, when each of them seeks his own ends at the expense of others and no one is concerned with the common good. When disorder is defined as the opposite of hierarchical order, it means that a person who should be ranked highly has, in fact, been given a lowly position. Disorder occurs when the ranking of individuals is based on principles which are not considered to be just. Finally, order as an absence of moderation means either disharmony or an attitude whch is not appropriate to the occasion. This is true of inner disorder which is manifest when unbridled passions hold sway in the heart of man. In such cases there is no harmony because the raging passions are in con-

---

[65] *Dictionnaire de l'Académie française*, 3rd edn. Paris, 1740.

flict with the rational part of the soul and so things are out of line because the passions should be subordinate to reason and not the other way round.

Rousseau's works provide several instances of this way of thinking about disorder and the most interesting examples are, perhaps, to be found in his autobiographical works. The experience of disorder and injustice is, in fact, one of the constant themes of the *Confessions* and Rousseau never loses an opportunity to express his feeling of moral revulsion at the detestable examples of inequality which one sees on every hand and which result in men being obliged to serve their fellows.

The best example of this – and one which is well known – is Rousseau's experience as the valet of the Count of Gouvon at Turin. During a sumptuous banquet in the Count's palace, the conversation turned to talk of the motto of the Solar family. Someone suggested that the motto contained a spelling error. Rousseau, who was standing behind the guests, smiled to himself, but said nothing. The Count noticed that his young valet would have liked to join in the conversation and told him he was free to express his opinion. Rousseau did not need to be asked twice and, thanks to his knowledge of French, he was able to interpret the motto correctly and explain that there was, in fact, no error. There was absolute silence and Rousseau writes: 'everyone was looking at me without saying a word', yet with so many eyes fixed upon him what struck him the most was the gaze of Mme de Breil, for it was the first time she had honoured him with her attention. 'This was', comments Rousseau, 'one of those all too rare occasions when the natural order of things is re-established and true merit, so long trampled underfoot by an unjust fate, is vindicated.'[66]

If one reads the *Confessions* carefully one notices that there are many occasions when a gaze such as this plays an important part in the narrative. Rousseau had already noted in the *Discourse on inequality* that this is the way men compare themselves with others, assessing their own worth in relation to that of others. Rousseau's elevation above the ignorant and overweening nobles who were present, though it lasted only a short time, was marked by this gaze they fixed upon him. For the first time others saw him as someone of note. The short-lived feeling of superiority Rousseau was now able to enjoy accords well with the natural order of things which requires virtue and merit to be held

[66] *Les Confessions, OC*, vol.1, pp.95–6.

in high repute. By contrast, the superiority enjoyed by the nobles, which was theirs by virtue of their birth and fortune was, for Rousseau, a mark of disorder, for it was an indication that something had gone awry.

In the episode from the *Confessions* referred to above, the link between disorder and inequality is straightforward enough, consisting as it does of a simple value judgement: the allocation of individuals to a specific place within a hierarchical system is an example of disorder because the principle on which it is based is deemed to be unjust.

However, the definition provided by the *Dictionnaire* implies yet another relationship between disorder and inequality. This disorder is no longer linked with the idea of hierarchy but with the notion of conflict. This relationship can best be expressed by saying that disorder consists in a state of disharmony amongst men, and this conflict springs from the quest for preferment. Rousseau holds that inordinate ambition comes to dominate the inner life of men from the moment when they acquire the habit of comparing themselves with others:

As soon as a man starts to compare himself with others, he automatically becomes their enemy, for when everyone is seized in his innermost being with the ambition to become richer, more powerful and happier than any of his rivals, then he cannot but view anyone who pursues the same goal as himself as a potential enemy, since he represents an obstacle to be overcome.[67]

Disorder is a by-product of the hatred and enmity generated when men engage in the struggle for pre-eminence. The prize they contend for here is not an absolute but a relative good. Wealth, esteem, respect and rank are valued by their possessors precisely because they have something which others do not have, or because they have a greater quantity of whatever it is they value than those they are comparing themselves with. Thus the concept of disorder embraces two subordinate ideas: the allocation of individuals to a particular level in the status hierarchy, and the notion of conflict:

As soon as we get used to comparing ourselves with others, allowing our gaze to move outwards from the self, but just to claim superiority over all others, it is impossible not to hate everything which excels us, everything which reduces our stature and restricts our scope, which by being something prevents us from being everything.[68]

---

[67] *De l'état de nature, OC*, vol.3, p.478.
[68] *Rousseau juge de Jean-Jacques, OC*, vol.1, p.806.

If men seek to surpass others, it is really in the hope that their superiority may be generally recognized. It is the reputation for excellence they hanker after rather than the quality itself. They desire, above all else, to be admired and looked up to. In the final analysis, the exalted position within society for which men are willing to sacrifice everything rests entirely upon the opinion of others and disorder is nothing other than competition for the high regard of others.

In Rousseau's opinion, the moralists considered self-interest to be the ruling passion of mankind. Self-interest here really refers to 'material self-interest', or the desire for material goods and wealth – to use the terms current at the time. As such, self-interest was not highly regarded. Rousseau, however, thought that this was going too far.[69] Correctly interpreted, material self-interest and the pursuit of wealth are not the dominant passion – there is something yet stronger which uses material goods and wealth as a means to an end, and this, says Rousseau, 'is the love of honour'.[70]

Thus, the cause of the state of mutual hostility, which so often characterizes men's relations, should be sought in the yearning for distinction rather than in the quest for material goods and wealth as such. The thirst for pre-eminence ('fureur de se distinguer') is not only the dominant passion, it is also the most universal. The portrayal of hostility and competition that society provides each day are a clear proof of this:

I could explain how much this universal desire for reputation, honours and advancement, which inflames us all, exercises and holds up to comparison our faculties and powers: how it excites and multiplies our passions, and, by creating universal competition and rivalry, or rather enmity, among men, occasions numberless failures, successes and disturbances of all kinds by making so many aspirants run the same course.[71]

The idea of man as a creature who craved esteem and good reputation above all else was current amongst the European moralists of the seventeenth and eighteenth centuries and once again the extent of Rousseau's indebtedness to them is apparent:

---

[69] See A. Hirschman, *The passions and the interests. Political arguments for capitalism before its triumph*, Princeton, 1977; see also J.A. Gunn, *Politics and the public interest in the seventeenth century*, London, 1969.   [70] *De l'honneur et de la vertu*, *OC*, vol.3, p.502.
[71] *Discours sur l'inégalité*, *OC*, vol.3, p.189 (transl. Cole, 1952, p.360).

All men in their hearts covet esteem, but are loath anyone should discover their anxiety to be esteemed . . . men are so full of themselves, that everything they do is connected with self; they like to be seen, to be shown about, even by those who do not know them.[72]

Moreover, when he observes that the antagonism between man and man springs from the fact that each strives to outdo the other, Rousseau is very close to Hobbes's viewpoint when he explains in *Leviathan* that 'men do not willingly live in society because they love their fellows, but because they desire honour and the satisfaction of their self-interest'. To use Hobbes's terms: 'profit or convenience' consists in 'pleasures conducing to sensuality'. But, above all, hostility between men arises from the craving for esteem, superior status and power, that is to say, for exclusive rewards which cannot be shared: 'Competition of riches, honour, command, or other power inclineth to contention, enmity, and war: because the way of one competitor, to the attaining of his desire, is to kill, subdue, supplant or repel the other.'[73]

For both Hobbes and Rousseau men value most those things which serve to set them apart from others, and it is the desire to be esteemed and respected more highly than one's fellows which is the root cause of most conflict. Pufendorf had also noted that the human spirit was afflicted by a moral 'sickness' and 'disease' which drove men to prize what was theirs and theirs alone and to pour scorn on those things which they shared with others: 'Generally we set a great value upon nothing but what raises us, in some measure, above the rank and condition of others.'[74]

Neither is Rousseau particularly original when he explains the desire for great wealth as an outward manifestation of the drive to achieve high status and respect, which he calls 'the hidden and ultimate goal which men pursue'. Great wealth is not an end in itself, but something sought after as a means to gain the respect of others and to enjoy the trappings of power: 'People do everything they can to get rich, but the real reason for this is that they want to be highly regarded.'[75]

[72] La Bruyère, *Les Caractères*, p.303 ('De l'homme') (transl. H. van Laun, 1929, p.295).
[73] Hobbes, *Leviathan*, Part 1, ch.11 and Part 2, ch.17; see also *De cive*, Bk 5, ch.5: 'man scarce esteems anything good, which hath not somewhat of eminence in the enjoyment, more than that which others do possess'.
[74] Pufendorf, *Droit de la nature et des gens*, Book 5, ch.1, s.6.
[75] *De l'honneur et de la vertu*, *OC*, vol.3, p.502.

Wealth is an object of esteem but of a kind which does not penetrate beyond surface appearances to make contact with the personal qualities of the one who possesses it. This is a very clear example of the way in which outward show can command respect. Montaigne, in a passage frequently quoted by writers in the eighteenth century, had noted how strange it was that men should be influenced by external trappings when judging their fellows, rather than see them as they really are.

It is quite extraordinary that, apart from ourselves, nothing else is valued otherwise than on the basis of its particular qualities. We praise a horse for its strength and agility . . . not for its harness; a greyhound for its swiftness, not for its collar, a bird for its wings, not for its harness and bells. Why should we not, in the same way, judge a man for his personal qualities? He has many servants, a fine palace, so much capital, he receives so much in rent; these things are all external to him, not part of his inner self.[76]

It is true that 'economic reward' may have come to someone as a result of his industry and thus may be considered as an indication of certain inner qualities. This is Pufendorf's view. He holds that wealth can be regarded as something that deserves respect in that the wealthy man could not have gained his wealth unless he had worked hard and also wealth may be used as an instrument of good.

Here Rousseau parts company with Pufendorf, for he holds that great wealth cannot be acquired through hard work, since the only thing to be hoped for by this means is a moderate degree of wealth. Even when profit is made in a perfectly legal way, it always comes at the expense of someone else who might have greater need of it; and as to the second point – the responsible use of wealth – this does not in itself merit the approval of mankind.

In the *Discours sur les richesses*, Rousseau comes down very firmly against 'Chrysophile', who advocated the pursuit of wealth as a means of doing good to those less fortunate than oneself:

I should like, you say, to be rich in order to make good use of wealth and if I desire to acquire possessions it is only for the pleasure that I derive from doing so and from helping those to whom fate has been unkind. As if the greatest virtue of all were not to avoid ill-doing. How is it possible to get rich without helping to impoverish someone else, and what can one find to say of a charitable man whose first act is to take all his neighbours' goods in order to have the pleasure of giving them alms.[77]

What lies behind the pursuit of a standard of living higher than is

---

[76] Quoted by Barbeyrac in his commentary on Pufendorf, *Le Droit de la nature et des gens*, Book 8, ch.4, note 4.   [77] *Discours sur les richesses*, ed. F. Bovet, Paris, 1853, p.13.

strictly necessary is the urge to excel over other people. So long as society is ordered in such a way that the wealthy are revered and the poor despised, men will never cease channelling all their efforts into the pursuit of wealth.

In the final analysis, Duclos had remarked in his *Considérations sur les moeurs de ce siècle*, the pride of the rich is well founded: 'If the rich come to believe that they are better than other men, are they so wrong? Is it not true that people show the same kind of regard, one might even say respect, for them, as for those whose rank enables them to command respect as of right?' Duclos arrives at a conclusion which seems to have been borrowed directly from Montaigne, which is that 'the judgements men make are entirely dependent on external appearances'.[78]

In a society in which gold meant nothing and wealth was not revered, no one would dream of devoting his time to the pursuit of either of these: after all, this was how it was in Sparta and in Rome during the republic. In these societies it was virtue and not the ostentation of wealth which attracted admiration, and this meant that men wanted to acquire virtue rather than wealth. But in so doing they were directed by self-interest just as much as those who, in another society, might place wealth before virtue. Deep down their motives are the same – self-interest or, more correctly, the desire for the esteem and respect of others. The only difference is the means adopted to attain these ends – means which vary in accordance with the particular criteria of excellence in vogue in the society in which they find themselves.

Duclos adds that 'men have but one unchanging inclination – the pursuit of their own self-interest: if this should go in the direction of virtue, they will be virtuous without effort, but if what they pursue is redefined in the light of new criteria, the disciple of virtue will become the slave of vice, without having to change his character: it is possible, while using the same colours, to paint either something beautiful or something monstrous.'[79]

Rousseau's debt to Duclos in this context cannot be questioned. For Rousseau, as for Duclos, the only way to incline men to virtue and to discourage them from the vanity of wealth is for there to be a transformation in the customs, that is to say, the criteria used by a community, in order to assess the relative worth of its members. Rousseau, also, when talking on this theme, makes reference to

[78] Duclos, *Considérations sur les moeurs de ce siècle*, 7th edn, Paris, 1780, p.198.
[79] Ibid., p.204.

Sparta and to the Roman republic as two models of communities where virtue was honoured and where men sought to be virtuous because this was the only way they could ensure that they would enjoy public esteem.

Duclos thought that the idea of a community along the lines of those which existed in Rome or Sparta was pure fantasy, while for Rousseau, this was by no means a Utopian dream:

What must be done, then, 'is to make sure that there is nothing to be gained, as far as creature comforts are concerned, by becoming rich, rather that this would entail a loss of esteem. This was the admirable result produced by law in Lacedemonia and custom in the early years of the Roman Republic; hence I conclude that these things are not beyond our reach.[80]

His conviction that a just society was possible rested upon the belief that by changing the ground-rules which govern the way rewards of status and esteem are meted out by society, individuals would also set themselves new goals, while still acting to further their own interests. This will be one of the topics for discussion in the third part of this study, but at present it is sufficient to note the important part played by such concepts as 'esteem', 'status' and 'honour' when Rousseau explains why disorder exists in society.

Men compete for goods which by general agreement are held to be valuable. Mutual hostility created by the necessity in which each individual finds himself to provide for his fundamental needs is not the source of disorder.[81] It is true that much human conflict is centred upon 'real' economic goods, such as land or cattle, but the unending conflict which blights men's social existence is not caused by the imperative laid upon man to satisfy his physical needs, nor is it caused by the pursuit of comfortable standards of living. The fundamental reason for this state of conflict is to be found in men's tireless pursuit of status, and the desire to be singled out from their fellows, to achieve which ends they seek to occupy those positions in society most likely to command such prizes.

Thus it is, that for Rousseau, as for other philosophers of his period,[82] human conflict and the unbridled pursuit of wealth, power and supremacy have almost nothing to do with the imperatives of nature. The individual, in his desire to improve his position on the

[80] *De l'honneur et de la vertu*, *OC*, vol.3, p.503.
[81] See on this subject the observations of V. Goldschmidt, *Anthropologie et politique. Les principes du système de Rousseau*, Paris, 1974, pp.542–65.
[82] It is interesting to compare Rousseau's arguments with what Adam Smith wrote in his *Theory of moral sentiments*, which appeared four years after the publication of the *Discourse on inequality*. For Smith, the desire to be placed in the highest rank may be

status ladder, is driven by a form of self-interest which has nothing to do with material goods as such. The benefits men hope to obtain for themselves when they strive so fiercely to rise on the social ladder are of a quite different kind, namely, the securing for themselves of the approval and respect of others.

It may be admitted that if others regard us highly we are more likely to be able to command 'material rewards'. Just as wealth frequently brings with it high status, so, too, high status is a gateway to the enjoyment of material goods.

Thus, conflict between men may take various forms. In the *Second discourse*, a distinction is made between the age dominated by competition for status alone and the following period in which the goal sought was not only social esteem but also material goods.[83] Rivalry in the first era was in a sense 'free' and it was characteristic of emergent society.

When private property was instituted, the 'innocent' form of competition for the respect of others was transformed into a competition for respect as a necessary means to obtain material rewards ('real goods'). Inequality, which had been based on esteem and honour alone, with the development of the institution of property rights now became real social inequality. The difference between these two forms of inequality is easy to describe: while the former is subject to variation and is still fluid, social inequality takes the form of a permanent structure. Chance may radically alter the situation of the individual – a man who is rich today may become poor tomorrow and vice-versa, but society itself will still be divided into rich and poor. The inequality which is based on wealth and 'economic goods' is much more firmly based than that which depends on personal qualities.[84]

explained by the pleasure men feel from being admired. It is because they seek to occupy the most elevated places that conflict arises between men: 'Of such mighty importance does it appear to be, in the imaginations of men, to stand in that situation which sets them most in the view of general sympathy and attention. And thus, place, that great object which divides the wives of aldermen, is the end of half the labours of human life and is the cause of all tumult and bustle, all the rapine and injustice, which avarice and ambition have introduced into this world' (ed. D.D. Raphael and A.L. Macfie, Oxford, 1976, p.57).

[83] See Goldschmidt, *Anthropologie et politique*, p.546.

[84] Another of Rousseau's contemporaries, J. Millar, wrote in his *Observations concerning the distinction of ranks in society*: 'The authority derived from wealth, as it is greater than that which arises from mere personal accomplishments, so it is also more stable and permanent. Extraordinary endowments, either of mind or body, can operate only during the life of the possessor and are seldom continued for any length of time in the same family. But a man usually transmits his fortune to his posterity, and along with it all the means of creating dependence which he enjoyed' (London, 1771, p.130).

This does not mean, however, that social disorder is the by-product of the competition for 'economic goods' rather than status. If men pursue material goods in an unrestrained fashion, this is because what they really desire is to obtain preferment which, once again, depends entirely on their reputation in the eyes of others.[85] Thus, the rivalry which sets men against each other, is, so to speak, a context in which the reward is recognition by others rather than the possession of material goods. The conflict is centred on personal identity and when men become rivals, determined that others will acknowledge their supremacy, what they really hope will happen is that others will grant them one identity rather than another.

This aspect of Rousseau's theory becomes even clearer if the famous distinction between self-love ('amour de soi') and egotism ('amour-propre') is looked at in greater detail.

While the former is an emotion which is 'always good and always in conformity with order',[86] the second is the cause of the disorder that afflicts mankind. The pursuit of preferment, which engenders hostility, first appears when what others think becomes something of prime importance:

[85] Kant was to use Rousseau's ideas in his description of the results produced by men's tendency to compare themselves with others, in *Die Religion innerhalb der Grenzen der blossen Vernunft* (1794) (*Immanuel Kants Werke*, Hildersheim, 1973, vol.6, pp. 165–6): 'The predisposition to humanity', writes Kant, 'can be brought under the general title of self-love ... which compares ('physischen, aber doch vergleichenden Selbstliebe'). That is to say, we judge our own happiness or unhappiness only by comparison with others ('sich nämlich nur in Vergleichung mit andern als glücklich oder unglücklich zu beurteilen'). 'Out of this self-love springs the inclination to acquire worth in the opinion of others.' From this arise all the vices which Kant calls the 'vices of culture' ('Laster der Kultur'): envy, jealousy, rivalry. All these passions are born, Kant thinks, from the fear that each of us has that others might gain a hated superiority over us and from the unjust desire to attain for ourselves such a position ('ungerechte Begierde'). As for the passions which make men hostile to each other, Kant does no more than spell out Rousseau's ideas: passions are not directed towards objects, but towards other men: 'Alle Leidenschaften aber sind immer nur von Menschen auf Menschen nicht auf Sachen gerichtete Begierden und man kann zu einem fruchtbaren Acker oder dergleichen Kuh zwar zur Benutzung derselben viel Neigung, aber keine Affektion ... haben; viel weniger eine Leidenschaft (*Anthropologie in pragmatischer Hinsicht* (1800), *Immanual Kants Werke*, Hildesheim, 1973, vol.8, pp.159). On the influence of Rousseau in Germany the reader will benefit from R. Trousson's study, 'J.-J. Rousseau et son oeuvre dans la presse périodique allemande de 1750 à 1800', *Dix-huitième siècle*, 1 (1969), pp. 227–64; on the relation between Rousseau and Kant see S. Ellemburg, 'Rousseau and Kant: principles of political right', in R.A. Leigh (ed.), *Rousseau after two hundred years*, Cambridge, 1982, pp.3–22; A. Levine, *The politics of autonomy. A Kantian reading of Rousseau's 'Social contract'*, Amherst, 1976; P. Pasqualucci, *Rousseau e Kant*, 2 vols., Milan, 1974–6.   [86] *Emile, OC*, vol.4, p.491 (transl. Foxley, 1974, p.174).

Self-love, which concerns itself only with ourselves, is content to satisfy our own needs; but selfishness, which is always comparing self with others, is never satisfied and never can be; for this feeling which prefers ourselves to others, requires that they should prefer us to themselves, which is impossible . . .[87]

A man can truly be called good if he has few needs and does not find it necessary to compare himself with others. If, on the other hand, he has many needs and 'sets great store on general opinion', he will have chosen the path of evil. In *Emile* the distinction between self-love and egotism corresponds to the opposition between 'having few needs' and 'having many needs'. In another work, written prior to *Emile*, Rousseau had distinguished between three kinds of need. The first refers to the means of subsistence: this kind, also known as 'physical needs', comes from nature and is limited to food and sleep. The second kind of need has nothing to do with survival, but with man's well-being. These needs are also known as 'appetites'. Though there is no absolute requirement that they should be satisfied, they are often more insistent than the first kind. While physical need can be defined as the body's need for food and sleep, the focus of our appetites is the luxury which gratifies the senses, comfort, sexual satisfaction and everything calculated to 'flatter our senses'. The third class of need is that which reflects our sensitivity to the opinions of others. The kind comes into existence only when the ones already mentioned have been gratified, but once it has appeared it soon becomes the focal point of a man's life. These needs are bound up with honour, a man's reputation, rank and nobility, that is to say, those objects of enjoyment which, in the last analysis, may be said to consist of enjoying the esteem of others and thus to be totally dependent on general opinion.

The last-mentioned category of needs is the only one which is the subject of egotism ('amour-propre') which Rousseau, in the *Discourse on inequality* defined as the 'true wellspring of honour'. As has already been noted, the individual acquires honour when others recognize his worth and grant him preferment. Now superiority, preferment, distinction are precisely the rewards coveted by the man ruled by egotism.

Rousseau holds that egotism is closely linked with ambition. We read in the *Dictionnaire de l'Académie française* that 'ambition is an inor-

[87] Ibid., p.493 (transl. ibid., p.174).

dinate desire for honour, glory, high status and distinction'. This definition exhibits a very close parallel with Rousseau's concept of egotism. Both ambition and egotism may be described as insatiable appetites. The anonymous *Dictionnaire philosophique*, for example, published in London in 1751, states that

ambition is a violent longing for honour and high standing. Of all the sicknesses which afflict the spirit, it is the one beyond all hope of cure: but the thirst of the man tormented by ambition is like that of the one who suffers from dropsy, it grows ever more acute even as the victim seeks to find some way of quenching it.[88]

and the same *Dictionnaire*, defines 'amour-propre' as the instinct which is responsible for the preservation and happiness of man. In Rousseau's terms, it corresponds to the concept of self-love; however, 'blind egotism' is there described, as it is by Rousseau, as the cause of all 'the evils which reign on earth'.

The link between ambition (or egotism) and honour is most clearly seen if we analyse the etymology of the word 'ambition'. The corresponding term in Latin is 'ambitio'. For this word the *Lexicon totius latinitatis* quotes two texts from Cicero: 'What shall I say concerning our ambition and desire for honours ('quid de nostris ambitionibus quid de cupiditate honorum loquar'); most wretched of all is the struggle for honours' ('miserrima omnino est ambitio honorum contentio': *Tusculan disputations*, 26.62). The definition of the word 'ambitiosus' is still more illuminating: 'he who seeks honour and canvasses support from individuals in order to gain support and favour is ambitious' ('ambitiosus est qui honores quaerit et prensat singulos ad captanda suffragia et favorem').

This definition of ambition may also be found in the writings of the modern moralists, and here the link between ambition and honour is clearly emphasized. In their case, the term 'ambition' refers to the same passion which Rousseau calls 'egotism' ('amour-propre'):

Ambition [says Charron] which is a hunger for honour and glory, an excessive and greedy desire for greatness, is the sweetest of passions . . . We think that we must embrace what is good and of all the things we value honour is valued the most highly, and that is why we pursue it with such fierce determination; the ambitious man longs to be the first, never looks behind him, always ahead at those who are before him, and the suffering he feels because one man takes

---

[88] (Chicaneau de Neuville), *Dictionnaire de philosophie ou introduction à la connaissance de l'homme*, London, 1751, p.8.

precedence over him is greater than the pleasure he gains from a thousand being left behind him.[89]

Ambition may produce good as well as evil results. It may impel men to heroic deeds or it may arouse enmity. In either case ambition works by comparison, and what it aspires to is a set of pure 'imaginary' rewards, to use Charron's definition. The connection between egotism and the pursuit of honour is also mentioned by Barbeyrac in his commentary on the *Droit de la guerre et de la paix* by Grotius. Rousseau was familiar with this work and it is very likely that he had read Barbeyrac's commentary.

In his treatment of 'the causes of war and particularly the right of self-defence and the protection of our possessions', Grotius had instanced slights on one's honour as a cause of war and as an offence calling for reparation. In this context Barbeyrac sees fit to make some comments on the 'disregard of honours'. The question was whether such disregard should be considered as a virtuous attitude or not. This issue was first raised in the interpretation of the passage in Aristotle (*Nicomachean Ethics*, Bk 4, ch. 9). According to Grenovius, one of the commentators on Aristotle's works, when Aristotle condemned the disregard of honours as evidence of the lack of civic spirit, he was not referring to civic honours, but to individual reputation. Here Grenovius agreed with Aristotle, because disregard for one's reputation with other people often leads the individual into dishonest ways, and causes him to adopt a disreputable and detestable mode of life.

According to Barbeyrac this was an erroneous interpretation. What Aristotle actually said was that those whose weakness it is to disregard any social recognition of their worth are not immoral; if they have a fault, it is that, though they deserve such recognition (which Aristotle regards as a good in itself), they deprive themselves of it because they do not consider themselves to merit it and fail to realize their true worth. They are not foolish, but merely indolent, held back by the modest opinion they have of themselves and their belief that they are incapable of admirable deeds.

Barbeyrac's view asserts the value of modesty. So long as one is ignorant of one's true worth, it is just as well not to lay claim too readily to the admiration of others. What usually happens is that men overestimate themselves rather than the reverse. It is at this point that Barbeyrac introduces the concept of 'amour-propre':

[89] Charron, *De la sagesse*, Bk 1, ch.20, p.70.

We will do well to think carefully about this to avoid the illusions that egotism ('amour-propre') may engender; there is every reason to believe that usually he who refuses to accept honours which he has earned does so out of modesty rather than through being indolent and disreputable.[90]

Rousseau does not consider that the effort involved in creating a good reputation for oneself is necessarily conducive to the attainment of the good life. In fact, men's opinions are often rendered suspect because of the existence of prejudice. They are the opinions of individuals who are also dominated by egotism. Others see only what they want to see. If a man desires to be just and morally upright, he should act not in conformity with the views of others, but according to the dictates of his conscience.[91] The only approval worth having is that of those who have learnt to judge wisely and are themselves virtuous. Like Barbeyrac, Rousseau sees egotism as an inordinate longing for social acclaim, something which he describes as the vanity of the world, being founded on nothing more solid than opinion. The distinction between real and imaginary goods plays an important part in Rousseau's explanation of social disorder. In fact, he emphasizes that disorder is completely artificial. Since the rewards for which men contend are based on nothing more substantial than opinion, the root cause of all social conflict is to be found in the warped judgements of mankind, not in any more fundamental flaw of nature.

Here, once again, Rousseau is borrowing the ideas of the natural law theorists, in particular Grotius. The distinction between 'real' and 'unreal' rewards was carefully set out in the *Droit de la guerre et de la paix*.[92] In the former category Grotius lists virtue and actions which are conducive to virtue. Other examples of 'real rewards' are things which are pleasant in themselves or likely to give pleasure. These he calls 'useful goods' and in the final analysis they may be described as the enjoyment of plenty. While the desire for rewards of the first variety produces no ill effects, the pursuit of the second kind may. Grotius includes among the 'imaginary goods' the desire for vengeance and the longing for preferment. Preferment, as Grotius notes, may mean that we are lifted above the common herd, but it has abolutely no connection with virtue and has no real use. The further these goods are from nature, the more shameful it is to harbour a desire for them.

[90] Hugues Grotius, *Le Droit de la guerre et de la paix*, 'new translation' by Jean Barbeyrac, Amsterdam, 1724, Bk 2, ch.17, s.22 (transl. anon., *The rights of war and peace*, London, 1738).   [91] *Emile, OC*, vol.4, p.671.
[92] Grotius, *Le Droit de la guerre*, Bk 2, ch.20, s.29 (transl. London, 1738).

The principle here is virtually the same as is to be found in Rousseau – the only difference being one of terminology: Rousseau calls 'goods of opinion' what Grotius calls 'imaginary goods'. In either case it is a question of relative or exclusive rewards which exist in the minds of others and which are based on comparison. These are the focus of enmity, hatred and jealousy. In this connection Grotius quotes St John, the apostle: 'the pride of life is a thirsting for vainglory and is quick to anger'. This passion is one of the main causes of the troubles which afflict humanity.

Ambition, or, to use Rousseau's term, egotism, is the real root of disorder because, of all passions, it is the most unrestrained and the greatest menace to human self-control. The desire for the things necessary to satisfy physical needs does not extend beyond a certain limit. By contrast, the 'urge to excel others' may drive men to extremes. Self-love is never a threat to order because, by its very nature, it is not given to excess. But egotism is inimical to order because it makes men intemperate, with the result that they live in a state of disorder.

Rousseau also makes the distinction between self-love – concern for the preservation of the individual – and egotism – obsession to attain superiority – on anthropological grounds. This is his theory of sensibility.

According to Rousseau there are two forms of human sensibility: physical (or organic) and moral (or active). Physical sensibility is governed by the ideas of pleasure and pain and is not merely concerned with self-preservation. This sensibility, like all natural needs, is common to all men, as members of the same species, quite independent of interpersonal relationships. Moral sensibility, on the other hand, is relevant to man in his relationships and is defined as 'the ability to direct our affections towards those whom we do not know well'.[93]

Moral sensibility may have negative as well as positive effects – positive when it leads us to expand and strengthen our innermost self, negative when it attempts to reduce and cause to contract the circle of the lived experience of others. Rousseau believes that the first kind of moral sensibility is quite natural and is the source of all our more human and gentle emotions.[94] The second is a product of reflection and breeds in man 'hateful and cruel' passions. The positive moral

[93] *Rousseau juge de Jean-Jacques*, *OC*, vol.1, p.805.   [94] Ibid.

sensibility is one of the fruits of self-respect, and its negative counter-part is the product of egotism. The latter is not concerned with those things which are necessary or useful for man's well-being. It is solely obsessed with gaining the upper hand and it is insatiable.

The negative moral sensibility, writes Rousseau,

is irked by the preferment it senses to be the just due of others, even though they might never obtain it: it is also irritated when someone excels us, yet is not appeased by the thought that there are those who are worse off than our-selves. A sense of inferiority in one direction turns to ashes the delight in being superior to others in a thousand other ways, and those areas where an advantage is enjoyed are soon forgotten when the mind focusses all its atten-tion on personal defects.[95]

The man guided by positive sensibility and self-love looks simply to his own well-being without concerning himself with that of others. But the man ruled by egotism directs his attention exclusively to others and only judges himself in comparison with them. It is not his own well-being as such that counts, but his well-being compared with that of others.

This is rather like the difference between a man who enjoys certain kinds of foods simply because he likes them, and another whose taste is limited to refined and exotic fare because he is the only one who can enjoy them and most men are excluded.[96]

Disorder and enmity are not created by men seeking their own happiness, but by those whose main end in life is to gain preferment: 'the man who lives through his senses is the natural man; the man ruled by his intellect is swayed by general opinion; he it is who is dangerous'.[97]

Rousseau disapproves of egotism because he sees it as the root cause of social disorder, and he uses the term 'degeneration' to describe the transformation of self-love into egotism. This process occurs as a result of the development of permanent social relation-ships, the evolution of ideas and culture.

Rousseau's study of disorder leads to the following opposition: on the one hand, there is self-love, species identity, but independence of opinion; on the other, society, egotism, subjection to the tyranny of opinion, but individual identity. Rousseau did not limit his reflection to the transition from the state of isolation to that of life in society; he also considered the reverse process, which leads from society and sub-jection to the general opinion to solitude and independence of thought.

[95] Ibid., p.806.   [96] Ibid., p.808.   [97] Ibid., p.805.

In his last works, in particular *Les Rêveries* and *Rousseau juge de Jean-Jacques*, he reflects on the situation of a man who has left society and freed himself from the tyranny of collective opinion. The feelings of this solitary man are no longer wasted on externals, on all the things which men value; he is able to allow his expansive sensibility free reign and no longer concerns himself with others. This man, withdrawn from society, is too preoccupied with his own well-being to be able to afford the time to think ill of others or to compare himself with them and thus he avoids the snare of jealousy.

The transition from the natural state to life in society is followed by the degeneration of self-love into egotism, accompanied by the corruption of the natural order into an artificial disorder. The contrary process changes egotism into self-love, and the quest for a happiness which is no longer dependent on opinion takes the place of the desire for preferment.

In the *Discourse on inequality*, Rousseau had analysed the way in which self-love was transformed into egotism. In the autobiographical writings he analysed the opposite process. It is very interesting to note that the same set of concepts is used in these two widely differing contexts: life in society subjugates men to the tyranny of opinion; this results in them leading lives which are alien to the natural order; when a man leaves society behind, it is possible for him to rediscover independence of mind and with this comes also the rediscovery of the natural order:

I never had much tendency to egotism ('amour-propre'); but this factitious passion was exalted in me by society, and above all when I was an author; even then I had perhaps less of it than others, but I had it prodigiously . . . By falling back upon my soul, by cutting the external relations which render it exacting, by renouncing comparison and preferences, it is content that I should suffice myself. Thus becoming again love of myself, it has returned to the order of nature, and has delivered me from the yoke of opinion.[98]

What Rousseau refers to as a liberation from the yoke of opinion goes hand in hand with his assertion in *Les Rêveries* that for his personal identity he is no longer dependent on what others think of him. Men can think of him as they please; this, says Rousseau, will affect his inner being not one iota: 'Let them do their worst, in spite of everything, I will continue to be what I am.'[99] In the solitude of nature he is beyond the reach of insults and feuds, wrongs and injustices, for his

---

[98] *Les Rêveries du promeneur solitaire*, *OC*, vol.1, p.1079 (transl. J.G. Fletcher, London, 1927, p.164).   [99] Ibid., p.1080.

status is no longer dependent on the esteem of others. Living in solitude the 'natural man' takes the place of the 'man fabricated by collective opinion'.

In his autobiographical writings, Rousseau suggests that it might be possible for the individual to develop a personal identity which is not dependent on social interactions, while in the *Discourse on inequality* he argued that individual identity could be formed only within the social context, through the individual's comparing himself with others. The reflections of the ageing Jean-Jacques revolve around the possibility that placing oneself outside the social order might be one possible way in which disorder is overcome. Once one has placed oneself on the outside of the social order equality ceases to be a problem. Words such as 'superiority' and 'inferiority' will be emptied of their content. Self-knowledge is no longer dependent on the perception others have of us and consequently it is no longer necessary to be constantly alert as to how they are reacting. Moreover, going beyond society means immersing oneself in the natural order, within which man may discover his true identity and find inner peace.

Another possibility open to the person who wants to bring order into his life is wisdom, that is to say, living as a natural man in a society but not obsessed by what others think. The wise man would be capable of living surrounded by disorder and yet remain untouched by the opinions of others. This is Rousseau's advice to Emile. If he wishes to live as a natural man, this does not entail his going to live in the depths of the forest. By all means he should enter the restless life of society if he so wishes, but, if he is going to be a natural man, he should beware of being swept away either by the strength of his emotions or by currents of opinion.[100] He must 'see with his own eyes, feel with his own heart and recognize no other authority beyond that of his own reason'. Emile is fully aware that the inane pursuit of social approval gnaws at the hearts of many, but he himself remains unaffected by it. He is free from pride and he has a balanced view of his own worth. He is not consumed by the urge to dominate others, neither does he get any pleasure from the misfortunes of others. Emile is 'well-balanced' and thus leads a well-regulated life.[101] He is well able to

---

[100] *Emile, OC*, vol.4, p.536.
[101] Ibid., p.536. The *Dictionnaire de l'Académie française* defines moderation as 'la vertu qui porte à garder toujours une sage mesure en toutes choses; et surtout à ne se point laisser aller à la colère, au luxe et à l'orgueil', that is to say, 'the virtue which ensures that we always keep a wise balance, in all things; and especially in not giving ourselves up to wrath'. The equivalent latin word is 'temperantia' (cf. *Lexicon totius*

satisfy the few needs which are his. He is a well-balanced person because he shows no desire for empty prestige: great wealth, ostentation, and self-display are of no interest to him. What he wants for himself is the things really worth having and he leaves to others the rewards that society offers.[102]

Emile must learn to behave in the same fashion in every situation, whether or not others are observing his actions. It is not that he scorns the approval of others, but it is a pride which has strict limits. The man who acts in harmony with nature and is not a slave of fashion desires preferment and the acclaim of others, but only for his true talents and not because of inherited wealth or any other externalities, and even less does he desire to profit from the prejudices of others.

In the race he desires to be the fleetest of foot, in combat the strongest, in work the most adept, in games of skill the most dexterous; but of little importance to him will be those talents which are not self-evident, but require confirmation through the approval of others, such as being wittier than his peers, and speaking better or being wiser than them, etc.; much less so those advantages which have nothing to do with the individual, like being of higher birth, being thought of as wealthier, having more influence and being able to put on a more magnificent display than others.[103]

It is easy to imagine Emile in Sparta or Rome during the republic or still more so the just republic envisaged by the social contract, but somewhat more difficult to imagine him living in the social turmoil which Rousseau himself described so effectively. But the most important thing to observe is that the alternative to disorder is, once again, to be identified with freedom from the uncontrolled desire for preferment at no matter what cost and for no matter what reason. This possibility involves removal from the distortion of perspective which leads men to value most highly those things which are theirs and theirs alone, as Pufendorf stated. Confronted by a world in which men are devoured by egotism, the wise man makes moderation the principle of his conduct. For him true pleasure is not negated by being shared. Anyone who enjoys good health and does not have to go without the basic necessities of life, may, provided that he is able to uproot any inner longing he may have for the acclaim of others, be considered wealthy enough: this is the 'aurea mediocritas' propounded by Horace.

latinitatis). On the importance of the concept of 'moderation' in Rousseau's theory of inequality, cf. R. Polin, 'Le Sens de l'égalité et de l'inégalité chez Jean-Jacques Rousseau', in *Etudes sur le 'Contrat social' de Jean-Jacques Rousseau*, Paris, 1964, pp. 158–9.   [102] *Emile, OC*, vol.4, p.666.   [103] Ibid., p.670.

The idea of 'moderatio', interpreted as 'nothing in excess', plays an essential part in Rousseau's reflections on the possible alternatives to disharmony. In the preceding pages two of these have been analysed. The first involved going beyond society to escape from disorder and to find peace, moderation, and the sweetness of life in direct communion with the natural order. It is of no consequence that this is not a very likely possibility, for what really matters is to consider it as an alternative to a life of disorder. The second possibility is to live in disorder in the midst of disorder without losing wisdom and moderation. One could describe this as speculation on two possible ways of avoiding the ill-effects of society.

The third idea that Rousseau proposes is completely different. It is no longer a question of defending oneself from the evil influence of society, but of transforming disorder into order. This time the order referred to is not the natural order which awaits those who leave the social world, but political order.

4

Political order

The social contract against disorder and superficial order

Rousseau's political doctrine, in particular his doctrine of the social contract, can be viewed as a quest for a rational solution to the problem of disorder. As I have attempted to show in the second part of this work, the term disorder has three connotations. Disorder occurs when men's station in society is not the one which is appropriate for them. Disorder is also inevitable when men regard each other as rivals in a contest for distinction, pre-eminence and preferment. Finally, disorder exists within the individual when his inner life is controlled by unregulated passions. The moral condition of men who live in a society without order is unenviable and wretched.

Driven by the insatiable desire to gain preferment, they seek happiness which will always remain beyond their reach. A man's desire will always exceed what he is capable of and he can never find the peace and self-discipline which alone can bring happiness. Imagination is for ever pushing back the frontiers of what is thought to be possible and so men are caught up in a quest which allows them no rest.

But the object which seemed within our grasp flies quicker than we can follow; when we think we have grasped it, it transforms itself and is again far ahead of us. We no longer perceive the country we have traversed, and we think nothing of it; that which lies before us becomes vaster and stretches still before us. Thus we exhaust our strength, yet never reach our goal, and the nearer we are to pleasure, the further we are from happiness.[1]

Nature, which always acts for the best, was careful to provide a balance between what a man might desire and what he is able to achieve, and he had it in his power to be happy if only he had not strayed far from his natural state, but, leading a life of disorder in a disordered environment, he deviated from his true nature and sacrificed his happiness. Thus, it is essential to restore order, if men are to live in a way which accords with true nature. This transformation makes it necessary to confront the problem of *politics*, that is to say, the organization of the community.

It was not mere chance that led Rousseau to study the 'Principes de droit politique' immediately after confronting the problem of inequality, at which time he had given his definition of social disorder. This casts a very specific light on his analysis of the problem of government, and his works provide many examples of the way in which his thinking goes beyond the issue of man's moral condition to embrace the dimension of politics. The break, as Derathé[2] has so aptly called it, between the two phases of Rousseau's thought occurs in the preface of *Narcisse* (1752):

What a bizarre and ill-starred constitution it is which permits accumulated wealth to provide the means of acquiring still more and where it is impossible for him who has nothing to gain anything at all; where the upright man has not the means to escape poverty, while the biggest scoundrels are the most highly regarded and where one must renounce virtue to become a man of repute! I know that the rhetoricians have said these things a thousand times; but they spoke only in a rhetorical way, while I am providing reasons. They saw the evil and I am uncovering the causes. Yet I also bring to light something which provides much hope and may be of great practical benefit in that I demonstrate that all these vices are not an integral part of man's nature but are typical only of man when he is ill-governed.[3]

It is clear that the 'bizarre and ill-starred' constitution is the very image of a society without order. When Rousseau says that 'scoundrels' are the most highly regarded and the upright man has no

---

[1] *Emile*, *OC*, vol.4, p.304 (transl. Foxley, 1974, p.44).

[2] Introduction to the *Contrat social*, *OC*, vol.3, p.94.

[3] *Narcisse ou l'amant de lui-même*, Preface, *OC*, vol.2, p.969; It is interesting to compare this extract from Rousseau with Book 3, ch.29, of Machiavelli's *Discorsi*, which opens with the following sentence: 'Princes ought not to complain of any fault committed by the peoples whom they govern, because such faults are due either to their negligence or to their being themselves sullied by similar defects' (Machiavelli, '*Il principe' e i 'Discorsi'* Milan, 1960, p.464; transl. Walker, London, 1970, p.483).

possibility of escaping from his wretched state, he is only repeating his assertion that a society which downgrades and humiliates those who ought to be looked up to and be highly esteemed is one which is contrary to the principles of justice. Thus, it will be impossible to find order in a society which makes it impossible for men to live together without always having to be one step ahead of the other, 'supplanting, deceiving, betraying and destroying one another', as he writes in the preface a few lines before the passage quoted above.

His study of the true foundation of the body politic can assist men in the task of correcting their institutions. The remedy for the disorder brought about by the actions of men left to their own devices or led astray by corrupt institutions lies in their converse – institutions which enshrine a high moral principle.[4] The study of politics finds its justification, therefore, in the fact that it promises a solution to the problem of disharmony. Rousseau, himself, makes the point in the concluding section of his preface to the *Discourse on inequality*, which ends with the revealing quotation taken from the *Satires* of Perse: 'Learn what it is God's will for you to be, and know your true situation in life' ('Quem te Deus esse jussit, et humana qua parte locatus es in re, Disce').

This does not mean that men should automatically accept the situation which chance or the judgement of others has made theirs, but they should be aware of the status which is most appropriate for them and they must strive to create an order in which they will be able to live in conformity with their moral nature.

Man's moral nature can be summed up in the single concept of virtue, which is identical with the love of order. This is a feeling which belongs to man alone. He is true to his nature when he has learnt to respect the love of order within him, without allowing himself to be carried away by uncontrolled passions. This, in Rousseau's view, is the only way in which men can attain true happiness. But it is impossible to be just and virtuous in a society in which the happiness of the one means the misfortune of the other. When the kind of rewards most sought after are those over which the individual finds it possible to exercise *exclusive rights* and which are, in fact, valued precisely because

---

[4] In the *Confessions, OC*, vol.1, pp.404–55, Rousseau recalls the thoughts which had led him to consider writing his work on 'Political Institutions'. This project was based on the belief that 'in the last analysis everything was connected with politics' and that the moral question could not be solved without first dealing with 'the great question of the best possible government'.

others either have none or have fewer of them, then it automatically happens that men come to hate their fellows. If the overriding ambition of each person is to gain preferment, then he will see others only as so many obstacles in his path. He therefore finds himself in the dilemma of being forced either to impose his will on others and treat them as means for the furtherance of his ambition, or be a victim of others and become, in his turn, a mere pawn in their larger strategy. Living in a corrupt society they must either act unjustly or become the victim of the injustice of others.

The text in which Rousseau expounds this idea most clearly is the chapter in the first version of the *Social contract* where he deals with the 'general society of mankind'. In this chapter he argues against the doctrine of the 'natural sociability' of men. According to this theory, men's needs have progressively increased to the point where they are no longer able to satisfy them individually without the assistance of others. This insufficiency on their part leads to the development of interpersonal relations, which, in turn, lead to the development of the universal society of mankind, which is not the same thing as 'particular civil societies'. This is envisaged as a 'state of independence' in which men are not subordinate to a sovereign authority. Rousseau does not deny that the needs of the individual serve to strengthen his relations with others, but he adds that the needs whose satisfaction requires the assistance of others are coupled with violent passions. While it may be true that needs bring men together, their passions divide them.[5]

   Thus, it cannot be argued that in this state reason is able to persuade men to co-operate for the common good since such a course of action is in their own interest. Quite the reverse, for the selfish interest of the one conflicts with that of his neighbours. A society which is no more than the sum total of the mutual needs of its members will never be a peaceful and stable community, but will rather take the form of: a multiplicity of relations without measure, order or consistency, which due to the agency of men are subject to continual variations; a hundred individuals are hard at work destroying them for every one who is working to build them up.[6]

   Such a situation where interpersonal relations are not subject to any kind of regulation and are totally lacking in stability may truly be

---

[5] *Manuscrit de Genève, OC*, vol.3, p.284.   [6] Ibid., p.282.

described as a state of disorder, one in which the strong become stronger and the weak lose all hope. Moreover, such conditions render it impossible for the individual to develop personal identity and live in a moral way, which activities, according to Rousseau, alone make true happiness possible, and which constitute a man's real worth:

As the relative existence of a man in the natural state depends on a thousand other relations which are continually fluctuating, he can never be confident that he will remain the same for any two moments in his life; peace and happiness are as momentary as the lightning flash; nothing is permanent save the misery which all these hazards bring in their train.

Clearly, the natural state Rousseau is referring to in the *Geneva manuscript* is not the same as the natural state he has described in the *Discourse on inequality*. The latter represented the hypothetical condition of man living completely outside society, whereas the natural state referred to in the *Geneva manuscript* portrays the 'general society of mankind'. In the first instance, Rousseau tries to imagine what the condition of man might be when he has no permanent relations whatsoever with any fellow beings; in the latter case he sets out to analyse the nature of the relationships obtaining where there is no political authority. In each of the two cases he is putting forward an abstract argument, but in the first it is society which is abstracted, while in the second it is the state.

Rousseau makes it quite clear that a society without political authority cannot be anything other than a multiplicity of relationships with no form or pattern. As a result no one in this perpetual flux could be sure from moment to moment that he was still the same person as he was the moment before. This thought brings us back to the problem of personal identity. Men who live in the isolation of the natural state cannot, as has already been noted, have a personal identity. Incapable of replying to the question 'who are you?', they have no means of identifying one another. The development of personal identity can take place only on the basis of mutual comparison and requires also that the individual should be identified by others. As these activities are not possible in a state of isolation, men in the natural state have not yet acquired individuality nor a moral character.

In 'the universal society of mankind' the problem of personal identity comes in a different guise. Now, men have formed more permanent relationships, ones which, primarily, have to do with the satisfaction of their needs. As the individual cannot satisfy his own needs by himself he is forced to call upon the assistance of others. Men have developed individuality. The distinction between strong and weak now makes its appearance and individual identity takes the place of simple 'natural identity'. This is, nevertheless, a form of identity lacking in stability, since it is dependent on relations with other men and these are in perpetual flux, since they are not governed by any kind of rule.

For Hobbes, also, men in the natural state have no means of telling what they will be from one day to another, since they cannot even be sure that they will still be alive. This, too, is very much how Rousseau understands the problem of personal identity. He emphasizes, as strongly as does Hobbes, that it is necessary to ensure that the conditions in which they live do not pose a threat to their survival. He, also, observes that in a hypothetical condition of perfect independence men would not be able to acquire a stable personal identity. To live in a society governed by no rules where men are in permanent conflict would mean that the individual could have no confidence that his personal identity would not change from one day to the next.

Within the context of their respective investigations into the nature of human society, Hobbes and Rousseau both confront the problem of personal identity. The former emphasizes the minimal conditions necessary for personal identity to emerge, that is to say, 'how to remain alive', while the latter focusses in a more comprehensive way on the problem of which kind of environment favours the development of personal identity, that is, not only by providing for the physical security of the individual but also by creating the necessary conditions for the development of social order. Men who live in a completely independent and unregulated way spend their days in misery:

The earth would be inhabited by men who would scarcely communicate with each other at all. There would be the occasional point of contact between us, but no real unity; each person would live alone surrounded by his fellows, no one would think of anyone but himself; our understanding would be incapable of developing; we would live without feeling; we would die without having lived; our hearts, our actions would be untouched by any moral considerations and we should never have experienced in our innermost being that most delightful of all feelings, which is the love of virtue.[7]

[7] Ibid., p.283.

In a society without order it is not possible for men to live in accordance with the love of order. The 'independent and enlightened man', whom Rousseau uses as a mouthpiece in the *Geneva manuscript*, attempts to justify his unregulated behaviour by suggesting that he can do no other.

The first consequence of the argument which Rousseau pursues in this text is the necessity of political institutions. Men cannot live in harmony with their moral nature if interpersonal relations are not regulated and this can only come about through a political authority. But this form of regulation cannot be selected at random and it is not true to say that any sovereign authority, provided that it has the power to enforce its will, may act as a bulwark against disorder.

Rousseau maintains that it is possible to imagine a situation where men are subject to laws and to a sovereign authority which is far worse than a state of anarchy. This is a state of disorder which gives the appearance of order, but it is only a superficial order. Since Rousseau's theory of political order aims to provide an alternative not only to the chaos of anarchic relations but also to an order which exists only on the surface, it is necessary to pause here to consider the latter concept.

The first work in which Rousseau speaks of 'a superficial appearance of harmony', which obscures a real division in society, is the *Discourse on inequality*. Here he describes how ambitious leaders whip up strife and hatred among their people in order to take advantage of the divisions within society. This is what Rousseau, in his account, calls the periods 'of chaos and revolution' which precede the imposition of dictatorship. In *Emile*, the dichotomy between a civil order which exists only on the surface and reality takes on a more general significance. The passage referred to is a familiar one but is quoted here for its importance to the argument:

In the civil state there is a vain and chimerical equality of right; the means intended for its maintenance, themselves serve to destroy it; and the power of the community, added to the power of the strongest for the oppression of the weak, disturbs the sort of equilibrium which nature has established between them. From this first contradiction spring all the other contradictions between the real and the apparent, which are to be found in the civil order.

And he adds the following note:

The universal spirit of the laws of every country is always to take the part of the strong against the weak, and the part of him who has against him who has not; this defect is inevitable and there is no exception to it.[8]

In his final autobiographical writings, Rousseau once again returns to the subject of superficial social order, and he notes that it is this superficial order which has always been the target of his criticism:

They accused him [Rousseau] of wanting to overturn the whole order of society because he was incensed by their daring through the use of this term to sanctify the most grievous inequities and thus to strip the suffering of humanity of all dignity by parading the most criminal injustices as if they were laws, when, in fact, such things are a cancer at the very heart of the system of law.[9]

Thus, superficial order characterizes any political constitution or government authority which does not protect all its citizens without fear or favour, but where instead some receive special treatment and the common good is sacrificed to private interest. Superficial order also exists if the highest ranks of society are occupied by individuals who claim to be working for the good of others, while, in fact, they only pursue their own interest.

In such a political constitution there is a form of order, since laws exist as does a sovereign authority. But this is a specious order, since the sovereign authority does not fulfil its proper function, namely, the protection of all citizens and the safeguarding of the common interest. Moreover, it is an order which exists in appearance only because men are not granted the status which is theirs by right: how many scoundrels, rogues and blackguards there are who rise to positions of highest authority in the state – which only goes to show the extent to which the state is built on injustice.

On this point, then, Rousseau's argument is that the worst fate which may befall men is not so much to live in anarchy, with no political authority and no laws, as to live with bad laws, under the heel of a tyrant, in a state where injustice is enshrined in its laws. The natural state in which there is no social order is nevertheless preferable, for most men, to what purports to be order in which they must struggle not only against nature but also against the institutions created by man.

It is far better to live in the independence of the natural state than in a society where the laws are framed to protect the interest of the rich

[8] *Emile, OC*, vol.4, p.524 (transl. Foxley, 1974, pp.197–8).
[9] *Rousseau juge de Jean-Jacques, OC*, vol.1, p.887; on the notion of superficial order see B. Baczko, *Rousseau. Solitude et communauté*, Paris, 1974, p.189.

and powerful. In such a society the goods, the freedom and the lives of the majority are dependent on the whim of those with power, against whom the law offers no protection. The citizens are encumbered with all the duties of the civil state without enjoying any of the rights of the natural state. In fact, they are not even in a position to use their own resources to defend themselves against injustice because the law forbids them that right: 'They would be in the worst condition in which free men could possibly find themselves.'[10]

To live in the civil state is not always preferable to a (hypothetical) life in the natural state. When private interests are allowed to come before the public good and the laws offer protection only to the rich and powerful, the civil state is, no doubt, preferable for those favoured by the system, but things are quite otherwise for those for whom the words 'the social order' or 'native land' are indelibly associated with duty, humiliation and submission.

The worst form of disorder is not the natural state but despotism. No government at all is still preferable to a bad government. Careful study of the fundamental idea which shapes and gives point to Rousseau's intellectual inquiry will reveal the most important aspects of his conception of political order.

In the *Second discourse* despotism is portrayed as the end-product of the process of social inequality. Rousseau makes this observation while developing a theme which recalls that part of the first book of the *Discorsi sopra la prima deca di Tito Livio*, where Machiavelli expounds the polybian theory of the *Anacyclosis*.

Despotism is the culmination of the 'ideal history' of social inequality. In fact, like the natural state which was the starting point of historical development, despotism is a condition of equality. In the natural state everyone has absolute equality since no one wields legitimate authority over anyone else. When tyranny reigns there is an end to inequality because all are as nothing before the tyrant. There is also another similarity between the natural state and despotism, and that is that the natural state (defined as the hypothetical condition of independence) is, as always in Rousseau, a condition in which interpersonal relations are not subject to any form of regulation. In despotism men are governed by the will of the master and the despot is, by definition governed only by his passions. But any man at the mercy of his passions is one who lives without discipline.

[10] *Economie politique*, *OC*, vol.3, p.256 (transl. Cole, 1952, p.374).

Thus, each of these two states have in common the fact that they are not governed by rules: in the first instance it is the passions of the individual which hold sway, while in the second it is those of the tyrant. Nevertheless, despotism is worse than the natural state since it represents the most extreme form of political corruption.

In the *Lettres de la montagne*, Rousseau makes this point even more clearly:

In making sure that every possible eventuality is provided for by some rule or other, you are destroying the most important rule of all, which is justice and the public good. When will men realise that there is no form of disorder as disastrous as the arbitrary power which they imagine to be the bulwark against chaos. This power is itself the worst form of disorder: using this as a way of preventing anarchy is like killing people to stop them having fever.[11]

Despotism is corrupt government, revealed unashamedly as such, and in this squalid form the interest of the dictator takes precedence over the common good. By arguing that a society dominated by the will of a single individual is the worst form of disorder and the most wretched state that can be experienced, Rousseau directly contradicts the view which states that arbitrary power is preferable to no authority at all.[12] This was Hobbes's argument in the chapter of *Leviathan* entitled 'Of dominion paternal and despotical'. Hobbes made a distinction between two forms of sovereignty: one which was acquired and the other which was instituted.

In a commonwealth *by acquisition* power was acquired by force. In other words, men, individually or collectively, confer legitimacy upon all the actions of the man, or of the assembly, which has, *by force*, made himself/itself master of their lives and liberty. The citizenry is led to do this through fear of death or of captivity. In the commonwealth by acquisition men 'choose' as their ruler the one they fear. In a commonwealth by *institution* men accept the authority of their ruler through fear of each other, not through fear of the ruler himself.

The classic form of despotic rule (rule 'by acquisition') occurs when one side gains victory in war. But, according to Hobbes's doctrine, the

---

[11] *Lettres écrites de la montagne, OC*, vol.3, p.828.
[12] On this issue Rousseau adopts the same view as Locke: 'It cannot be supposed that they should intend, had they a power so to do, to give to any one, or more, an *absolute Arbitrary Power* over their Persons and Estates and to put a force into the Magistrate's hand to execute his unlimited Will arbitrarily upon them: this were to put themselves into a worse condition than the state of Nature . . .'; *Essay concerning the true original, extent, and end of civil government*, s.137, in *Two treatises of Government*, Cambridge, 1970, p.377ff.

rights that exist – together with the practical consequences – under despotic rule are exactly the same as those which exist under institutional rule: 'the rights and consequences of sovereignty are the same in both'.[13] In each case there is no limit to political power and, even though the unfortunate consequences of this situation may be a cause for concern, they are, nevertheless, to be preferred to the results of general warfare where every man's hand is raised against his neighbour, as occurs in the natural state. Hobbes's answer to the charge that the condition of the citizens is wretched because they are at the mercy of the whims and the 'irregular passions' of the person or persons whose power knows no bounds is straightforward: 'not considering that the state of man can never be without some incommodity or other; and that the greatest, that in any form of government can possibly happen to the people in general, is scarce sensible, in respect of the miseries, and horrible calamities, that accompany a civil war, or that dissolute condition of masterless men, without subjection to laws, and a coercive power to tie their hands from rapine and revenge'.[14]

For Rousseau, the situation is quite the opposite, for the worst fate that may befall anyone is to be totally subservient to others, in other words to be ruled by a tyrant.[15] When Rousseau grapples with 'the great question of what constitutes the best possible form of government', he takes it for granted that, while the condition in which each individual lives as an isolated entity is not particularly to be desired, to be forced into subservience to a tyrannical ruler is worse still.

When men live quite independently of one another they are the prey of anxieties with regard to their personal identity and they also fear what the future may hold; they cannot vouch that any continuous thread will link their future selves with what they are now, and they lack the capacity to live in accordance with the love of order. Where social order is merely superficial and the sovereign will resides in an individual, men are forced to act to further the selfish interests of their leaders; they have a personal identity but one chosen by others. Rousseau believes that political order cannot be based on a concord which by natural means alone brings the conflicting interests of men

---

[13] T. Hobbes, *Leviathan*, Part 2, ch.20.

[14] *Leviathan*, Bk 2, ch.18. For Pufendorf, also, absolute power can be justified as the lesser of two evils: 'absolute power is not as contrary to Nature as those people imagine, who claim that Nature gives them a clear right to rid themselves of it at the first possible opportunity, even when it has been imposed upon them to avoid a greater evil which might befall them', *On the law of nature and nations*, Bk 7, ch.8, s.6

[15] *Discours sur l'inégalité, OC*, vol.3, p.181.

into harmony. This happy state of affairs can be instituted only by a sovereign authority: order can arise only when some authority is in a position to give 'orders' or, more precisely, to create a body of laws. However, the existence of an authority which has the might to ensure that the law is respected, and to impose peace on the warring factions within a society, is not of itself a sufficient condition for this. A just political order must satisfy another requirement:

It is a great thing to preserve the rule of peace and order through all the parts of the Republic; it is a great thing that the State should be tranquil, and the law respected: but if nothing more is done, there will be in all this more appearance than reality; for that government which confines itself to mere obedience will find difficulty in getting itself obeyed.[16]

Political order is therefore not to be equated either with the untrammelled freedom of men, living in isolation or with the bare existence of political authority and a code of law. The problem now is to hit upon the rule which should inform the will of the sovereign authority in such a way that this authority will not create worse disorder than that which would have existed if there were no sovereign authority at all.

The definition of this rule and of the sovereign authority capable of establishing a 'well-ordered society' is the subject and purpose of the doctrine of the social contract.

Utility and justice

The word 'rule' makes its appearance at the very beginning of the *Social contract*: 'I mean to inquire if, in the civil order, there can be any sure and legitimate rule of administration, men being taken as they are and laws as they might be.'[17]

In the *Geneva manuscript*, Rousseau had spoken of the 'maxim of Government and the rules of civil law' and had noted that 'it is not here a question of the administration of this body but of its constitution'. The different expressions used in the two versions are not as contradictory as they seem. The rule which must be found is, in fact,

---

[16] *Economie politique*, OC, vol.3, p.251 (transl. Cole, 1952, p.372).
[17] In the first version of the *Social contract* Rousseau notes that he is referring to the 'constitution of the body politic' and not its administration. As Derathé has correctly pointed out, by 'administrative rule', 'one should not understand the administration itself, but the element which regulates administration, that is to say, the general will which is the ground rule of government', *OC*, vol.3, p.1432, n.1.

the rule which should inspire the government's conduct. As an analysis of this text shows, administration is simply another term for the activity of the government.[18]

When Rousseau explains that he is concerned with the *constitution* of the body politic and not its *administration*, he intends to emphasize that he does not wish to deal here with the management of public or private business but to concentrate on the order of the state, that is to say, the political or constitutional laws which have to do with the relations between the governed and those who govern and also the relations between the different administrative bodies of the state.

What Rousseau is concerned with here is that there should be order in human relationships. He thinks that for men to live in order the state itself should be well ordered. Thus the task is to hit upon the rule which ought to provide the backbone of a *just constitution*.[19]

Rousseau has thus set himself to solve a problem which may, not without reason, be judged to be insoluble by its very nature, namely, how is it possible to define a political order which does not rely exclusively upon force and which is intended to serve the needs of individuals who, left to themselves, are capable only of producing disorder. The aim of this chapter is to follow Rousseau in his 'great enterprise', of which he speaks in a *Fragment politique* which clearly reveals the finality of his political doctrine:

Though it is not easy for us to describe in precise detail the constitution of a sound and legally constituted government, provided that my zeal does not cloud my judgement as I embark on this great enterprise, I am confident that with a resolute and upright spirit, this enemy of the human race will abjure hatred and error and, repressing the urge to prey upon the weak, will, through a better understanding of the direction in which his self-interest truly lies, become a just, virtuous and moderate well-doer, a friend to his fellow men and the most upright of citizens.[20]

The real difficulty in the way of what Rousseau hopes to achieve is the potential conflict which exists between the individualism of his premise and the idea of a political order which requires, if it is to

---

[18] *Economie politique*, OC, vol.3, p.250.
[19] When Rousseau speaks in the *Geneva manuscript* (Bk 1, ch.2) of 'the well-ordered society', he is referring to the state which has a sound constitution. In fact, in a fragment where he reiterates somewhat more ornately the idea which he develops in the *Manuscript*, he speaks of the 'true, sound and legitimate constitution'. The object of Rousseau's analysis is to discover which social conditions give rise to good institutions ('gli ordini buoni'), for, to use the terminology of Machiavelli, one of the political writers whom Rousseau most admired, 'good institutions make men virtuous'. It is in the hope of making men virtuous and happy that Rousseau, as has already been stated, reflects on politics.   [20] *De l'état de nature*, OC, vol.3, p.480.

endure for any length of time, that its citizens should be virtuous. For men who only obey the dictates of their egotistic nature, it is not possible to conceive a political order in which sovereign authority is directed by the general will and seeks only the common good. These corrupt men, must, sooner or later, fall under a tyrant's sway.

Men whose one aim in life is to subject others to their will and who do not find it repugnant to bend others' necks to the yoke, if that will make it possible for them to dominate them, have little defence against the establishment of a dictatorship. But it would be impossible to impose a tyranny on men who are not driven by an insatiable appetite for social acclaim.

Rousseau develops this argument in the *Discourse on inequality*: 'Besides, individuals only allow themselves to be oppressed so far as they are hurried on by blind ambition, and, looking rather below than above them, come to love authority more than independence, and submit to slavery, that they may in turn enslave others.'[21] A nation, whose citizens are corrupt and ambitious cannot hope for good government; instead it will inevitably succumb to tyranny. On this point Rousseau is the faithful disciple of Montesquieu. In *The spirit of the laws* we read that democracy is corrupted when, 'No longer will there be any such thing as manners, order, or virtue.' Leaders who seek to have absolute power contribute their part to the corruption of the people by exalting ambition: 'The people fall into this misfortune when those in whom they confide, desirous of concealing their own corruption, endeavour to corrupt them. To disguise their own ambition, they speak to them only of the grandeur of the state; to conceal their own avarice, they incessantly flatter theirs.'[22]

Another classic of modern political theory which it is appropriate to quote alongside Montesquieu is Machiavelli. The pages of the *Discorsi*, in which the Florentine scholar explains how the ambition of the great of this world has given birth to tyranny, are written from a theoretical perspective which is very close to Rousseau's. For both writers, a society of men consumed by their ambition or weighed down by egotism cannot but end in tyranny.[23] Above all else, tyranny

[21] *Discours sur l'inégalité*, *OC*, vol.3, p.188 (transl. Cole, 1952, p.360); see also the *Lettres écrites de la montagne*, *OC*, vol.3, p.842.

[22] *Esprit des lois*, Bk 8, ch.2 (transl. T. Nugent, revised by J.V. Prichard, *Great books*, vol.38, Chicago, 1952, p.51).

[23] See Machiavelli, *Discorsi*, in '*Il principe*' e i '*Discorsi*', Milan, 1960, pp.139–41, 179–83. One of the most eloquent texts in the *Discorsi* is to be found in Bk 3, ch.8. After having quoted the passage in which Livy observes that there is a big difference when it

represents the state of affairs where private interests (whether of the tyrant or of his immediate circle) take preference over the public good, and this is directly contrary to the situation which exists with a good political constitution, where the principle of the general good comes before the individual's private interest. But Rousseau says that he considers men as they really are, that is to say, ambitious. How, then, can such men create a just society and what possible reason do they have for submitting to an authority which has in view only the public good and which has – and this is the most important point of all – the necessary might to command obedience to its will?

Any attempt at answering these questions will involve an analysis of the doctrine of the social contract. We begin by setting the scene, so to speak, for this analysis, by stating as a premise that the doctrine of the social contract is from start to finish a theoretical construct whose sole function is a normative one. This is, perhaps, an unnecessary point to make, but it is worth noting that this is a doctrine whose only claim is to provide a solution to normative problems and which does not pretend to offer a historical reconstruction of the way in which political societies evolved. Rousseau's purpose is to discover a *rule* which has *moral validity* and not to provide a description of actually existing rules. It is not surprising to find Rousseau depicting the condition of men before the contract came into existence in a fashion which has all the hallmarks of a rational construct:

I suppose men to have reached the point at which the obstacles in the way of their preservation in the state of nature show their power of resistance to be greater than the resources at the disposal of each individual for his maintenance in that state. That primitive condition can then subsist no longer; and the human race would perish unless it changed its manner of existence.[24]

In this passage from the *Social contract*, it seems that Rousseau is alluding to the description of the wretched state of warfare which he had already depicted in a more summary fashion in the *Second discourse*. The state of things prior to the contract resembles Hobbes's picture

comes to acquiring prestige between a corrupt polity and one which is soundly based, he writes: 'from the words of the historian cited above, it may without hesitation be inferred that, had Manlius been born in the days of Marius or Sulla, when the material was corrupt and it would have been possible to impress on it the form to which his ambition looked, he would have met with the same success that attended the actions of Marius and Sulla and others who, after them, aspired to tyranny' (transl. Walker, 1972, p.428).

[24] *Contrat social*, *OC*, vol.3, p.361 (transl. G.D.H. Cole, 1952, p.391).

of the natural state in which no one can be sure that they will not be killed by their neighbour. For Rousseau, also, the peril, which weighs equally upon each man and woman, is the threat of the destruction of the human race. In conditions where warfare is endemic no one can escape the curse of insecurity: 'there was no safety to be found in poverty nor in wealth'.[25] In the *Geneva manuscript*, Rousseau precedes the description of the social compact with an account of the disorder caused by the 'independent man' who is always seeking to have his own way heedless of what others might want. The 'independent man' is well aware that his actions will inevitably lead to social chaos, but he does not allow this knowledge to deter him: 'I am aware that I cause turmoil and chaos everywhere I go . . . but I am faced with the choice of being unhappy myself, or bringing unhappiness to others, and no one is dearer to me than myself.'[26]

The human condition as depicted in the *Geneva manuscript* differs very little from the account in the *Second discourse*: in each case we are presented with a 'society' in which men are totally independent of one another and, though they need others for their survival, they are nevertheless in conflict when it comes to acquiring goods that confer status.

But having said this, it is necessary to be aware of the difference between the two texts. The account given in the *Discourse* is first and foremost a hypothetical reconstruction of the origin of the political state as 'in all likelihood' it was first instituted. The chapter in the *Geneva manuscript*, on the other hand, elaborates an argument which is not concerned with hypotheses concerning the real or probable origin of political institutions but, rather, with the answer to the question 'why are political institutions necessary?' The *Discourse* deals with matters of fact, the *Manuscript* with questions of law. Beyond this observation of a philological nature which suggests that this comparison should not be made without due caution, there is another difference to be pointed out. In the *Discourse on inequality* Rousseau notes

---

[25] *Discours sur l'inégalité*, *OC*, vol.3, p.177.
[26] The whole discussion in the chapter in the *Geneva manuscript* on the 'universal society of mankind' is, as many commentators have noted, a direct answer to the article entitled '*Droit naturel*' by Diderot. The context Rousseau provides shows a remarkable similarity with the condition of the troglodytes whom Montesquieu mentions in the *Lettres persannes*. As does Rousseau, he imagines a society of wicked and fierce men who do not recognize any principle of equity or justice. The rule of conduct for each of them is to obey nobody and pursue only their own interest without bothering about anyone else; *Lettres persannes*, in *Oeuvres complètes*, ed. A. Masson, 3 vols., Paris, 1950, vol.1, p.27.

that among the motives prompting men to accept the 'contract' offered by the wealthy are the emotions of fear and uncertainty. The advantages of the political constitution offered by the wealthy are consequently peace, harmony, protection, defence against common enemies and the enjoyment of property rights. These inducements have been sufficient to persuade men to renounce their innate (natural) liberty: 'As a wounded man has his arm cut off to save the rest of his body.'[27]

In the *Geneva manuscript* Rousseau sets himself a different task: namely, to show that a just political order may even be accepted by individuals who seek only their own interest and that these self-same individuals may become 'just' while pursuing their interest 'properly understood'.

The problem Rousseau confronts here is, primarily, the issue of justice. It is possible to read the *Social contract* and *a fortiori* the *Geneva manuscript* as an attempt to prove that in certain circumstances it is in men's interest to be just. The precondition for this is that society must be just – a well-ordered state. When Rousseau writes in the opening lines of the *Social contract*, 'In this inquiry [he refers here to the inquiry whether there can be a sure and legitimate rule of administration] I shall endeavour always to unite what right sanctions with what is prescribed by interest, in order that justice and utility may in no case be divided', he is referring back to the argument of the second chapter of the *Geneva manuscript*. In fact, the fundamental problem which Rousseau is raising in this passage is whether it is possible to reconcile justice with the interest of the individual. This is, in fact, the problem of the 'independent man' who must be convinced that it is better for him to submit to the rule of law rather than to continue to pursue his own interests at the expense of others: 'It is not just a matter of teaching what justice is, says the independent man; you must show me why it is in my interest to be just.' Rousseau hopes to prove that people may be persuaded to accept the rule of law on the basis 'of self-interest, properly understood'. On the theoretical level, and also, very probably, with regard to the literary sources, the theory of the social contract may be envisaged as an attempt to rebut the position defended by Trasimaco against Socrates, in the first book of Plato's *Republic*.[28] What Rousseau is anxious to demonstrate is that justice

[27] *Discours sur l'inégalité, OC*, vol.3, p.178 (transl. Cole, 1952, p.355).
[28] Plato, *Republic*, 343–344 c.

does not necessarily require the sacrifice of one's private interest. In fact, he does not ask the 'independent man' to subordinate his individual will to the general will, a process defined as 'a pure act of the understanding which, when passion is silenced, reasons concerning what a man may require from his neighbour, and what his neighbour may legitimately require of him.'[29]

It is Diderot, not Rousseau, who demanded that the 'passionate man' should obey the inner voice of reason, which instructed him concerning the law of humanity and the principles of justice.

You have the most sacred natural right to anything which is not prohibited by the whole species. The general will will guide you concerning the nature of your thought and your desires. Provided that it is in accord with the general and common interest, all your reasoning and all your thoughts will be good, great, elevated and sublime. There is no quality which is essential to your species other than what you require in all your fellows for your happiness and for theirs. It is this fundamental likeness which exists between you and them, and all others and yourself, which can never be erased whether you leave your fellow men or remain with them . . . Often repeat to yourself: I am a man and I have no other truly inalienable natural rights than those of humanity in general.[30]

According to Diderot's reasoning, the passionate man should cease to act as an individual and should behave instead as a *man*. Rousseau, on the other hand, states that it is not enough to explain the principle of the general will and the natural law to convince the independent man that he should place the general will of mankind before his own private interest. By definition such a man attends only to his own interest and so it is necessary to go beyond Diderot's argument to prove 'how it is that such a man's personal interest can best be pursued by his submitting to the general will'. In his attempt to discover the fundamental principle which is the key to a just political order, Rousseau does not forsake his premise of individualism. For Rousseau, the problem of political institutions and of good government arises precisely because he adopts as his premise the view that men do not follow the precepts of justice. If they did so we should have no need of governments or law.[31] He does not deny the validity of natural law but only its effectiveness, and especially he does not accept that it is sufficient to provide the basis for social order.

[29] *Manuscrit de Genève, OC*, vol.3, p.286.
[30] *Droit naturel*, in *Encyclopédie ou Dictionnaire raisonné des sciences, des arts et des métiers*, Neufschatel, 1765, vol.5, pp.97–8.   [31] *Manuscrit de Genève, OC*, vol.3, p.326.

The fundamental reason why men are unjust is, as has already been noted, that it is more profitable to do what is wrong than it is to lead a moral life. And to this it is necessary to add, if Rousseau's dilemma is to be truly understood, that it does not pay to treat others well if they are not willing to deal honestly with us. If he is to act in accordance with the principles of justice and humanity the individual man will require some kind of guarantee against the wrongdoing of others:

It is useless me trying, he might add, to reconcile my interest with my neighbour's; everything you tell me about the advantages of the social law would all be very well if, while I was scrupulously obeying it, to the great profit of my fellows, I could be sure that they would be doing the same for me; but how can you guarantee this?, and what could be worse for me than to find myself the object of the malice of those stronger than me while being unable to get my own back on my weaker brethren? Either guarantee that I will suffer no injustice, or do not expect me to refrain from evil-doing in my turn.[32]

The same argument reappears in the chapter of the *Social contract* devoted to the law,[33] and this goes to show that, even from the point of view of philology, the fundamental problem which lies at the heart of all Rousseau's thinking about good government is the question of justice or, more precisely, whether it is possible to reconcile justice with the interest of the individual.

Even though it was not included in the final version, the chapter entitled 'concerning the general society of mankind' contains compelling evidence of the nature of the problem that the theory of the social contract is seeking to address. But it is also necessary to note that there is an important theoretical relationship between this chapter in the *Geneva manuscript* and the depiction of disorder in the *Second discourse*. Men who heed their individual interest are, it is true, 'enlightened', but they are also men who act only in accordance with what passion dictates. They are quite capable of calculating and comparing the advantages and disadvantages inherent in each situation. Nevertheless, they are still men who are dominated by their passions.

This means that they are also ruled by egotism and ambition. For Rousseau, these are, without doubt, the most extreme of passions, and the root of disorder because they drive men to extremes, and

---

[32] *Manuscrit de Genève, OC*, vol.3, p.285.
[33] 'Humanly speaking, in default of natural sanctions, the laws of justice are ineffective among men: they merely make for the good of the wicked and the undoing of the just, when the just man observes them towards everybody and nobody observes them towards him', *Contrat social, OC*, vol.3, p.378 (transl. Cole, 1952, p.399).

make them eager to dominate others, rather than recognizing the rights of their fellow beings. The 'independent man' of the *Geneva manuscript*, like the one described in the *Discourse on inequality*, always seeks a higher status and greater wealth than others, to be looked up to and admired. This is why his interests run contrary to those of his neighbours and the latter thus represent a threat to his well-being. This clash of interests is (more than anything else), the result of intense rivalry for the benefit of status, that is, the desire to be thought of as well as possible by other men, and, according to Rousseau, the thirst for the rewards of high status is all consuming and insatiable. The law of nature which imposes on independent man the duty of respecting the rights of others as fellow human beings, requires him, in effect, to temper his desire;[34] when he demands a guarantee against the injustices of others, what he is really seeking is that others should also moderate their own desires. Careful examination of the reasoning of the individual man leads to the conclusion that it is necessary to have some power capable of restraining anarchic passions.

The logic of this argument also raises another issue – if justice is not to conflict with individual self-interest, it is necessary that the principle of reciprocity should be built into the system of justice. A just political order must, according to Rousseau, provide a solution to these two requirements. The just society is a body politic animated by the general will, that is, a will which always seeks the greatest good for each and all. In other words a society is based on sound foundations if the general will is central to the process of government. Now, the essence of the social contract is that individuals should defer to the authority of the general will: 'Each of us puts his person and all his power in common under the supreme direction of the general will, and, in our corporate capacity, we receive each member as an indivisible part of the whole.'[35]

[34] This interpretation may, perhaps, be supported by certain philological observations. The independent man is well aware that obedience to the natural law will entail moderation; but he adds that, even if he acted moderately, he could not be sure that others would do the same: 'I do not see how my moderation can guarantee me like treatment' (*Manuscrit de Genève, OC*, vol.3, p.285). There is another text which demonstrates that controlling the passions is a central aspect of the problem of justice, as Rousseau presents the matter in the *Geneva manuscript*, and this is the fragment *De l'état de nature*, several passages from which found their way, after varying degrees of revision, into the chapter in question in the *Geneva manuscript*. In this text Rousseau twice states that the problem is how to transform a violent and predatory creature into a man who practises moderation.

[35] *Contrat social, OC*, vol.3, p.361 (transl. Cole, 1952, p.392).

The principal consequence of the social compact – according to the beginning of the second book of the *Social contract* is that 'the general will alone can direct the state according to the object for which it was instituted, i.e. the common good', but Rousseau himself had stated in the *Geneva manuscript* that 'independent and enlightened' men would have no interest in obeying the general will, and as they heed only their own self-interest, they will never agree to be governed in this way. Why, then, does he suggest in the *Social contract* that the contrary is the case?

Rousseau has not abandoned the individualism which is at the heart of his theory, and yet the definitive text of the *Social contract* is not at all in conflict with what he had written in the *Geneva manuscript*. The reason for this is that the general will he refers to in the *Geneva manuscript* is not the same as the one referred to in the *Social contract*. The difference lies in the source from which the will emanates. In the first case, it is the will of the individual which acts to promote the good of mankind as a whole, rather than the self-interest of the individual himself. In the second instance it is the sovereign authority, that is, the citizens assembled as the sovereign body. The social contract is a compact agreed between the body of the people in its entirety, as sovereign and the individuals who comprise that body. Through this compact, each individual becomes a *citizen* and, as such, a member of the sovereign authority. At the same time he becomes a *subject*, one who must obey the laws of the state. The sovereign body to which each citizen pledges his loyalty in the social compact is formed only of individuals. This is the fundamental condition which ensures that it is in the interest of each individual to submit to such a political authority: 'In this lies the key to the working of the political machine; this alone legitimizes civil undertakings, which, without it, would be absurd, tyrannical and liable to the most frightful abuses.'[36]

When citizens pledge their loyalty to the sovereign authority formed by themselves which is, in its turn, pledged to work for the common good, they have made a completely rational choice. The guarantee that the sovereign authority will not pursue its own ends at the expense of the interest of individual citizens is the fact that the sovereign body is made up of those self-same individuals 'because it is impossible that the body should ever wish to harm its members'. While it is true that it is difficult to imagine the body desiring to inflict

[36] Ibid., p.364 (transl. ibid., p.393).

suffering on all its members – such an action would be in contradiction with the premise that this body is comprised of individuals who seek only their own interest and these individuals would be incapable of contemplating an action which would be inimical to the interests of them all – it might decide upon a course of action which would harm certain of its members and work to the advantage of others. This would be completely illegitimate but there is no reason why it should not occur. Thus our 'independent and enlightened man' would still not have the guarantee concerning the reciprocity of rights and duties that he had demanded as the price of his agreeing to subordinate his own private interest to the general will. It would not be in his interest to submit to a sovereign authority which might be more severe in its treatment of one citizen than another or be biased towards one rather than another, even if this were done in the name of the common good. No one could be sure that he would never be numbered amongst those whose interest might be harmed by the deliberations of the sovereign, and the fact that he was a member of the sovereign body would not serve to protect him against injustice.

In addition to the requirement that the members of the sovereign body and the subject should be one and the same, the other basic condition to be respected if individuals are to find it in their interest to accept the fundamental social compact is that the links binding the individual with the body politic should be reciprocal. Rousseau holds that it is only mutual agreements which can be binding. If each citizen only accepts the authority of the sovereign on the condition that the same is true of all the others, he will find that by fulfilling his obligations 'he cannot work for others without working for himself'.[37]

The social compact means that all citizens enjoy 'equality before the law'. They are all committed to accepting the same conditions and they equally 'all enjoy the same rights'.[38] Every citizen has a symmetrical relation with regard to the deliberations of the sovereign authority. Enjoying, as he does, equality before the law and having a system under which agreements made between individuals are held to be mutually binding, each citizen as a member of the sovereign body must seek the common interest in order to advance his own interest. Since the deliberations of the sovereign body apply with equal relevance to all citizens, it is the self-interest of the individual citizen which prompts him to seek the common good. For this reason

---

[37] Ibid., p.373 (transl. ibid., p.397).   [38] Ibid., p.374.

Rousseau writes that, 'the Sovereign, for its part, cannot impose upon its subjects any fetters that are useless to the community, nor can it even wish to do so'.[39] The condition of equality under the law established by the compact is, according to Rousseau, justice: 'It is in everyone's interest that all should have an equal chance in life, and justice is no more than an expression of this equality.'[40]

At this point it is appropriate to introduce the concept of law into the discussion. In the theory of the social contract, the principle of the sovereignty of law is entailed by the principle of equality under the law, that is to say, the principle of justice. On this matter, Rousseau is quite clear: 'It is thanks to the law, and to the law alone, that men can have justice and liberty.'[41]

Law is able to guarantee justice through its universality. By the term 'law' Rousseau always means the public deliberation of the legitimate sovereign body, which applies equally to all individuals (or to all the individual members of a social whole) always judging the actions of citizens in an abstract way. The law cannot 'judge a man or a deed as if they were unique'.

The law is universal both from the point of view of its subject and of its object. It is this universality which distinguishes law from a mere order or decree:

We see further that, as the law unites universality of will with universality of object, what a man, whoever he be, commands of his own motion cannot be a law; and even what the Sovereign commands with regard to a particular matter is no nearer being a law, but is a decree, an act, not of sovereignty, but of magistracy.[42]

The sovereign will can express itself only through laws, that is, through universal and abstract norms and not through orders and decrees. This norm is the fundamental condition to be fulfilled if the acts of the sovereign body are to have legitimacy:

Thus, from the very nature of the compact, every act of Sovereignty, i.e., every authentic act of the general will, binds or favours all the citizens equally; so that the Sovereign recognises only the body of the nation, and draws no distinctions between those of whom it is made up.'[43]

If the sovereign body allows itself to display partiality or unfairness in favouring one citizen at the expense of another, its deliberations

[39] Ibid., p.373 (transl. ibid., p.397).   [40] *Lettres écrites de la montagne, OC*, vol.3, p.891.
[41] *Manuscrit de Genève, OC*, vol.3, p.310.
[42] *Contrat social*, Bk 2, ch.6 (transl. Cole, 1952, p.400).
[43] Ibid., Bk 2, ch.4 (transl. ibid., p.397).

are void of authority, since they violate the principles of the social contract, according to which equality under the law and the acceptance of the authority of universal laws is what constitutes justice, and justice thus interpreted coincides with the public interest. For Rousseau, the notion of the common or public good has a formal character which really means that justice is here to be equated with equity. In the *Lettres de la montagne*, he makes this point very clearly: 'The first and the most outstanding public interest is always law.'[44] By this he means to emphasize that it is in the interest of everyone to be governed by universal laws. With this point we reach the heart of the social contract. This doctrine consists of a series of interrelated arguments, which set out to define the common interest in terms of the self-interest of individuals. The main criterion adopted by Rousseau as he develops his argument is that of rational choice.[45] The doctrine of the social contract proposes to explain why, if individual men were wiser and better able to see in which direction their true interests lay, they would create a political constitution in which the subjects participate in sovereignty on the condition that the sovereign body may carry out its deliberations only by means of universal and abstract laws.

Thus, the doctrine of the social contract assumes a society of 'independent and enlightened men', as described by the *Geneva manuscript* – men who are able to calculate how best to satisfy their interests, not the kind of men as represented by the poor savage who in the morning sells his cotton bed, and comes back whining in the evening hoping to buy it back, all because he has failed to realise that he would need it again the next night.[46]

Thus, the state constituted by the social contract is rational in two senses of the word. The first is the rationality of calculation, the second is rationality defined as universality. The legitimate state is rational in the first sense because individuals who are well able to calculate what is in their best interest would be willing to give their rational consent to a political constitution of this kind and to no other. It is rational in the second sense because it is governed by universal and abstract laws which are the highest expression of reason, namely 'public reason'.[47]

---

[44] *Lettres écrites de la montagne*, OC, vol.3, p.891; see also *Economie politique*, OC, vol.3, p.251.   [45] See S. Veca, *Questioni di giustizia*, Parma, 1985, p.37.
[46] *Discours sur l'inégalité*, OC, vol.3, p.144 (transl. Cole, 1952, p.339).
[47] *Economie politique*, OC, vol.3, p.248.

Rousseau's theory of the state may be thought of, somewhat schematically, as a hybrid located somewhere between Hobbes and Hegel, the first having the role of the theoretician of the rational state in the sense of the rationality of calculation, and the second being the advocate of the doctrine which sees the rationality of the state as an aspect of the rule of universal reason embodied in the law.[48]

As we shall see, these two forms of rationality are likely to come into conflict: on the one hand, the rational calculation of the private interest of the individual leads the individual citizen to act in a way that is contrary to the law and to seek to gain preferment;[49] on the other, the public good may degenerate into an abstract reason of state opposed to the interests of its citizens.[50] In Rousseau's view, it is worthwhile stressing this point; a state depends for its legitimacy on its capacity to reconcile private and public interests – a harmony which is often fragile. The *Social contract* is quite clear on this point:

... for if the clashing of particular interests made the establishment of societies necessary, the agreement of these very interests made it possible. The common element in these different interests is what forms the social tie; and, were there no point of agreement between them all, no society could exist.[51]

Rousseau never said that political society – still less the just political constitution – forbids its citizens to have their own private interests: men without private interests would not be individuals. According to his doctrine, individuals have their private interests and they continue to do so even after the institution of the body politic. At the same time they define for themselves a formal common interest, which is for each of them the necessary condition if they are to be free to pursue their own private interests. The 'individual and enlightened man' was willing to submit to the general will only on condition that rights and duties should be reciprocal. The sovereign body instituted by the social compact is able to provide the necessary guarantee. In fact, if they are to be legitimate, the deliberations of the sovereign body must respect the two principles of universality and reciprocity.

Moreover, in cases where citizens may be tempted to resist its will, the sovereign authority has at its disposal the means of compelling

[48] See G.W.F. Hegel, *Vorlesungen über die Philosophie der Geschichte*, p.41 (transl. Sibree, 1956, p.39).   [49] *Contrat social*, Bk 2, ch.1.
[50] *Economie politique*, *OC*, vol.3, p.258.
[51] *Contrat social*, Bk 2, ch.1 (transl. Cole, 1952, p.395).

obedience.[52] The 'individual and enlightened man' is therefore able to accept the social compact, and in so doing he accepts the principle of equality under the law, which is justice, and thus also agrees to lead an upright life – out of self-interest, correctly understood.[53] When Rousseau speaks of the 'admirable harmony between self-interest and justice', he does not choose these terms by chance. He is concerned to demonstrate that the just society instituted by the social compact is the reply he was seeking to the objection voiced by the 'independent man' who demanded to know what advantage it could be to him to act justly. The individual man who insisted on a guarantee against the misdeeds of others, was, in effect, asking that law should be sovereign, and it is the case that the social contract institutes a political constitution in which men should be ruled by law. If the law is to be sovereign it must be a will exercised by a sovereign power which has the means to command obedience,[54] and not a mere law of reason or of nature. It is not a question of explaining a law to men who do not understand it. The problem is to moderate their conduct, ruled as they are by their passions, and for this it may be necessary to use compulsion. But, if this situation arises, justice will be served only if the force employed is sanctioned by law and is at the behest of a legitimate authority which respects the principle of equality under the law and makes sure that each person respects the rights of others. The legitimate authority which acts *per leges* may curb men's passions, and, by tempering their desires, impose limits on their more extravagant ambitions. In a word it is law and law alone which can bring order to human affairs.

This is not to say, however, that civil laws can be in contradiction with natural law. Rousseau states several times very clearly that there is a natural law, described also as the 'Law of Reason', which is distinct from civil law, and that the natural law is superior to civil law. The

[52] Ibid., Bk 1, ch.7.
[53] Ibid., Bk 2, ch.4; This is why the social contract is not, as Vaughan believes (Vaughan, *Political Writings*, Oxford, 1962, vol.1, p.440), 'discredited in advance' because the citizens who subscribed to it have no sense of moral obligation, as Rousseau himself stated in the *Geneva manuscript* (Bk 1, ch.2). But, to agree to this compact, such individuals have no need of the natural law; all they require is the ability to see what is in their interest, which is what they are able to do because they are 'enlightened'. Even if they do not value moral obligation, this does not make the contract impossible: they undertake certain obligations towards a sovereign out of self-interest and the sovereign will ensure that these obligations are adhered to, but, once again, appealing to the citizens' self-interest (the fact that it is in their interest to avoid the punishments which should be theirs if they disobeyed the law).
[54] *Contrat social*, Bk 2, ch.4.

point is made most explicitly, and this is something worthy of note, in his 'Constitutional' writings on Corsica and Poland. The fact that he built his case on the foundation of natural law in texts dealing with problems of positive legislation, bears witness to the importance of natural law in Rousseau's political theory: 'Noble people, it is not my wish that you should be provided with a set of artificial and systematic laws invented by men; but rather that your lives should be directed solely by the laws of nature and of order which speak directly to the heart and do not curb the freedom of the will.'[55]

In the *Considérations on the government of Poland*, he appeals to the natural law, in order to criticize the *positive* laws according to which it is only the senate, the king and the order of knighthood who have the authority to pass laws:

Such is, or should be the law of the State of Poland: but the law of nature, that holy and imprescriptible law, which speaks to the heart of man and to his Reason, will not allow legitimate authority to be thus restricted – a situation which would result in the law controlling the actions of citizens who had not voted for them personally, like the nuncios, or at the very least had not approved them through their representatives – as happens with the body of the nobility.[56]

Contrary to Hobbes, Rousseau holds that there is an authority which transcends that of kings themselves and this authority is none other than the natural law. Rousseau's reply to the anonymous 'Gens de Loi' who reproved him for recognizing authorities superior to the king of France himself, was that he believed there were three such: God, the natural law, deriving from the very nature of man, and honour. These authorities, he added, 'are not only independent, but superior. If the sovereign authority were ever to contradict any of these, then it would be the former which would have to yield.'[57]

It is possible to find texts which proclaim the superiority of natural law over other systems of law, even in the *Discourse on inequality*, where Rousseau makes a far-reaching attack on the doctrine of natural right and natural law, and allows that Hobbes 'had seen clearly the defects of all the modern definitions of natural right'.[58] Even here, he has recourse to natural law when he condemns as totally unacceptable

---

[55] *Projet de constitution pour la Corse, OC*, vol.3, p.950.

[56] *Considérations sur le gouvernement de Pologne, OC*, vol.3, p.973.

[57] Rousseau to the 'Gens de Loi', 15 October 1758, in *Correspondance complète de Jean-Jacques Rousseau*, ed. R.A. Leigh, Geneva and Oxford, 1965–84, vol.5, letter no.712, pp.177–81; the editor comments: 'this important text, which is by no means unique in the work of Jean-Jacques, shows that in Rousseau's contractual State, positive law does not suppress natural law' (p.180).

[58] *Discours sur l'inégalité, OC*, vol.3, p.153 (transl. Cole, 1952, p.343).

most forms of moral inequality permitted by the systems of positive
law in force in civilized societies:

Moral inequality, authorised by positive right alone, clashes with natural
right, whenever it is not proportionate to physical inequality; a distinction
which sufficiently determines what we ought to think of that species of inequality which prevails in all civilised countries, since it is plainly contrary to
the law of nature, however defined, that children should command old men,
fools wise men, and that the privileged few should gorge themselves with
superfluities while the starving multitude are in want of the bare necessities of
life.'[59]

Should we conclude, then, that for Rousseau the natural law is
always the final arbiter of what constitutes justice and that the
legitimacy of the political authority will be in proportion to the
extent that it conforms with natural law?

On this issue commentators on Rousseau are divided. According to
Vaughan, for example, Rousseau's great merit consists precisely in
the critical attitude he maintains towards the political philosophy of
his time, amounting as it does to a rejection of the very foundations of
the latter.[60] In Rousseau – the argument here is still Vaughan's – the
natural law is no more than a synonym for a shared sense of what is
just, which has developed in human society through a long history of
moral discipline and submission to positive law. This law, which
Rousseau prefers to call the law of reason rather than the law of
nature, can be envisaged as the principle of human conduct only in
the natural state, as was the opinion of Locke.[61] In a situation where
there are no moral relations, and in which men follow their instincts
or their inner feelings, it is a contradiction to suppose that a law
exists, and even more so a law of reason. In the absence of moral
relationships and prior to the development of reason, it is impossible
to conceive any rational principle which could direct men along the
path of true morality: 'In this cardinal point, therefore,' writes
Vaughan, 'the work of Rousseau opens a new era in political

[59] Ibid., pp. 193–4 (transl. ibid., p.363); for Rousseau, the natural law is superior from
the moral point of view to the civil laws because it is more general. The civil laws
indicate what the citizens' duties are; the natural law indicates the duties which
everyone has in as far as he is a man: 'his duties as a man come before his duties as a
citizen'. See *Economie politique*, *OC*, vol.3, p.246.
[60] C.E. Vaughan, Introduction to Rousseau's *Political writings*, 2 vols., Oxford, 1962,
vol.1, pp.16–19. See also A. Cobban, *Rousseau and the modern state*, London, 1934.
[61] On the idea of natural law in Locke, see C.A. Viano, *John Locke. Dal razionalismo
all'illuminismo*, Turin, 1960, pp.70–101; J. Dunn, *The political thought of John Locke*,
Cambridge, 1969, pp.27–42, 187–202; P. Laslett, Introduction to John Locke *Two
treatises of government*, Cambridge, 1970, pp.79–120.

philosophy. And it is a point for which he is entitled to more credit than he has received.'[62]

However, with the argument for the natural law fatally undermined, the theory of the social contract faces serious difficulties. If the idea of natural law is abandoned then it follows that the citizens involved in the social compact are void of all sense of moral obligation. But then it becomes very difficult to imagine how a state founded on a social compact formed between its citizens who have no idea of moral obligation can ever come into existence. The legitimacy of the political authority would not then lie in a social compact emptied of all moral content, but in the common interest of the members of the political community. This is the route that Rousseau, according to Vaughan, was very close to taking. Moreover, Rousseau's unwillingness to accept the doctrine of the law of reason should have led him to totalitarian conclusions. If the natural law is not recognized as a set of principles which are morally superior to any positive law, then the only touchstone of what constitutes justice will be the will of the state, and this is something against which there can be no appeal. Should the individual citizen find himself in opposition to the will of the state he can no longer have recourse to any higher law. As Rousseau states in the *Economie politique*, the general will is 'for all members of the State, in their relations to one another and to it, the rule of what is just and unjust'.[63]

According to this view, Rousseau's arguments threaten the very foundations of the classical conception of natural law, since it undermines both its claim to be a principle of conduct universally recognized, accepted and obeyed (at least in the natural state) and also its claim to moral superiority in comparison with positive law.

Vaughan's interpretation has been contested in Derathé's *J.-J. Rousseau et la science politique de son temps*.[64] Derathé agrees that Rousseau rules out the possibility of men living in the natural state in harmony with the precepts of reason but he adds that this does not mean a fundamental break with the classical conception of natural law. Rousseau's argument does not preclude the possibility that natural law is encapsulated in the maxims of right reason, but merely shows that it can-

---

[62] Vaughan, Introduction to the *Political writings*, Oxford, 1962, p.18.
[63] *Economie politique*, *OC*, vol.3, p.245 (transl. Cole, 1952, p.369).
[64] R. Derathé, *J.-J. Rousseau et la science politique de son temps*, Paris, 1970, pp.151–7. See also F. Haymann, 'La Loi naturelle dans la philosophie politique de J.-J. Rousseau', *Annales de la Société Jean-Jacques Rousseau*, 30 (1943–5), pp.65–109.

not, *in this form*, be applied to the natural state, since it is not possible, of course, for man to know the maxims of reason before he has the use of his reason.[65]

The argument which Rousseau develops in the *Discourse on inequality* is about the place of the natural law in the temporal order, but it has nothing to do with its superiority as a norm. In particular, as far as relations between the civil and the natural law are concerned, Rousseau comes to the same conclusion as others writing from within the tradition of natural law, notably Locke and Pufendorf. Abstracted from the natural state, the natural law now reappears in the civil state. This confusion of chronological with normative order has caused writers such as Vaughan to fail to understand Rousseau's thought.

On the issue, raised by Vaughan, of the moral foundation of the social compact, Derathé acknowledges that this cannot be provided by the natural law. This does not, however, mean that in the natural state there is no rule whatsoever. In addition to natural law founded on reason ('secundum motum rationis') instituted by the general will, Rousseau also accepts that there is 'a natural law properly speaking' ('secundum motum sensualitatis')[66] which is appropriate to the natural state. This latter form of natural law exists prior to the development of reason and it is ultimately founded on the feeling of natural pity associated with the quest for survival. The basic precept here is, as has already been noted, 'look after your own interests, causing as little harm to others as possible'. This maxim of natural morality is, however, rendered ineffective by the flood of pride and other passions occasioned by the formation of civil society. In the final analysis, what is necessary is to prevent injustice dominating men's lives, and this means transforming the natural law into civil law which now has the power to inflict punishment as well as the guarantee of reciprocity. The purpose of the basic social compact, which has its moral basis in the prior maxims of reason, is to institute a legitimate authority to force men, since they are not capable of doing this themselves, to put into practice the precepts of natural law by guaranteeing the reciprocity of duties and rights.

Rousseau [writes Derathé] has not, therefore, totally rejected the idea of natural law. On the contrary, all his arguments are intended to show that natural law does exist in the natural state and that it persists in civil society. But, while his predecessors see natural law as something unique, maintaining

---

[65] Derathé, *Rousseau et la science politique*, p.164.   [66] Ibid., p.166.

that the laws of Nature and of Reason are one and the same, Rousseau is led to make a distinction between primitive natural law, which exists prior to Reason, and the natural law established by Reason. As it passes from the natural to the civil state, natural law undergoes the same metamorphosis as do the human beings to which it refers. In the natural state it merely took the form of instinct and goodness, in the civil state it becomes justice and Reason.[67]

The fundamental social compact does not do away with the rights which individual citizens have as men; they retain these rights in their dealings with the state. For Rousseau, concludes Derathé, the distance between the natural and the civil state is minimal. Unlike Hobbes, Rousseau holds that man is by his very nature inclined to live peacefully with his fellows. The voice of reason enjoins him to lead an upright and peaceful life. Civil society is not therefore the polar opposite of the natural state. When the natural law is given added weight by the legitimate authority which guarantees the reciprocal nature of rights and duties, it is transformed into civil law. Here Rousseau distances himself from Hobbes, and in so doing comes close to the position of Locke and the school of natural law.

In my view, the best way to set about answering the questions raised by Vaughan and Derathé is to ask what, in practice, is the place of natural law at the heart of Rousseau's doctrine of political order?

As has already been made clear, Rousseau accepts the idea of a moral order based on innate principles recognized by all men, without the aid of reason, and which is independent of all human conventions, customs and education:

Observe all the nations on earth, search all the histories, amidst all those in-human and weird cults, amidst that prodigious variety of customs and charac-ters, you will find everywhere the same notions of good and evil . . . There is, therefore, in every man's innermost soul an innate principle of justice and moral truth prior to all national prejudices and all the maxims of education. This principle is the involuntary rule according to which, in spite of all our merely local standards, we judge our actions and those of other people as being good or evil, and this is the principle to which I give the name of conscience.[68]

The fact that these moral rules exist in nature indicates that man may be thought of as a social creature thanks to his 'innate feelings for his species'. In another passage Rousseau uses these same innate prin-ciples as a foundation for his ideas concerning natural law, but on this

[67] Ibid., p.168. [68] *Lettres morales, OC*, vol.4, p.1108.

occasion he rejects the notion that it is necessary to include natural sociability:

> Throwing aside, therefore, all those scientific books, which teach us only to see men such as they have made themselves, and contemplating the first and most simple operations of the human soul, I think I can perceive in them two principles prior to Reason, one of them deeply interesting us in our own welfare and preservation, and the other exciting a natural repugnance at seeing any other sensible being, and particularly any of our own species, suffer pain or death. It is from the agreement and combination which the understanding is in a position to establish between these two principles, without its being necessary to introduce that of sociability, that all the rules of natural right appear to me to be derived.[69]

The argument that Rousseau believes that man is by nature suited to social life because he has certain innate qualities is open to question. Even if we admit that man has latent within him the possibility of living peaceably with his fellows, that potential is not one of the premises of natural law. Moreover, the precepts of natural law are not the principles which actually regulate men's conduct in society. These precepts are in conflict with other maxims which reduce the voice of nature to silence. Once reason in its successive stages of development 'has stifled the voice of nature', it is necessary to find other grounds for the rules of justice. It is not clear that Rousseau considers that all that needs to be done to strengthen the natural ideas of justice, already accepted and followed by the majority of mankind, is to add the threat of punishments, for the real problem is that men's behaviour is almost as a matter of course in conflict with the precepts of natural justice.[70] It is not natural man, nor the man who behaves in accordance with the principles of natural justice, who needs to be persuaded that he should give his wholehearted consent to a society which aims to model itself on the principles of justice. It is, in fact, the 'individual and enlightened man' who must be convinced that it is better for him to obey laws rather than to break them. If every man followed the principles of natural justice, the creation of a just society would present no problem. But the difficulty which Rousseau's politi-

---

[69] *Discours sur l'inégalité, OC*, vol.3, pp.125–6 (transl. Cole, 1952, p.330).
[70] See L. Strauss, *Natural right and history*, Chicago, 1953, p.283. On Rousseau's understanding of natural law the key work is V. Goldschmidt, *Anthropologie et politique*, Paris, 1974, chapters entitled 'Natural law and history' and 'The problem of law'. Goldschmidt notes that in the *Discourse on inequality* Rousseau intends to present a counter theory to that of the natural-law theorists. This intention, he says, is clear from the very beginning from the approach Rousseau adopts in the *Discourse* which in general conforms with the norm for the treatises on natural law.

cal theory must confront is to make credible a just social order whose starting point is not men whose behaviour is for the most part already morally acceptable, but men whose lives are riddled with unjust acts and who, nevertheless, believe that basically their behaviour is not subject to condemnation. On this subject the most important test is the chapter in the *Geneva manuscript* on 'General society of mankind', the original title of which was: 'Natural law and the general society'. When men organize themselves into a social whole by freely forming links with others, they do not seek to work for a common happiness which may then become the source of each man's personal satisfaction, but, rather, each of them hopes to gain pleasure from the misfortunes of others, which is a procedure totally contrary to what natural law prescribes. It would, therefore, seem that a contented and harmonious society where men order their interpersonal relations in accordance with the natural law has never existed:

Thus, the gentle voice of nature is no longer our infallible guide, neither is the state of independence which she granted us a desirable one; peace and innocence have flown from us for ever, before we could taste their delights. Even in the earliest times man was insensitive and dull of mind and so that happy life of the golden age has always been foreign to the experience of our race, either because we failed to recognize it when it was within our reach or through having lost it when we had the capacity to recognize it.[71]

In other passages we find similar conditions with regard to the natural law. This so-called social treatise, states Rousseau 'is a veritable chimera; since the conditions for it have always been unknown or impracticable, and so we are condemned either to remain ignorant of what is necessary or act against our true interest'.[72]

Rousseau's reflections on this subject start from the assertion that it is almost impossible to say with any degree of confidence what is artificial and what is natural in man's make-up. The very notion of the natural state is not something that can be thought of as having actually existed in the past, nor will it in the future. It is a hypothetical reconstruction which has a role to play in the context of a study of normative principles. The hypothesis of the natural state helps to form a clearer judgement concerning the present condition of mankind, and this is why it must be worked out in a painstaking way. Rousseau, like Burlamaqui,[73] considered that when the definition of

[71] *Manuscrit de Genève, OC*, vol.3, p.283.
[72] Ibid., p.284. [73] *Discours sur l'inégalité, OC*, vol.3, p.124.

natural law was obscure this was a result of the difficulty of forming an exact idea of the nature of man. The lack of agreement between those who have attempted theoretical definitions of natural law is not surprising. On this issue, Rousseau emphasizes an important difference between the conception of natural law adopted by the Roman natural-law theorists and modern ideas on the subject.

This has to do with the difference between the two very different terms 'law' and 'rule'. The former is related to the ideas of the ancient natural-law theorists, the latter to more modern ideas. By the term 'natural law' the natural-law theorists of the ancient world meant the law which nature prescribed for itself, rather than a law imposed by some authority. According to this interpretation, natural law applies equally to man and animal. It is quite simply the expression of the 'general relationship which nature has established between all animate beings, for their common life'. The modern meaning of the term – the natural law – is applicable only to the one animal endowed with reason: man. It is the rule which has been prescribed for a free, moral and intelligent being, considered in his relations with others. This rule may also be disobeyed. Ignoring those areas where modern definitions of the natural law are at variance, they nevertheless all suffer from one very important contradiction.

To qualify as natural, a law must be recognizable as such without any need for a complicated process of reasoning. But none of the definitions of natural law which philosophers have been able to produce could be understood by other men without a long and complicated series of arguments and much profound reflection on questions of metaphysics. This means that it is impossible for untutored men of the kind who live in the natural state to discover for themselves the principles of a law. How then can one imagine them being able to obey rules which they are in no position to understand? To understand a law – and even more so, the ability to define a law – requires the capacity to follow an abstract argument. A mode of thought which is in conformity with law requires the ability to think in universal terms – something which is manifestly impossible for men who have only their instincts and feelings to go by. Thus, to speak of 'law' in connection with men living in the natural state is a contradiction. It might be possible to talk of certain very simple principles of natural law but not of a 'law of reason'.

For Rousseau, the instinct of self-preservation and the desire for happiness, the fear of pain and pity for one's fellow-beings who are suffering, all originate in the realm of feeling, not of reason.[74] These promptings influence men directly in the natural state, while the principles of law have no such immediacy. The voice of nature does not speak the language of law, but of instinct and feeling.

Deprived of the knowledge that is necessary to understand the principles of natural law as defined by modern theorists, men would not be in a position to grasp the advantages and benefits it provides, so long as they live in isolation and in the independence of the natural state.

The principles of natural law have often been justified on the grounds that it is to everyone's advantage if they are generally obeyed.

Modern writers begin by inquiring what rules it would be expedient for men to agree on for their common interest, and then give the name of natural law to a collection of these rules, without any other proof than the good that would result from their being universally practised. This is undoubtedly a simple way of making definitions, and of explaining the nature of things by almost arbitrary conveniences.[75]

Now, it is difficult to imagine that people living in isolation without needing each other's help who have no enduring social bonds could formulate the idea of a 'common good' or of universal obedience to a single set of principles. Even if it is allowed that man is capable of forming 'by highly abstract chains of reasoning, maxims of reason and justice, deduced from the love of order in general or the known will of his Creator', these maxims would not be of any use to him:

In a word, were we to suppose him as intelligent and enlightened, as he must have been, and is in fact found to have been, dull and stupid, what advantage would accrue to the species, from all such metaphysics, which could not be communicated by one to another, but must end with him who made them? What progress could be made by mankind, while dispersed in the woods among other animals? and how far could men improve or mutually enlighten one another, when, having no fixed habitation, and no need of one another's assistance, the same persons hardly met twice in their lives, and perhaps then, without knowing one another or speaking together?[76]

In the natural state the natural feelings of self-respect and pity take the place of law and virtue and contribute to the preservation of the species. It is not the concept of law, but the feeling of pity which pre-

---

[74] Ibid., p.143.
[75] Preface to *Discours sur l'inégalité*, *OC*, vol.3, p.125 (transl. Cole, 1952, p.330).
[76] *Discours sur l'inégalité*, *OC*, vol.3, pp.145–6 (transl. ibid, pp.339–40).

vents a strong man from depriving a child or an old person of the basic necessities of life. On those very few occasions when the preservation of the one demands the sacrifice of the other, the feeling of pity comes to moderate the conflict. The preservation of the one does not necessarily mean that the other must perish nor that the weak should be sacrificed for the well-being of the strong. The maxims of natural goodness influence the conduct of uncivilized men in such a way that all, whether they are weak or strong, are able to live in peace. This is how Rousseau imagines the order created by natural right (droit naturel), for he sees it as providing the ground for a harmonious 'order' for those living in isolation, not an order where each part of the whole is linked to all the others.

Considered from the point of view of order, that is, from the point of view of the links existing between the various parts and also between these parts and the whole, the natural condition represents an absolute limit:

Furthermore, even if this state of perfect independence, this liberty which knows no rule, had continued to be closely associated with primeval innocence, it would still have had one essential flaw, inimical to the unfolding of our most excellent faculties: namely, the lack of connections between the parts which make up the whole. The earth could be inhabited by men between whom there would be scarcely any communication; there would be momentary contact between us, but no degree of unity; each person would live alone surrounded by his fellows, everyone would think only of himself; our understanding would be incapable of developing, we should live without feeling and die without having lived. . . .[77]

While 'order' as defined by natural law prior to reason can only be this primitive condition, a hypothetical order founded on the law of nature would be quite different.

In the *Geneva manuscript* Rousseau asks himself what kind of society it would be in which everyone complied with a system of justice based on reason. 'Let us suppose', he writes, 'that the human race is a moral individual and that this person had an awareness of a shared existence with others which endowed him with individuality and in fact made him in all respects an individual.' This individual would be endowed with an organizing principle, a universally shared sense of purpose which ensured that each of the entities of which the human race is actually comprised, in their turn defined as moral persons, would pur-

[77] *Manuscrit de Genève, OC*, vol.3, p.283.

sue a goal shared by all other members of the human race. That sense
common to all, and therefore existing within the moral person we are
considering, belongs to humanity itself. The active principle which
sets each part in motion in a way which harmonizes perfectly with the
whole is the natural law. If the natural law were really obeyed by all
men, there would be a harmonious order, in which all parts would find
their own well-being and happiness in pursuing the common good.

This hypothetical moral person would be more than the sum of his
parts, since he would have his own distinct qualities. Contrary to what
we know to be the case, there would be a universal language which
would make it possible for men to communicate freely with each
other and there would be 'a kind of 'sensorium' which would enable
all the parts to communicate with each other. The public good or
harm would not merely represent the sum of all the good or evil which
befell specific individuals, as is the case with an aggregate, but would
reside in the links which unite them; it would thus be greater than the
sum of the parts; and, far from the happiness of the community being
built upon the private happiness of individuals, it would, itself, be the
source of their happiness.'[78]

The law of reason would provide the foundation for an order far
more harmonious than the order founded on the maxims of natural
law. The hypothetical society for which the law of nature is sovereign
is a whole whose parts are reciprocally linked together and where the
interest of the individual does not come into conflict with the general
good. Each person respects the laws of society which have been drawn
up for the well-being and the preservation of the whole. The maxim of
rational justice, which runs as follows, 'do to others as you would be
done by', can, in theory, be the fundamental principle which governs
the actions of men in a society where justice and order reign. The normative principles of a just society will be deduced from the law of
reason and not from the precepts of natural right.[79]

[78] Ibid., p.284.
[79] The distinction between natural right and the law of reason is not, in Rousseau's
case, the same as the one Hobbes made. To be sure, the distinction is present in
Hobbes, but the connotation he gives the term is quite different. In *Leviathan*,
natural right is defined as the freedom each man has to use his powers in whatever
way he thinks best to safeguard his nature, that is to say, to preserve his life. Natural
right, then, consists in using any method which his reason tells him to be suitable
for that purpose. The concept of natural right, which may be interpreted as the can-
celling of any obligations owed by one party to another as soon as they are in conflict, is therefore quite different from the definition Rousseau gives, which includes
the right to self-defence but also natural compassion. The difference between
Hobbes and Rousseau, here, is a consequence of a difference in their understanding

Nevertheless, such an order is not only inconceivable in the natural state, but is widely transgressed by men who live in society. These men do not behave as members of the universal society of mankind. They act as if each of them was, himself, a sovereign society; the principle which directs their actions is 'self' and they have no respect for the laws of humanity. On the contrary, each of them does his utmost to ensure that others fulfil their duties as defined by the laws of society without applying those laws to himself. The precepts of rational justice are based on reason, as the very name suggests, but no sooner has reason developed than it becomes apparent that the passions opposed to the precepts of natural law have also developed and act with far greater force than reason itself.

Let us now observe [says Rousseau, who has just depicted a society whose members all obey the law of nature] what are the consequences of our human nature as it affects our relations with our fellows; and, contrary to what we have supposed, we find that the progress of society stifles all that is best in us, by awakening selfishness, and we also find that the notion of natural law which it would be more apt to call the law of Reason, begins to develop only at the moment when the passions which have already developed make all its precepts impotent.[80]

of the natural state, which, for the former, is characterized by conflict, while for the latter it is essentially peaceful. There is, however, a broad comparison to be made between their respective conceptions of the natural law. For each of them the law of nature (or of reason) represents a code of law which, if obeyed by everyone, would make it possible for them to lead a peaceful and well-balanced life (see *De cive*, ch.2, s.2; *Leviathan*, Part 1, ch.14). Hobbes considers that these rules, however, are not in themselves sufficient to bring peace, and here Rousseau is in agreement with him. Where he parts company with Hobbes is when he claims that the natural laws are mute in the natural state (*De cive*, Bk 5, ch.2). For Rousseau it is, in fact, with the coming of the social state that the law of reason is stifled, whereas in the natural state it is as yet unknown.

[80] *Manuscrit de Genève, OC*, vol.3, p.284; according to Haymann, 'La Loi naturelle', p.77, Rousseau not only recognizes the validity of the natural law but also that it places an obligation on mankind. The truth is quite the opposite. Rousseau holds that natural laws are clear examples of laws that lack authority: in the *Ecrits sur l'Abbé de St-Pierre*, he spells it out – 'as for what is commonly known as the rights of peoples, it is certain that, unless they are backed up by the threat of punishment, these laws are mere make-believe with even less force than the natural law', *OC*, vol.3, p.610. In the writings of one of the major theorists of natural law, R. Cumberland, the natural law is seen as possessing the power to compel obedience, and he spends a whole chapter, ('De la loi naturelle et de l'obligation qui l'accompagne') in trying to show that the man who seeks the common good (and thus who respects the natural law) will be rewarded, while he who acts against natural law cannot hope to go unpunished. See R. Cumberland, *Traité philosophique des lois naturelles*, Leide, T. Haak, 1749, transl. from the Latin by J. Barbeyrac, pp.206–333. For Rousseau, as has already been stated, no punishment awaits the person who breaks the natural law, and often it is very advantageous to do so.

The 'enlightened man' living in society does not find it 'natural' to subordinate his own private interest to the common interest. From his point of view it is 'natural' to work for his own advantage without concerning himself with the rights of others or the common good.[81] It is not natural for men to act and think as so many parts of a common whole. It would be more accurate to describe as 'natural' the conduct of the person who thinks of himself as a perfect and isolated whole. 'Natural', as has already been observed, becomes a synonym for 'individual' or 'private' as opposed to 'general' or 'public'. Rousseau's theory of the just society takes as its starting point the 'independent and enlightened man', not the man who obeys the maxims of natural law, much less the man who reverences the law of reason. The man Rousseau is thinking of knows very well that his behaviour runs contrary to the precepts of natural law, but he nevertheless believes that he has more to gain from wrongdoing than he can hope for by honest and plain dealing. It is not possible to ground a moral code in the precepts of rational justice because they lack persuasiveness when it comes to influencing men's conduct. Moreover, they lend themselves because of their formal character, to conflicting interpretations, which would be the cause of never-ending disputes:

It is a precept both admirable and sublime that we should do to others as we would that they should do to us. But is it not obvious that, far from serving as the foundation of justice, it is, itself, in need of a foundation? For, what obvious and sound reasons are there for me, being myself, to act as if I were someone else? Furthermore, it is clear that this precept admits of a thousand exceptions which have never been satisfactorily explained.'[82]

With regard to the other classical axiom of natural law 'cuique suum', Rousseau refers to Hobbes. Without going so far as to accept the interpretation of natural law as 'jus in omnia', Rousseau says the following: 'Why, at least, should I not recognize as mine, in the natural state, anything which is useful to me, and which I am able to get hold of?'[83]

Instead of providing the basis for an ordered and peaceful community, the natural law would actually lead to disorder. The natural

---

[81] *Manuscrit de Genève, OC*, vol.3, p.284.
[82] Ibid., p.329; see also *Emile, OC*, vol.4, p.523, where Rousseau explains that the maxims of natural law cannot be justified by reason, but only by the feelings which drive men to identify with their fellow men.
[83] *Manuscrit de Genève, OC*, vol.3, p.329.

law as such has no place in Rousseau's political theory: in the natural
state it is neither understood, nor adhered to; in civil society it is
understood but it is, with a few exceptions, flouted; in the just society
its function as a rule of conduct is replaced by the will of the legitimate
sovereign and by the civil law. Wherein, therefore, lies the much-
vaunted superiority of natural law in comparison with civil law?

The former is superior to the latter in that natural law is a standard
by which the fairness of civil laws may be judged, and, if they are truly
to have the status of law, they must respect the fundamental principle
of natural law: do to others as you would be done by. Good civil laws
dictated by the legitimate authority, and having in view the greatest
possible good of each and everyone, satisfy the principle of rational
justice in that they guarantee the reciprocal nature of rights and
duties. As has been already stated, when the civil law permits or pro-
hibits a certain course of action, it is universal in its scope and will not
tolerate the situation in which certain citizens have only rights or,
alternatively, only duties. A law which allows one person to do what is
forbidden to another would be a law which tolerates the existence
of privilege; but a law which does this is not, for Rousseau, a true law.
By contrast, the sovereign law which applies to all without exception
satisfies the requirement of reciprocity, which forms part of the system of rational justice, but which the latter was not capable of
guaranteeing.

What is well and in conformity with order is so by the nature of things and
independently of human conventions. All justice comes from God, who is its
sole source; but if we knew how to receive so high an inspiration, we should
need neither government nor laws. Doubtless, there is a universal justice
emanating from reason alone; but this justice, to be admitted among us, must
be mutual. Humanly speaking, in default of natural sanctions, the laws of justice are ineffective among men: they merely make for the good of the wicked
and the undoing of the just, when the just man observes them towards
everybody and nobody observes them towards him. Conventions and laws are
therefore needed to join rights to duties and refer justice to its object.[84]

The social compact, which establishes sovereignty, not only does
not contradict the natural law[85] but also translates its principles into
fundamental laws which should guide the actions of the legitimate sovereign will. In fact, the social contract establishes the principle that the sovereign authority must seek the greatest good of

---

[84] *Contrat social, OC*, vol.3, p.378 (transl. Cole, 1952, p.399).
[85] *Lettres écrites de la montagne, OC*, vol.3, p.807.

each and everyone and act *per leges*, that is, by means of abstract and universal precepts. The significance of this is that it thereby fulfils two principles of the natural law: the duty to seek the general law[86] and the prohibition against treating others in a fashion that we would not find acceptable if the same were done to us.

Thus those who, in their exposition of Rousseau, have, like Vaughan, emphasized the radical nature of Rousseau's critique of the doctrine of natural law are right, but not entirely so. They are right to say that Rousseau rejects the idea that the natural law is a principle of conduct universally recognized, accepted and obeyed (at least in the natural state): they are wrong, however, when they claim that Rousseau does not, in his political theory, recognize the moral superiority of the natural law in comparison with positive law.

By contrast, while Derathé has accurately observed that Rousseau never questions the normative superiority of the natural law, he is less convincing when he writes that civil justice is, in the last analysis, nothing other than the restoration of natural justice and that consequently the difference between the natural state and civil society is minimal. It seems to me that the truth is quite the reverse and that there is a notable difference between natural and civil justice. For Rousseau, it is not just a question of adding an element of compulsion to the commands of natural (or rational) justice – something which was lacking in the natural state. The rules of civil justice are different from the precepts of natural justice both in their ground and also in the kind of obligation which they entail. While rational justice is grounded in reason and conscience, civil law is grounded in the legitimate political authority which must, through the fundamental social compact, seek the greatest good for all. Men have a moral obligation towards the natural law while citizens have a juridical and political obligation towards civil law. The citizen is juridically obliged and may, at the same time, feel himself to be morally obliged to respect the civil law. This is how things stand with regard to a civil law

[86] For example, the definition of the basic principle of natural law provided by R. Cumberland is presented in the following words: 'The task of advancing, as far as lies in our power, the common good of the whole order of rational agents, serves to procure, inasmuch as it depends on us, the good of each of the parts, which also contributes to our own happiness, since each of us forms one of those parts: from which it follows that actions contrary to this desire produce contrary results, and consequently bring down suffering on our own heads as well as on our fellow beings'; Cumberland, *Traité philosophique des lois naturelles* (1749), 'Discours préliminaire', p.11.

which citizens deem to be just: it may be imposed by force, since it is a civil law, but it is obeyed quite irrespective of the element of compulsion. However, it may also happen that the juridical obligation is not accompanied by any feeling of moral obligation. An example of this is provided by the unjust law which receives obedience because citizens fear the punishment that may befall them even though they do not feel morally obliged to respect this law because they hold it to be unjust.

The citizen may very well refuse inwardly to give his consent to the civil law, but he cannot refuse to obey it by appealing to the natural law. The laws which have been duly authorized by the general will must be observed for the simple reason that they are the expression of the legal authority. In the just society instituted by the social contract, the supreme judge is the general will; the natural law is still the supreme authority, but its jurisdiction does not reach beyond the inner life of man.

The social contract does not codify the rights or the liberties which (in the logical, not in the chronological sense) exist independently of the institution of the legitimate political constitution. Whether it is a question of the rights which citizens enjoy with respect to the sovereign,[87] or of property rights, most sacred of all the rights possessed by citizens,[88] or of the 'inviolable rights of all citizens within the state, with regard to their person',[89] these are all rights founded on the social contract, the true cornerstone of all rights.[90] Individual citizens do not enjoy these rights to liberty before (in the logical sense) the political society is instituted. These liberties are born with the advent of the political constitution and the laws which act as its bulwark. If the just political constitution did not exist there could only be natural independence, obedience to the passing whim, but not liberty.

Liberty and the republic

The sovereignty of law and equality under the law represent for Rousseau the only rational response to the argument that justice is always opposed to private interests. The whole theory of the social

---

[87] *Economie politique, OC*, vol.3, p.242.   [88] Ibid., p.263.
[89] Ibid., p.257.   [90] *Contrat social, OC*, vol.3, p.365.

contract is, ultimately, no more than a rational justification of a law-governed society.[91] Contrary to the thesis referred to above, it is not in the true interest of men to live in a condition of complete independence or under a political constitution where the sovereign will resides in one person alone and where equality under the law is not respected.

The sovereignty of law and equality under the law are central to Rousseau's response to the problem of the relation between justice and utility. It was not by chance that he appended certain lines of Virgil to the frontispiece of the *Social contract*: 'let us provide them with equitable laws' 'foederis aequas dicamus leges': Aeneid, Bk 11). This same frontispiece provides other important clues. For example, it also contains one of Rousseau's favourite symbols, the cat – the most independent of animals and the one who resists most determinedly any attempt to curtail its liberty.[92] With Virgil's lines and the image of the cat, Rousseau, who was particularly fond of symbols which he would often select for the frontispiece of his works, provides the key to the interpretation of the *Social contract*. If we follow Rousseau's hint we will find that the cardinal point of his political doctrine is the relation between the sovereignty of law and liberty.

Moreover, in his defence of the *Social contract* against the criticism levelled against it, he makes it clear that the basic theme of the book is the necessary relation between the sovereignty of law and liberty.

Just read it, Sir, this book which has been so fiercely criticized, but which is so timely; you will find on every page that it claims the right of freedom, but always under law, without which freedom is not possible, and under which one is always free, whatever form of government there may be.[93]

Rousseau adds that, 'liberty always follows the fate of law, it reigns or perishes with it; I know of nothing more certain.'[94] As law is identified with the general will, liberty is possible only through obedience to the general will.[95] In the fragment entitled '*Des loix*' Rousseau explains the connection between liberty and the sovereignty of law in an unambiguous way:

---

[91] On Rousseau's conception of law see P. Pasqualucci, 'Il soggetto e la legge secondo Jean-Jacques Rousseau', *Rivista internazionale di filosofia del diritto*, 60 (1983), pp. 382–406.

[92] The same symbol appears in the frontispiece of the *Discours sur l'origine de l'inégalité*.

[93] *Lettres écrites de la montagne*, *OC*, vol.3, p.811; see also the Dedication of the *Discours sur l'inégalité*, *OC*, vol.3, p.112.

[94] *Lettres écrites de la montagne*, *OC*, vol.3, p.842.   [95] Ibid., p.811.

I am free when I am subject to the laws, but not when I am forced to obey my fellow man, because in the latter case I am doing the will of just one individual, but when I obey the law I act at the behest of the common will, which is as much mine as it is anyone else's.[96]

The liberty which consists in submission to the law is, in the first place, the liberty which comes from belonging to the sovereign body.[97] However, Rousseau's interpretation of the relation between liberty and law (still defined as the expression of the general will) does not only consist in a simple assertion of the principle of positive liberty, but also implies a negative liberty, meaning by this protection for the individual from outside interference.

For Rousseau liberty is the opposite of the servitude which occurs when one man is subject to the whims of another. Liberty is not the same as being independent. The citizen who is subject to the general will is not independent since he is subject to the sovereign authority, but he is free because he is not forced to obey the will of any other individual. Men who live in the natural state (as described in the *Geneva manuscript*) are independent because they are not subject to any political authority, but they are not free because either they must do the bidding of another or they themselves command the obedience of those around them. On this issue, Rousseau does no more than go over the ground already covered by Montesquieu in the *Spirit of laws*, where he defines political liberty in the following words: 'It is necessary to grasp', he states, 'the difference between independence and liberty. Liberty is the right to do everything which the laws allow: and if a citizen were able to do what is forbidden, there would be no more liberty because the others would also have this same right.'[98]

In his defence of the *Social contract* which appears on the *Lettres de la montagne*, Rousseau makes direct use of this ideal of political liberty:

One should never confuse independence and freedom. These two things are so different that they are actually mutually exclusive. When everyone does what he likes that often means doing something which annoys others and they cannot fairly be described as being free. Liberty is not so much a question of

---

[96] *Des loix*, *OC*, vol.3, p.492.
[97] According to Isaiah Berlin, Rousseau, in fact, 'does not mean by liberty the "negative" freedom of the individual not to be interfered with within a defined area, but the possession by all, and not merely by some, of the fully qualified members of a society of a share in the public power which is entitled to interfere with every aspect of every citizen's life'; 'Two concepts of liberty', in *Four essays on liberty*, London, 1969, pp.162–3; see also N. Bobbio, *Il futuro della democrazia*, Turin, 1984, p.156.
[98] *Esprit des lois*, Bk 11, ch.3.

doing what you want as not being forced to do what others want; even less so does it involve making others subservient to ourselves.[99]

The general will makes men into free citizens because it protects them from the fate of being subjected to the whim of some other individual. In the original compact each citizen continued to obey the general will, and in thus pledging obedience to all the others he owes obedience to no single individual since the situation in which the general will and equality under the law are supreme removes none of men's freedoms even though they are no longer independent. In the political constitution where law and the public good are sovereign, citizens obey but no one gives the orders; they are subjects but they have no masters. They appear to be in subjection but in fact they are free and, by agreeing that this republic should be instituted, 'each loses no part of his liberty but what might be hurtful to that of another'.[100]

Moreover, these passages which are often used to present an image of a 'totalitarian' Rousseau opposed to freedom must, on the contrary, be considered as so many affirmations of the principle of liberty as total independence of the will of any other individual. Rousseau writes, 'whoever refuses to obey the general will, will be constrained to do so by the whole body: which means nothing more nor less than that he will be forced to be free'; he also adds that this is what is involved when the fate of each citizen is entrusted to his country while at the same time he receives a guarantee that he will never become personally dependent on another.

If being free means the absence of any constraint preventing the individual from acting as an independent being seeking to attain his own personal goals, it is clear that to speak of a constraint being necessary for freedom to exist is a contradiction in terms. But if 'being free' means not being subject to the domination of others and making no attempt ourselves to control their actions, it is not a contradiction to say that he who is forced to obey the general will is 'forced to be free'. He who refuses to obey the general will is unwilling to obey the deliberations of the sovereign body of which he forms part and has as its goal the common good. By his refusal he seeks to promote his selfish interests at the expense of the good of others and thus dispenses with the principle of equality under the law. Therefore he considers that the duties imposed by the law should be respected by

---

[99] *Lettres écrites de la montagne, OC*, vol.3, p.841.
[100] *Economie politique, OC*, vol.3, p.248 (transl. Cole, 1952, p.370).

others but not himself. If he achieves his goal the consequence is that
the will of one individual has triumphed over the will of all the others
who thus become the means to the attainment of his personal ends.
But this means that neither he nor any of his fellow citizens is now
free: he, because he has attained a position of dominance, and the
others because they must obey. He who refuses to obey the general
will refuses to obey the law, and he places himself above the law. He
violates liberty for, according to Rousseau, there is 'no freedom
without law, neither can freedom exist so long as any one person is
above the law'.

The same considerations apply in the other passage where
Rousseau explains that the fundamental clause of the social compact
is 'the complete submission of each member with all his rights to the
will of the community'. This text has been interpreted as proof that
the theory of the social contract ultimately assumes the complete
subordination of the individual with all his rights, to the state.[101] In
this context it is necessary to point out that the total abrogation of all
rights is, according to Rousseau, a necessary condition to be met if the
body politic is not to degenerate into tyranny. The reason for this is
clear: if each one retains this natural liberty and unrestricted right to
anything that catches his fancy or that lies within his grasp (for it is
precisely these rights being referred to here), he can always resist the
general will by appealing to his own rights. This would mean that
individual interests might prevail against the general interest, and
there would be certain individuals who were above the law, and this,
of course, would mean tyranny. Rousseau holds that the sovereignty
of law makes the people free: 'a free people obeys, but it does not
serve, it has leaders but no masters; it obeys the laws, but it obeys only
the laws, and it is due to the strength of the laws that it does not find it
necessary to obey men.'[102]

[101] It is on this point that the theorists of 'negative liberty' have always relied to criticize
the *Social contract* as a book which provides arguments for those who advocate
tyranny. 'What can be the significance of rights that one enjoys in proportion as
they are taken away from one? What is the meaning of a form of liberty by virtue of
which one's freedom is enhanced as the ability to choose is steadily taken away? The
supporters of despotism can derive great advantage from Rousseau's principles'; *De
l'esprit de conquête et de l'usurpation*, in *Oeuvres*, Paris, 1957, p.1049. See also R. Chapman, *Rousseau totalitarian or liberal?*, New York, 1968, pp.74–88.

[102] *Lettres écrites de la montagne*, *OC*, vol.3, p.842. The argument that liberty is not incompatible with obedience to rational laws intended for the common good is also to be
found in Spinoza (*Tractatus Theologicus-Politicus*): 'Admittedly action done by order,
i.e. obedience, does destroy freedom in a sense, but it does not of itself make a man a
slave; what makes a man a slave is the object of his action. If its object is not the
benefit of the agent himself, but of the man who gives the order, then the agent is a

Hobbes, in the *Leviathan* (Bk 2, ch. 21), had been careful to distinguish between individual liberty and the liberty of the state ('the liberty of particular men' and 'the liberty of the commonwealth'): 'The Athenians, and Romans were free; that is, free commonwealths: not that any particular men had the liberty to resist their own representative; but that their representative had the liberty to resist, or invade other people.'

For Hobbes, the liberty of the subject is dependent on the obligation that each one accepted when he submitted to the sovereign authority. It consists of the right of self-defence and the right enjoyed by each citizen that he should not be forced to do anything that might be for his harm. But, above all, the liberty of the subject is expressed in those things which are not forbidden, in the things not mentioned by the sovereign, that is, where the law is silent. Hobbes lists such things as the freedom to buy and sell, the choice where to live and to give one's children the education considered appropriate. At the same time he reproaches the Greek and Roman writers on politics for having allowed the liberty of the state to become confused with the liberty of the individual. By contrast, Rousseau relies directly on these same writers to argue for the identity of the liberty of the citizen and the liberty of the polity.

Man, like the polity, is free when he does not have to depend on anyone else. The analogy between individual liberty and the liberty of the polity had already been made by Machiavelli who, at the beginning of the *Discourses*, distinguished between the 'cities' which 'in their early days were subordinate to a foreign power' and those 'cities' which 'from the very beginning were free from external control but immediately became a self-governing State', in the same way he distinguished between 'free men' and men who were 'dependent on others'.

Everything points to the fact that the liberty which Rousseau is referring to here is political, that is to say, the liberty of the people or of the polity. The principle that the best form of government is the one where law has sovereignty over men and checks their desires is to be found, supported by other argument, in Aristotle (*Politics*, 1286a)

slave, and useless to himself. But in a state where the welfare of the whole people, and not of the ruler, is the highest law, he who obeys the sovereign in everything must not be called a slave, useless to himself, but a subject. Thus the state whose laws are based on sound reason enjoys the greatest freedom; for in it everyone can be free whenever he wishes, i.e. can live with a sound mind under the guidance of reason' (transl. A.G. Wernham, *Benedict de Spinoza, The political works*, Oxford, 1958, pp.135–7).

and in Plato (*Laws*, 715d; *The Statesman*, 294ab – 196e). With regard to the idea that obedience to the law is the one and only guarantee of liberty, Rousseau was very probably influenced by the well-known passage from Cicero:

The State without laws is like the body when it is deprived of the mind and can no longer cause its constituent parts – the nervous system, the blood and limbs – to function. The magistrates are ministers of the law, the judges its interpreters: through the laws we are all made servants in order that we may be free.[103]

The people, or the polity, are free when they are not subject to the will of a despot who governs in his own interest or for the benefit of a foreign power. 'Liberty', wrote Cicero, 'is the right of the people which opposes *slavery* and *domination*.'[104]

[103] *Pro Cluentio Avito*, Oratio quartadecima, L 111, 53, 146, in Marci Tullii Ciceronis, *Opera quae extent omnia*, Studio atque industria Jani Guglielmii et Jani Grutari, additis eorum notis integris nunc demo recognita ab Jacobo Grenovio, Laudanum, 1690, 'Pars Quarta', vol.2, p.1269 (transl. W. Peterson, London 1895, p.84). The Laudanum edition is very probably the edition owned by Rousseau: see Rousseau to J. Barillot, a bookseller in Geneva, April–October 1736, in *Correspondance complète*, ed. R.A. Leigh, vol.1, n.13, pp.37–42. For the history of the idea of government by law see F.A. Hayek, *The constitution of liberty*, Chicago, 1960; see also: N. Bobbio, *Il futuro della democrazia*, Turin, 1984, in particular the final chapter, 'Governo degli uomini o governo delle leggi?'.

[104] Cicero's text states: 'That the Roman people should be slaves is contrary to divine law; the immortal Gods have willed it to rule all nations. Matters have been brought to the utmost crisis; the issue is liberty. You must either win victory, Romans, which assuredly you will achieve by your loyalty and such unanimity, or do anything rather than be slaves. Other nations can endure slavery, the assured possession of the Roman people is liberty' ('Populum Romanum servire fas non est; quem dii immortales omnibus gentibus imperare voluerunt. Res in extremum est adducta discriminen; de libertate decernitur. Aut vincatis oportet, Quirites, quod profecto et pietate vestra et tanta concordia consequemini, aut quidvis potius, quam serviatis. Aliae nationes servitutem pati possunt, populi Romani est propria libertas': 6 *Phil*, s.7, par.19; transl. Walter C.A. Ker, London, 1921, p.333), in *Opera Omnia* (1690), 'Pars Quarta', vol.3, p.2043. Cicero was not the only writer in the republican tradition who in all probability influenced Rousseau on the issue of liberty. Political liberty, interpreted as law having sovereignty in human affairs, is also present in Livy and Sallust, two writers with whose work Rousseau was familiar. 'Now', writes Livy (*Ab urbe condita*, Bk 2, ch.1) 'I will describe the deeds of the Roman people, freely delivered of all servitude both in war and peace, and its dignitaries appointed each year and its empire, more powerful by law than any force of people' ('Liberi, iam hinc populi Romani res pace belloque gestas, annuos magistratus, imperiaque legum potentiora quam hominum peragam'). The commentary in the Lémaire edition, Paris, 1822, vol.1, pp.170–1, reads as follows: 'That is the state of a free people, bound by law, whose strength is very great and of great effect, even divine and immutable; in which there is no place, as occurs in the powers of men, either for leniency or wrath, strong desire or caprice, and, finally, they cannot be deflected by the workings of chance'. Rousseau probably also derived from Livy the idea that political liberty requires moderation: 'Libertate modice utuntur' (Bk 34, ch.49).

Moreover, if a people is not free, neither are the individual members. If the polity is ruled by a tyrant who subordinates the common good to his own private interest, that indicates that most citizens cannot protect their interests as they would like. But if they cannot achieve what they want, it follows that they are prevented from acting as they would like. This, in turn, means that individuals are not free, in the sense of 'being free from hindrance'. They are faced with obstacles which do not allow them to pursue their own goals. Hobbes's distinction between the freedom of the state and the freedom of the individual subject is not, therefore, applicable to Rousseau's conception of freedom.[105] If a people is not free, and it is only free when it obeys the law, it has been enslaved by a single man (or a foreign power); and if a people is enslaved, so also are the individuals who together form that people.

The liberty of the citizen does not consist only in the exercise of the right of sovereignty. It also implies protection from all wrongs and injustices. The limits of the liberty of each individual also mark the point at which the liberty of his neighbour begins. The guarantee of these reciprocal limits is provided by the finality of law. The sovereignty of law provides encouragement for each citizen to respect his neighbour's rights, thanks to the principles of universality and reciprocity which are its essential characteristics. Since law does not allow one person to do what is forbidden to another, it ensures that no one can enlarge the sphere of his freedom at the expense of others. When one person's liberty is infringed by another, the latter imposes his will on the former. Consequently, the will of one has become subject to another, which is for Rousseau the very opposite of liberty. Without the limits set by the boundaries of their neighbour's exactly equal space of freedom, citizens may not be called to account for anything: 'In the republic', and here Rousseau reiterates what the

---

On the idea of liberty in republican Rome, see G. Crifo, 'Di alcuni aspetti della liberta in Roma', *Archivio Giuridico Filippo Serafini*, 33 (1958), pp.1–72. On Rousseau's reading of Livy and Sallust see *Les Confessions, OC*, vol.1, p.1352, n.2; *Emile, OC*, vol.4, pp.29 and 529.

[105] See on this subject Q. Skinner, 'The idea of negative liberty: philosophical and historical perspectives', in R. Rorty, J.B. Schneewind, Q. Skinner (eds.), *Philosophy in history*, Cambridge, 1984, pp.193–221, especially pages 212–13, where the author points out that 'Hobbes has either failed to grasp the point of the classical republican argument . . . or else (a far more probable hypothesis) is deliberately attempting to distort it.'

Marquis d'Argenson had said, 'everyone is perfectly free to act as he wishes providing that he does no harm to others.'[106]

Like Hobbes, Rousseau praises the civil state. But his praise is reserved for the civil state governed by the general will and by law. With the social contract man loses his 'natural liberty and an unlimited right to everything he tries to get and succeeds in getting', but he gains 'civil liberty and the proprietorship of everything he possesses.'[107] In exchanging their natural liberty for civil liberty, men have improved their circumstances. Natural liberty seems to be unbounded but its only guarantee lies in the individual's strength. It is, in reality, very fragile and may at any moment be transformed into servitude. By contrast, civil liberty is limited and has very precise limits set by civil laws and the rights of others. But it guarantees, for each person, a right which social union makes absolutely certain: security and the protection of his life and property.[108] In the first place, therefore, the legitimate state guarantees security, and herein lies its superiority over the natural state. Moreover, men accept the social compact precisely because they prefer a 'better and more secure' life than 'one which is uncertain and precarious'.

To this point, Rousseau adds the following:

To the list of advantages provided by the civil state one could add moral liberty, which alone makes man truly master of himself; for to be driven by one's appetites alone is slavery, and obedience to a law which one has prescribed for oneself is freedom. But I have already said enough on this topic and the philosophical sense of the word 'liberty' is not my subject here.

Even though from this extract it might appear that Rousseau does not attach great importance to moral freedom, it would seem that this very concept plays an important part in his theory of political order and, in this context, it will be of interest to compare the passage from the *Social contract* quoted above with another one in *Emile* in which Rousseau mentions a form of liberty which is specifically moral and which is not the same as civil liberty:

[106] Rousseau's quotation does not correspond exactly with what the Marquis d'Argenson had written in his *Considérations sur le gouvernement ancien et présent de la France*, Amsterdam, Michel Rey, 1764. The passage by which Rousseau was most probably influenced reads: 'perhaps nobody has ever contemplated the degree of liberty which I have just described; this is what the laws must allow for those who are subject to them in order that they may conserve all their natural energy which leads to great things, but also so that they may be able to suppress, where necessary, the licence which disturbs the general order; often there is too much repression or too much disorder' (p.22).   [107] *Contrat social, OC*, Bk 1, ch.8 (transl. Cole, 1952, p.393).
[108] Ibid., Bk 2, ch.4 (transl. ibid., p.398).

If the laws of nations, like the laws of nature, could never be broken by any human power, dependence on men would become dependence on things. All the advantages of a state of nature would be combined with all the advantages of social life in the commonwealth. The liberty which preserves a man from vice would be united with the morality which raises him to virtue.[109]

The strength of the general will and the sovereignty of law remove the need for men to be dependent on others and this is the first step towards virtue, for being dependent on others is a form of 'disorder' and is an unending source of corruption. Moreover, the civil laws are able to restrain men's selfishness through the threat of retribution and this prevents them from wronging their fellows.

But this is not yet moral liberty, for this is an inward quality; while civil liberty has to do with social relations, moral liberty is relevant to a man's relations with his inner self. To attain moral liberty a man must control his inner passions and live in harmony with a law which he has imposed on himself. Only the man who is willing to obey the inner voices of conscience and reason is 'really free', that is, morally free.[110] The man who is morally free obeys an inner law, not one that is external to him. He is just and moderate, because he loves justice and moderation, not because he fears the retribution of civil law. Even if there were no civil laws or political authority, and no courts, the man who was morally free would still act in the same way. It is possible to force a man to be free defined in the sense of civil law, but it is not possible to force anyone to be morally free. A people which has moral liberty is one whose customs are all that is necessary to make the citizens just and moderate. Moral liberty is the prerogative of the man who can find the necessary strength to tame his inner passions and this only the virtuous man is able to do:

The word 'virtue' is derived from a word signifying strength, and strength is the foundation of all virtue. Virtue is not the heritage of a creature weak by nature but strong by will; that is the whole merit of a righteous man; and though we call God good we do not call Him virtuous, because He does good without effort.[111]

The virtuous man is not one who has succeeded in rooting out his passions, but he has learnt how to control them. According to Rousseau, it is not that certain passions are to be allowed and others not. Passions are always reprehensible when they take control of a

---

[109] *Emile OC*, vol.4, p.311 (transl. Foxley, 1974, p.49).
[110] Ibid., p.818. [111] Ibid., p.817 (transl. ibid., p.408).

person; they are good when they are governed by reason: 'To feel or
not feel passion is beyond our control, but we can control ourselves.
Every sentiment under our own control is lawful; those which control
us are criminal.[112]

Rousseau has clearly been influenced here by the ideal of moral virtue put forward by Plutarch in his moral works. Moral virtue is a
quality imprinted on the irrational part of the human soul through a
long process of maturation and this is why, says Plutarch, philosophers
have talked of 'Ethos' or of 'Customs'. In fact, moral virtue does not
bring about the sudden destruction of passion but works slowly and
requires patience. Reason is not concerned to

eliminate or uproot our passions, because such a course is neither possible
nor desirable, but only provides them with some kind of limit and thus
establishes a degree of order, with the result that moral virtues are no longer
impassivity, but are rather achieved by the control and moderation of our
passions and the affections of our soul; this is achieved by prudence which
reduces the power of the sensual and feeling part of the self to make it adopt
an honest and praise-worthy way of life.[113]

In the virtuous man reason reigns over the passions, but it does so
by persuasion not by enforcing obedience. It reigns as a wise monarch, not as a despot. The temperance of the virtuous man is not at all
the same thing as continence:

When reason governs and shapes the sensual and passionate part of the self, as
with an animal which has been thoroughly broken in and has become completely accustomed to the bridle, it is now found to be very ready to obey and
quite willing to accept the bit. And self-control is when reason is the stronger,
but lust arrives, and it brings with it grief and sorrow because it is not willing
to obey: thus it goes along in a disorderly manner, driven by blows, forced
along by the bit, and resisting reason as much as it can and thus causing it
much labour and trouble.[114]

When Rousseau describes the man who is morally virtuous as 'well-
balanced' he is using the words in the same sense as Plutarch.[115] The
virtuous man is the one who can govern his passions and keep his
desires proportionate to what he is capable of achieving. By leading a
life which is 'well-ordered' ('bien ordonné'), man can be reconciled to
his true nature, since, as Rousseau points out in his *Lettre à l'Archevêque
de Beaumont*, 'man is a creature who, by nature, is good, loving justice

---

[112] Ibid., p.819 (transl. ibid., p.409).
[113] Plutarch, *Les Oeuvres morales et meslées*, transl. Jacques Amyot, Geneva, published by
   Françoise Estiene, 1582, ch.3, 'On virtue', p.32 (transl. F.C. Babbitt, *Plutarch's
   'Moralia'*, London and Cambridge, Mass., 1962, vol.2, pp.93–101.
[114] Plutarch, ibid., p.33.   [115] *Emile*, *OC*, vol.4, p.304.

and order'.[116] Although the hold egotism has gained over him has warped his nature, contact with moral freedom restores a man to harmony with himself. Only a man who is morally free can be truly himself and completely free from 'appearance'. The liberty which is appropriate to the nature of man is not merely a question of living independently of the will of others, but is realized through a very particular mode of conduct, namely, when the individual's behaviour bears the imprint of order.

Inner order is not to be compared with a polity where one man or some section of the populace has reintroduced order after an uprising. A better comparison would be with the 'well-regulated society'. Communal reason controls men's passions through the civil law; when a man's life is well balanced, his passions are subject to a law which he has imposed upon himself in accordance with reason and conscience. In the former case, order vanishes as soon as the uncontrolled passions of one man or of a social faction (or still more the greed of citizens in general) place themselves above the law; in the latter case order is destroyed because the individual is enslaved by his passions and his desires. The polity is free because it owes obedience only to the laws which it has chosen for itself; the individual retains his liberty so long as he obeys the law he has chosen for himself and is not controlled by his passions. But when order is lost, liberty and happiness go too – and this is as true of the individual as it is of the polity.

A just political order provides the best possible conditions for the growth of moral liberty. In a well-regulated republic, as we shall see in the next chapter, virtue is encouraged and the wicked receive no rewards. By contrast, in a society where injustice reigns, inward moral liberty is the only form of freedom that the wise man may hope for. In a society where private interests and human passions go by the name of 'law', the just man is forced to submit to laws of which he, himself, would never approve and he cannot avoid becoming dependent on the will of those persons who rule the polity.[117] The only laws to which he can appeal are the 'eternal laws of nature and of order', which, for the wise man, 'take the place of positive law'.[118] They are written on his heart by conscience and reason and it is these he must obey if he wants to be free. When Rousseau states that 'liberty does not reside in any particular form of government, but in the heart of the free man;

---

[116] *Lettre à l'Archevêque Christophe de Beaumont*, *OC*, vol.4, p.935.
[117] *Emile*, *OC*, vol.4, pp.857–8.
[118] Ibid. (transl. Foxley, 1974, p.437).

he carries it everywhere with him', he is referring to moral liberty which is the final court of appeal of the self-disciplined man forced to live in disorder. Nevertheless, Rousseau also notes that the 'mere appearance of order' leads the upright man to a knowledge and love of order. The mere existence of civil laws, even if they are not respected, helps man to become virtuous. They 'give him the courage to be just, even when surrounded by evil doers'.[119] In an unjust society, where laws are not respected, there can be no civil liberty since these laws do not provide protection against injustice, but they point the upright man towards moral liberty. If superficial order can provide encouragement for the upright man who wants to acquire moral liberty, true political order is able both to guarantee civil liberty and encourage moral liberty.

True order is, according to Rousseau, a 'Republic'. He means by this term 'every state that is governed by laws, no matter what the form of its administration may be; for only in such a case does the public interest govern, and the res publica rank as a reality. Every legitimate government is republican.'[120]

If the law is sovereign, it is certain that the common interest 'governs'. In the first place, the sovereignty of law guarantees liberty and equality under the law which is the 'greatest good of all' and must be 'the goal of every system of law'.[121]

Moreover, in a republic the 'common interest is something important' because every government which allows itself to be guided by the general will has as its goal the greatest good of each and every one and not the satisfaction of the private interests of an elite few, however powerful they might be.[122] The purpose of law should be the well-

---

[119] Ibid., p.858.
[120] *Contrat social, OC*, vol.3, pp.379–80, transl. Cole, 1952, p.40. In *Politics*, III, 6–7, 1279a, Aristotle calls 'a *republic* properly speaking' the form of government where the many administer the State with a view to the common interest; while 'a republic' is at the same time 'the name common to all true constitutions'. There is the same ambivalence here that also exists in Machiavelli and Rousseau. On the issue of the legitimacy of political authority in the thought of Rousseau and in modern theories of democracy see W. Maihofer, *Prinzipien freiheitlicher Demokratie*, Handbuch des Verfassungsrechts, De Gruyter, 1982, pp.186–194.
[121] *Contrat social, OC*, vol.3, p.391.
[122] In *Economie politique*, instead of the word 'republic', Rousseau uses the phrase 'legitimate or popular public economy'. The sense is, however, the same since he had in mind a government 'whose object is the good of the people, and therefore . . . to follow in everything the general will', *OC*, vol.3, p.247 (transl. Cole, 1952, p.370); the distinction between legitimate and illegitimate government recalls the distinction made by Aristotle between good and bad political constitutions: 'the conclusion is evident: that governments which have a regard to the common interest are constituted in accordance with strict principles of justice, and are therefore true

being and security of each individual as well as the good and security of the republic. In formulating his conception of law, Rousseau uses for the purpose the principle that Cicero had expounded in Bk 2 of *De Legibus* (lines 12–13): 'Without question it is agreed that laws are framed to preserve the State from harm, for the safety of the citizens and to ensure a tranquil and happy life for all'.

In a state where justice reigns, the public good, which is the purpose of all law, does not require the sacrifice of the individual's private interests. For Rousseau the 'public good' is not a kind of 'summum bonum' or 'Reason of State' which should be allowed to ride roughshod over the interests of the individual citizens. The public good is to be equated, rather, with the 'utilitas publica' or 'communis utilitas' to which Cicero referred.[123] Now, the 'utilitas publica' does not conflict with the 'utilitas singulorum'; it is opposed only to 'cupiditas'. Thus, for Rousseau, in a state ruled by just laws, the public good is incompatible with the extravagant desire for wealth or power, but it does not militate against the citizens' well-being and security. If political activity is to have moral validity, it should aim to bring the public good, that is the interest of the polity as an entity, into harmony with the interests of citizens as individuals.[124] This notion of morally valid political action was borrowed, in all probability, from the Marquis d'Argenson, who had described politics as a 'difficult art whose practice requires both moderation and severity', and whose purpose must be the bringing together, on to the common ground of the general good, of those different interests within the republic which so easily enter into conflict, not only with each other but with the common good.[125]

The most difficult problem to be solved, if a just political order is to be preserved, is that of ensuring that the deliberations of the sovereign body would in actual fact be working for the public good, that is to say, that they should be 'de jure'.[126] Rousseau commented more than once that the deliberations of the people might not necessarily embody the general will:

forms; but those which regard only the interests of the rulers are all defective and perverted forms, for they are despotic, whereas States are a community of free men.' *Politics*, 1279a (transl. B. Jowett, *Great Books*, vol.9, 1952, p.476).

[123] See J. Gaudemet, 'Utilitas publica', *Revue historique de droit française et étranger*', 29 (1951), pp.465–99.   [124] *Lettre à Monseigneur de Beaumont, OC*, vol.4, p.937.

[125] Marquis d'Argenson, *Considérations sur le gouvernement ancien et présent de la France*, Amsterdam, 1764, pp.26–7; *Contrat social*, Bk 2, ch.3.

[126] See *Contrat social*, Bk 2, chs.1, 2, 3; Bk 4, chs.1, 2, 3.

It is not impossible that a Republic, though in itself well governed, should enter upon an unjust war. Nor is it less possible for the Council of a Democracy to pass unjust decrees, and condemn the innocent; but this never happens unless the people is seduced by private interests, which the credit or eloquence of some clever persons substitutes for those of the State: in which case the general will will be one thing and the result of the public deliberation another.[127]

It is always possible that 'factions' and 'cliques' may form within the sovereign body and succeed in getting the assembly to agree to their wishes and thus allow their private interests to prevail. In order that the public deliberations should be in conformity with the general will, Rousseau proposes various ways in which collective decisions might be made, the precise one used being dependent on the gravity of the problem under discussion.[128] The more serious the problem that the collectivity faces, the greater must be the unanimity if the measure is to be passed. But still more important than questions of procedure is the requirement that the deliberation of the sovereign body should be 'de jure', that is, the members of this body should not heed their 'hidden motives' and their private interests. For Rousseau, public decision-making should be something more than merely quantifying the individual preferences of the members of the sovereign body.[129] If this were to happen, the majority vote would represent the interests of one part of the polity and the minority would be forced to accept a decision imposed on them from outside, and thus they would no longer be free. A just political order requires that in the discussion of public policy, the citizens exercising their sovereignty should not attempt to advance their personal interests, nor the interests of a party or any other group, but that they should deliberate as citizens, that is, keeping in mind the public good and the long-term interests of the community.

The different procedures for decision-making can be of assistance in the task of recognizing the general will and ensuring that the deliberations of the public assembly do not become invalid. Rousseau thinks that preventing 'partial associations' and factions from forming, will make less likely the degeneration of the general will into the pursuit of merely personal goals. Yet the *Social contract* seems to rely

---

[127] *Economie politique*, *OC*, vol.3, p.246 (transl. Cole, 1952, p.369).
[128] *Contrat social*, Bk 4, ch.2.
[129] On this point, see K.J. Arrow, *Social choice and individual values*, New Haven and London, 1963, pp.81–91; J. Elster, *Sour grapes, Studies in the subversion of rationality*, Cambridge, 1983, in particular pp.33–42.

on the civil virtue of citizens and the openness of the deliberations of
the sovereign body as the main bulwark against the corruption of the
body politic. The appeal to civic virtue reveals just how difficult it is to
make sure that the sovereign will and the general will coincide. The
selfish interests of individuals are continually acting as an obstacle to
the realization of the general will. Consequently, as we shall see, the
liberty of citizens and the sovereignty of law are under threat and in
danger of being dissolved.

In Rousseau's terminology the 'Republic' is not a form of government
in the same sense as a monarchy or aristocracy is. In principle,
Rousseau's theory does not rule out a monarchy which is also a
republic as being a contradiction in terms. The opposite of a republic
is a tyranny, the former being a legitimate and the latter an
illegitimate form of government. While in the republic the general will
is sovereign, by definition, a tyranny is control exercised by a private
will (even if the private will in question emanates from more than one
single individual). In Rousseau's theory there is a fundamental opposition between the republic and despotism and this fact merits a number of further observations. In the *Social contract* he takes pains to spell
out the distinction between the tyrant and the despot:

In order that I may give different things different names, I call him who usurps
the royal authority a tyrant, and him who usurps the sovereign power a despot. The tyrant is he who thrusts himself in contrary to the laws to govern in
accordance with the laws; the despot is he who sets himself above the laws
themselves. Thus the tyrant cannot be a despot, but the despot is always a
tyrant.[130]

Despotism, therefore, has two distinguishing characteristics:
sovereign power is wielded by usurpers, and it is not exercised for the
public good.[131] There is also another aspect of despotism which illustrates even more clearly the fundamental contrast with the republic.
The state becomes despotic the moment that certain of its members
are unfairly treated in comparison with others, or when the government sacrifices one person for the benefit of the majority.[132] These are
characteristics which resemble closely those which Locke mentioned
in the chapter of his *Second treatise* devoted to tyranny. In each case,

---

[130] *Contrat social*, *OC*, vol.3, p.423 (transl. Cole, 1952, p.419).
[131] *Economie politique*, *OC*, vol.3, p.427.
[132] *Economie politique*, *OC*, vol.3, p.256.

despotism is the opposite of a state where law is sovereign: 'Where-ever Law ends', says Locke, 'Tyranny begins'.[133]

In order to have a clearer idea of the opposition between despotism (illegitimate power) and the state where the law is sovereign (legitimate power), it should be pointed out that the law in question is the fundamental or constitutive law – the law which constitutes the body politic by uniting all the members of the state under a sovereign authority whose purpose and limits are spelt out by this same law.[134] For Rousseau, this fundamental law is grounded in the social compact. This is why the latter is also described as the 'fundamental compact'.[135]

[133] John Locke, 'An essay concerning the true original extent, and end of the civil government', ch.18, §2 *Two treatises of government*, text annotated and edited by P. Laslett, Cambridge, 1970, pp.416–18.

[134] 'Going back to the origins of political right, we find that before there were leaders, by the very nature of things, laws must have existed. At least one was necessary to establish the public confederation, a second would have been needed to set up some kind of government and these two suppose the existence of various intermediary laws of which the most solemn and sacred was the one through which each citizen pledged to obey all the others', *Des loix, OC*, vol.3, p.491.

[135] Very probably Rousseau was influenced here by the definition of the *Lex fundamentalis* given by Althusius: 'for under this law the universal association has to be constituted in the realm. This law serves as the foundation, so to speak, of the realm and is sustained by the common consent and approval of the members of the realm. By this law all the members of the realm have to be brought together under one head and united in one body. It is indeed called the pillar of the realm' ('Sub hac enim lege, universalis consociatio in regno est constituta, qua tanquam fundamento nititur, atque ex communi consensu et approbatione membrorum regni sustinetur, atque haec omnia regni membra sub uno capite collecta et in unum corpus sunt conjuncta, quae dicitur etiam columna regni'), Johannes Althusius, *Politica methodice digesta*, Caput XIX, 49, reprint of the third edition of 1614, Cambridge, Mass., 1932, p.169; transl. by Frederick S. Careny, *The politics of Johannes Althusius*, London, 1965, p.123. It is interesting to note that in the chapter 28, 'De tyrannide eiusque remediis', Althusius defines tyranny as the opposite of an 'upright and just administration' ('rectae et justae administrationis') and as a violation of the fundamental law (paras. 5 and 6). Derathé emphasizes Rousseau's debt to Althusius in *J.-J. Rousseau et la science politique de son temps*, Paris, 1970, pp.130, 135, and he here rejects the idea that Rousseau ever accepted the notion that sovereignty was limited by any fundamental laws. It is true that Rousseau says that 'there is not, nor could there ever be, any form of fundamental law which is imperative for the whole body of the people, not even the social contract' (*Contrat social*, Bk 1, ch.8). This, however, only means that (cf. *Contrat social*, Bk 2, ch.12) the sovereign may change the fundamental laws if he thinks it would be beneficial to do so. But the point which, I would argue, should be particularly noted, is that by virtue of the fundamental laws the people must obey the magistrates, who in their turn are subject to the fundamental laws: 'these are the conventions which are the source of the sovereign's rights and which make his position secure, and no one would be obliged to obey the magistrates if it were not for the fundamental laws of the State, laws which the magistrates themselves are obliged to obey', *Des loix, OC*, vol.3, p.491; on the use of the term 'fundamental laws', see also *Economie politique, OC*, vol.3, p.270, and *Discours sur l'inégalité, OC*, vol.3, p.185. It is interesting to compare what Rousseau writes on the 'fundamental laws' with Hobbes's account in *Leviathan*, Part 2, ch.26.

The sovereignty of law means, therefore, that the sovereign power is entrusted to the ruler on the basis of fundamental or constitutive laws (if it were not so the power would have no legitimacy); the exercise of sovereign power must respect the rules set by those same fundamental or constitutive laws; legislator, subjects, magistrates or ordinary citizens, all are equal before the law, and no one is above the law. Rousseau aligns himself with Aristotle here against Hobbes. The English philosopher had criticized Aristotle for having supposed that 'by reason of human infirmity' the supreme power 'is committed with most security to the laws only', and had instead argued that the sovereign cannot be restricted by the laws he has created, since no one owes any obligation to himself. Consequently, laws 'are set for Titus and Caius, not for the ruler'.[136] For Rousseau, if the prince is above the law, 'he lives in the pure state of nature and is not obliged to account for his actions to his subjects or to anyone else'.[137] By contrast, the highest magistrate in the land and the lowliest citizen are equally subject to law, for the sovereign body itself, which has the power of course to change all the laws, is obliged to respect the fundamental laws, and if these laws are to be changed a unanimous vote is required. But so long as the fundamental laws are in force, the sovereign body is obliged to respect them. Respect for the fundamental laws and the laws passed in harmony with these, are, according to Rousseau, the surest defence against tyranny. When the constitution is a just and sound one, he reminds his fellow citizens of Geneva, everyone's liberty is protected and rendered all the more secure because in reality it has finite limits and 'It is the laws alone which rule, and rule over everyone; the highest citizen in the land is no less subject to law than the lowliest; no one may go against them, no private interest is permitted to change them and the constitution is as firm as a rock.'[138]

By contrast, the violation of the constitution leads to despotism. The fundamental law created by the social compact establishes that the people is sovereign and that every citizen should submit to the general will, which is to be equated with the sovereign will. As despotism involves a usurpation of sovereign power and this power is exercised on behalf of private interests, it is evident that despotism represents a denial of the fundamental law. It is through this law that men are united in the body politic and a multitude becomes a

---

[136] *De cive*, ch.12, s.4.
[137] *Etat de guerre, OC*, vol.3, p.603.
[138] *Lettres écrites de la montagne, OC*, vol.3, pp.894–5.

people.[139] When this law is flouted, civil society is dissolved. The citizens are now united only by force; but, now, what was once a people with its leaders has become a band of slaves with a master. When the despot no longer has sufficient power to impose his private interests on others, all bonds uniting the citizens in the body of the nation are broken.[140]

Through participation in the fundamental compact, each citizen submits to the general will and, should the interests of a private individual usurp the general will, the duty of obedience by which each citizen was formerly bound is now removed. The relation between subject and despot has become like those of two sovereign powers. With the removal of all duties towards the sovereign, the political bond uniting all citizens is dissolved. By his acceptance of the fundamental social compact, each citizen has proclaimed his willingness to submit to the general will. When despotism undermines the constitution it also dissolves the body politic since this body depends for its existence on the constitution.

Rousseau takes from Montesquieu the idea of despotism as a corruption of the principle of political government and, in this respect, a comparison between the *Spirit of laws* and Rousseau's works is very enlightening. Despotism is a prime example of corrupt government (*Discourse on inequality*, 191; *Spirit of laws*, Bk 13, ch. 10). Under despotism all have equality because, as far as their political master is concerned, they have no status at all (*Disc. on In.*, 191); since men are all slaves, they are all equal (*Sp. of L.*, Bk 3, ch. 8). In states ruled by a despot 'the form of government requires total obedience' (*Sp. of L.*, Bk 3, ch. 10); when despotism reigns 'the only will which a slave can acquire is blind obedience' (*Disc. on In.*, ibid.). The master is 'ruled only by his passions' (ibid.); 'the despot obeys no rule and his whims destroy all others' (*Sp. of L.*, Bk 3, ch. 8). The purpose of despotic government is to satisfy 'the desires of the prince' (*Sp. of L.*, Bk 11, ch. 5); the goal of despotic government is to benefit the tyrant (*Social contract*, Bk 3, ch. 10). For Rousseau, as for Montesquieu, despotism is the form of government where laws count for nothing or are no more than the passing whims of the sovereign (*Sp. of L.*, Bk 26, ch.2).

[139] 'What is it that holds the State together? It is the union of its members. And where does this union come from? From the obligation which links them to each other. Everything is in agreement up to this point' (*Lettres écrites de la montagne*, *OC*, vol.3, p.806).
[140] *Manuscrit de Genève*, *OC*, vol.3, p.303; *Contrat social*, *OC*, vol.3, p.359. See on this point Spinoza, *Tractatus politicus*, 4, 4–6.

In a republic men obey only the law and not other men; in a despotism 'Man is a creature who obeys a creature who commands' (*Sp. of L.*, Bk 3, ch. 10). Rousseau envisages a just political order as one in which the law is the rule which curbs passions and gives them self-discipline and makes them moderate; on the other hand, despotism cannot survive long when it is forced to conform with some kind of order and obey a set of rules (*Sp. of L.*, Bk 8, ch. 10).

As Rousseau makes clear, his conception of despotism is very different from Hobbes's. The latter had maintained that prince and subjects are bound by the same interests. Thus, Aristotle's distinction between the king who governs in the common interest and the tyrant who pursues his own interest is not valid.[141] Hobbes defends this position in *De cive*.[142] In the French translation of *De corpore* (1652), the same thesis appears again, but in a way calculated to attract Rousseau's criticism even more strongly:

Avouons, que cette division des gouvernemens, à scavoir qu'il y en a un qui regarde l'avantage du Souverain, et l'autre celu des Subjects, dont le premier s'appelle Despotique, c'est à dire Seigneural, l'autre un gouvernement d'homme libres, est fausse et tout à fait vaine.[143]

Rousseau does not limit himself to reasserting, against Hobbes, the distinction made by Aristotle, but goes further to include the monarchy amongst those forms of government where the interest of those who govern takes precedence over the interests of the governed. If, says Rousseau, we accept Aristotle's definition, it follows that 'from the beginning of time, there would never yet have been any kings but only tyrants'.[144]

It is true, as Hobbes argues, that it is in the king's interest that the people should prosper. It is also true that a king who has learnt to gain the love of his people will be more powerful than any other. But it should not be forgotten that the people's prosperity is a secondary matter as far as the king is concerned. What comes first and what really counts for him is being able to assert his authority. If kings were to heed the voice of reason they would seek the good of the people, but it is a mistake to think that a king, any more than other men, is

---

[141] *De cive*, ch.10, s.2. [142] Ibid.
[143] Thomas Hobbes, *De corpore politico, or The elements of law, moral and politik*, London, 1652. I am quoting from the edition published in the collection 'Images et témoins de l'âge classique', Saint Etienne, 1972, p.102.
[144] See *Contrat social*, Bk 3, ch.10 (transl. Cole, 1952, p.419, n.1); *Jugement sur le projet de paix perpetuelle*, *OC*, vol.3, p.952.

swayed by reason. Like all other men he is swayed by his passions,[145] and a king's all-consuming passion is to wield authority.

In this context, one of the political writers who most strongly influenced Rousseau is, without doubt, Machiavelli. Machiavelli's name appears in two texts which are particularly important for the question of the opposition between the republic and tyranny. The first is *On political economy* in which Rousseau explains the difference between the legitimate or popular 'public economy', where the people and those who govern them are bound by common interests and a common will, and the 'tyrannical' political economy, where the interests of those who govern and the people run counter to each other.

'The people's maxims', says Rousseau, 'are inscribed at length in the archives of history and in Machiavelli's satires.'[146] The second relevant passage is in the chapter of the *Social contract* which deals with monarchy and comes immediately after Rousseau's criticism of Hobbes's argument about the identity of interests between king and people. According to Rousseau, Machiavelli makes it clear that the

---

[145] See the letter to Mirabeau dated the 26 July 1767: 'It is demonstrated that the real interest of the despot is to govern according to the laws – that has been accepted from all time; but who is it who allows himself to be led by his true interest? The wise man alone, if such a person exists. You are making, Sirs, your despots into so many sages' (*Correspondance complète de Jean-Jacques Rousseau*, ed. R.A. Leigh, vol.33, p.243).

[146] *Economie politique*, *OC*, vol.3, p.247 (transl. Cole, 1952, p.370). The interpretation of Machiavelli as a republican had already appeared in Spinoza (*Tractatus politicus*, 1677, ch.5, s.7) and in Alberico Gentili, *De legationibus*, Bk 3, ch.9, to which P. Bayle also refers in his *Dictionnaire historique et critique*, 2nd edn, Rotterdam, published by Reiner Leers, 1702, 3 vols. (article 'Machiavelli', note 'o'). Rousseau's position was also shared by Diderot, who in the article 'Machiavelisme', wrote that 'it was the fault of his contemporaries if they misunderstood what he was getting at: they took a satire for a eulogy', *Encyclopédie*, Neufschatel, vol.9, 1765, p.793. It is likely that Rousseau had read Machiavelli during the period of his collaboration with the encyclopédistes. Besides his influence on *On political economy*, there are traces present in the *Discours sur l'inégalité* (*OC*, vol.3, p.113, notes 2 and 3, and p.191). Machiavelli's name also appears in *La Reine fantastique*, *OC*, vol.2, p.1910, a work which Rousseau referred to as 'a trifle' (see M. Launay, *Jean-Jacques Rousseau écrivain politique*, Cannes, 1971, p.202). There is another possibility – that Rousseau may have read Machiavelli already when he was living in Geneva, during his childhood. Machiavelli's works were to be found in the small library of the craftsmen of Geneva who lived near the Rousseau family and were on good terms with them (see Launay, *Jean-Jacques Rousseau écrivain*, who relies on P. O'Mara, 'Geneva in the eighteenth century. A socio-economic study of the bourgeois city-state during its golden age', unpublished thesis, University of California, 1952. We also know that between 1610 and 1650 five editions of Machiavelli's works were printed in Geneva; see G. Bonnant, 'Les Impressions genevoises au XVIIe siècle de l'édition dite de la 'Testina' des oeuvres de Machiavel', in *Annali della scuola statale superiore per archivisti e bibliotecari dell'Università di Roma*, 5 (1965), n.1, pp.83–9.

prime interest of the king is that the people should be weak, wretched and unable to resist his will. This is why, 'while appearing to instruct Kings he has done much to educate the people. Machiavelli's *Prince* is the book of Republicans'.[147]

In some respects the two references to Machiavelli mean more or less the same thing, but in other ways there is a distinct difference. They are the same when it comes to the definition of tyranny as a form of government in which the interests of people and sovereign are opposed. The difference lies in the fact that in *On political economy* Machiavelli is referred to as a writer who satirized tyranny, while in the *Social contract* he is mentioned as the one who revealed to the people the truth about kings. In the first text, the main contrast is between the legitimate (or popular) government and monarchy.

Here we have an important problem which must be resolved if Rousseau's republicanism is to be fully understood: does being a republican mean supporting the republic as the legitimate constitution (the opposite of which is tyranny), or does it mean supporting the republican government? Taken by itself, the definition of the republic might lead one to conclude that Rousseau's republicanism involves support for the republican constitution without making any pronouncement on the actual form of government. This interpretation could be supported by the fact that Rousseau does not consider democracy, defined as the form of government under which the people exercise both legislative and executive power at the same time, as the best form of government.[148] By contrast, in the republican constitutions, sovereignty (legislative power) is held by the people, but it would be an indication of the corruption of the body politic if, at the same time, the people performed the role of executive and if it 'turned its attention away from the broader issues to concentrate on

[147] Cf. the words of Albericus Gentilis, quoted by Bayle in his *Dictionary*, art. 'Machiavelli', note (o): 'Machiavelli, a strong supporter and enthusiast for democracy, was born in that Republican state; he was extremely hostile to tyranny. Therefore he did not help the tyrant; his intention was not to instruct the tyrant, but by making all his secrets clear and openly displaying the degree of wretchedness to the people . . . He excelled all other men in wisdom and while appearing to instruct the prince he was actually educating the people'. ('Machiavellus Democratiae laudator et assertor acerrimus: natus, educatus, honoratus in eo Reip: statu; Tyrannidus summe inimicus. Itaque Tyranno non favet; sui propositi non est Tyrannum instruere, sed arcanis ejus palam factis ipsum miseris populis nudum et conspicuum exibire. (. . .) Hoc fuit viri omnium praestantissimi consilium, ut sub specie principalis eruditionis populos erudiret.')

[148] *Contrat social*, Bk 3, ch.3; *Lettres écrites de la montagne*, *OC*, vol.3, pp.838 and 844.

specific matters'.[149] On the other hand, the most suitable form of government for the continuance of the republican constitution cannot possibly be the monarchy. In fact, Rousseau's choice rests on a form of 'mixed government', half way between a monarchy and democracy, that is to say, the aristocracy, interpreted as the form of government where the people are sovereign and the executive power is entrusted to a small number of magistrates chosen by the people by virtue of their wisdom, and their upright character.[150]

Rousseau's notion of the republican constitution has a remarkable affinity with Machiavelli's concept of 'vivere libero' ('self government').[151] For Machiavelli this notion consists essentially of the common good being placed above individual self-interest. The reason why the people of the ancient world placed such value on the 'vivere libero', notes Machiavelli in the *Discorsi*, is

easy to understand for it is not the well-being of individuals that makes cities great, but the well-being of the community, and it is beyond question that it is only in Republics that the common good is looked to properly in that all that promotes it is carried out; and however much this or that private person may be the lower on this account, there are so many who benefit thereby that the common good can be realized in spite of those few who suffer in consequence.[152]

While the contrast between 'vivere libero' and tyranny is quite clear, that does not mean that for Machiavelli 'vivere libero' can only exist under a republican government. Certain passages in the *Discorsi*, like the one quoted above, support the argument that 'vivere libero' can become a reality only under a republican government, but other

---

[149] *Contrat social*, Bk 3, ch.4. [150] *Lettres de la montagne, OC*, vol.3, p.808.

[151] In the 1782 edition of the *Social contract*, the following note from the manuscript is preserved in the Library of Neuchâtel, n.7842, folio.52: 'Machiavelli was a proper man and a good citizen; but, being attached to the court of the Medicis, he could not help veiling his love of liberty in the midst of his country's oppression. The choice of his detestable hero, Caesar Borgia, clearly enough shows his hidden aim; and the contradiction between the teaching of *The prince* and that of the *Discourse on Livy* and the *History of Florence* shows that this profound political thinker has so far been studied only by superficial or corrupt readers. The court of Rome sternly prohibited his book. I can well believe it; for it is that Court it most clearly portrays'; *Contrat social, OC*, vol.3, p.1480 (transl. Cole, 1952, p.413, n.1). Rousseau, on the other hand, carefully distinguished between 'Machiavelism' (which he detested) and the thought of Machiavelli (which he admired). In a letter to Lenieps, dated the 4 December 1758, he wrote, with regard to Frederick II: 'I am unable to esteem or have any sympathy for a man without principles, who tramples underfoot all the human rights, who does not believe in virtue, but sees it as a delusion fit only for fools and who begins his Machiavelism by refuting Machiavelli' (quoted from *OC*, vol.1, p.1567, n.4).

[152] *Discorsi sopra la prima deca di Tito Livio*, Bk 2, ch.2, p.280 (transl. by L.J. Walker, revised by Brian Richards, London, 1970, pp.275–6).

passages allow one to entertain the possibility that the 'vivere libero' may be realized, at least in part, even under a monarchy.[153] Machiavelli's republicanism, therefore, is characterized by the principle of the sovereignty of the common good which, with liberty, constitutes the essential quality of 'vivere libero'. This is the same characteristic which Rousseau embodies in the concept of the republic. In each case, 'vivere libero' or a republic governed by a king is presented as an abstract possibility. But history proves that it is very difficult for this to be attained and that the condition of 'vivere libero' or the republic is that the people should be sovereign. While the opposition between monarchy and republic exists *de facto*, the incompatibility of the republic with any form of tyranny is something which exists in principle.

It is now possible to answer the question posed above, concerning Rousseau's republicanism. For Rousseau, to be a republican means, in the first place, being inspired by the ideal of the republic defined as the political constitution where law is sovereign over men and the common good is placed before individual self-interest. In the second place his republicanism includes a preference for government by a small elite of wise and virtuous men as the best way of realizing the republican ideal. To be a republican means being opposed to tyranny and to monarchy, but does not include a commitment to democracy as government (in the sense of the exercise of executive power) by the people. Rousseau's republicanism is therefore a theory centred upon the just political constitution, and in particular concerns itself with what is the best form of government and when this latter problem presents itself it is in the context of deciding upon the most suitable means to achieve a just political constitution.

The fundamental principles of the just political constitution are, therefore, that men's lives are to be governed by law, and sovereignty is to reside in the people. The other principles all derive from these two cardinal doctrines: the common good is to take precedence over

[153] *Discorsi*, Bk 1, ch.2, where he observed that Romulus and the other kings 'made many good laws quite compatible with liberty', but they were unable to frame all the laws which were necessary for 'vivere libero' because 'their aim was to found a kingdom not a republic' (transl. ibid., p.110).

[154] See Bk 1, ch.9, where Machiavelli, speaking of the 'first institutions' ('primi ordini') of Rome, notes that they were more suited to 'a civil, self-governing State than to one which was absolute and tyrannical' ('uno vivere civile e libero che a uno assoluto e tirannico'); Bk 2, ch.37, where the opposition between 'liberty' and 'tyranny' is particularly clear and corresponds to that between 'vivere libero' and 'vivere servo' (416); see also Bk 2, ch.24, p.455.

the self-interest of the individual and men's passions – ambition and egotism, in particular – are to be kept in check. The very definition of the law enshrines these qualities. It is the expression of the general will which by its nature works to safeguard the interests of all and which is bound by the principle of equality under the law. If it proves necessary, the general will employs force to impose this principle and thus the citizens' ambitions are tempered by law. If this were not so ambition would cause men to ride roughshod over the legitimate rights of others in order to advance their own interests.

An analysis of the two antithetical concepts of 'the Republic' and 'despotism' illuminates the theoretical affinity between Rousseau and Machiavelli. After explaining in Bk 2, ch. 2 of the *Discorsi* that only in the 'republica' does the common good take precedence over private interests, Machiavelli goes on to say: 'On the contrary, it happens, when there is only one leader, that for the most part his actions are against the interest of the city, and the actions of the citizens in general run contrary to his interests.' When the interests of those in power are allowed to come before the interests of the people at large, the result is that tyranny replaces the self-rule of the people. The antithesis between 'vivere libero' and tyranny is made clear in several other passages of the *Discorsi*.[154] 'La tirannide' is born the moment a social faction within the polity, abandoning moderation, attempts to bend others to its will.[155] As is the case in Rousseau with regard to despotism, 'la tirannide', as Machiavelli conceives it, takes root when the sovereign governs in a fashion that is contrary to law. Anyone who usurps the sovereign will does not, either for Machiavelli or for Rousseau, by virtue of this fact alone, become a despot. Even if a man takes to himself 'istraordinaria autorita', this does not necessarily imply that he is using this authority 'tirannicamente'.[156] By contrast, a tyrant is one who acts like Tarquin the Proud, who had violated the laws of the kingdom and had 'governatolo tirannicamente'. His government was tyrannical because he had succeeded in gaining for himself a monopoly of authority and because he took privately decisions which should have been made openly before the public. The laws he violated were political or fundamental laws – the one which required that the sovereign authority should be divided between the king and the senate and also the one which required that deliberations on certain issues should be held in public. The 'vivere libero', like the

[155] *Discorsi*, Bk 2, ch.40, pp.227–8.   [156] *Discorsi*, Bk 3, ch.3, p.386.

concept of 'liberty' for Rousseau, is preserved as long as the fundamental laws retain their sovereignty. It perishes when 'they begin to break the laws and to disregard the ancient traditions and customs under which men have lived'.[157] When law is sovereign, princes are moderate, prudent,[158] and reliable. The people of a republic in which the law is respected have no desire either to humiliate others or to fall under another's domination. But it is precisely the people which is neither in a state of servitude nor corrupted by the arrogance of power which is free: 'Such was the Roman populace which, so long as the republic remained uncorrupt, was never servilely obsequious, nor yet did it ever dominate with arrogance: on the contrary, it had its own institutions and magistrates and honourably kept its own place.'[159]

This definition of liberty appears again in Rousseau and he calls it the 'Republican' conception of liberty[160], that is, the freedom of men who have no desire to serve or dominate others. The republican is willing to obey, but the objects of his obedience are limited to the law and the general will. He can, therefore, only be at liberty in a republic.

The sovereignty of law is therefore a necessary condition if political liberty is to exist.[161] So long as the general will is sovereign, the citizens need not fear for their liberty and men are ruled by law.[162] The rule of law requires that individual wills should be in harmony with the general will.[163] Now, as it is this process which imbues the individual will with virtue, the sovereignty of law and the just political constitution, in their turn, cannot exist without virtuous citizens and magistrates: 'It is not only upright men who know how to administer the laws; but at bottom only good men know how to obey them.'[164]

The virtue that the republic requires of its citizens and magistrates is civic virtue; the virtues of those in authority are no different from the virtues of those under that authority. Just as the magistrates must

---

[157] *Discorsi*, Bk 1, ch.33, p.208.   [158] *Discorsi*, Bk 1, ch.58, p.262
[159] *Discorsi*, Bk 1, ch.58, p.262 (transl. ibid., p.253).
[160] *Lettres écrites de la montagne, OC*, vol.3, p.842; see also how the same concepts reappear in the autobiographical writings: *Rousseau juge de Jean-Jacques, OC*, vol.1, p.891.
[161] *Contrat social*, Bk 2, ch.11; see also *Projet de constitution pour la Corse, OC*, vol.3, p.946. It is interesting to note that for Locke also political liberty is opposed to enforced submission to the arbitrary will of another man and consists of obedience to the law established by the legitimate sovereign (*Second treatise*, ch.IV, s.22, pp.301–3).
[162] *Contrat social, OC*, vol.3, p.393. The problem of the corruption of the well-ordered society will be dealt with in greater detail later in this chapter.
[163] *Economie politique, OC*, vol.3, p.252.
[164] *Economie politique, OC*, vol.3, p.252 (transl. Cole, 1952, p.372).

be fair but strict in their dealings with others, bold but not rash, and moderate in their behaviour, so the citizens must seek to be just in their obedience to the laws, moderate in their pursuit of honour and wealth, bold in the face of all enemies (whether within or without) and must exercise care in their choice of magistrates. These are not virtues which co-exist with the love of humanity, for this calls into existence other virtues, such as gentleness, moderation, charity, fairness and tolerance. Civic virtue is born with the love of one's country and inspires courage, firmness of purpose and sometimes even heroism.[165] Christianity inculcates the former virtues: the ancient masters of the republican tradition preached the latter. Rousseau stands within the second tradition. He attacks St Augustine fiercely for daring to criticize Brutus, the outstanding example of republican virtue, and praises Cato, who stands for 'energy and virtue'.[166] Amongst the moderns his masters are Montesquieu and Machiavelli. Montesquieu had argued that virtue was the principle which should provide the inspiration for democratic government. Rousseau takes Montesquieu's idea further: virtue should not only be the core of democracy but of every state founded on justice.[167] Though virtue plays a role whose importance varies with the form of government, it must, nevertheless, direct men's consciences in every state ruled by law. The just political order cannot hope to remain true to its founding principle – the universal liberty and the common good, if the citizens do not fulfil their civic duties. If they are not 'proud', passionate and impetuous the republic cannot survive and neither can virtue.

Machiavelli had held Christianity responsible for the way in which love for 'vivere libero' had lost its power. This love, so strong amongst the ancients, now, in the modern world, had died out. The Christian religion preached a form of virtue which had little in common with the ideas of the ancient pagan religions.[168] Christianity values most highly 'humility, abnegation, and contempt for mundane things. For pagan religion the highest good is magnanimity, bodily strength, and everything else that conduces to make men very bold.' Christianity has 'made the world weak' and has, consequently, 'handed it over as a prey to the wicked'.[169]

---

[165] *De la patrie, OC*, vol.3, p.536.
[166] *De l'honneur et de la vertu, OC*, vol.3, p.506; see also n.2, p.1525.
[167] *Contrat social, OC*, vol.3, p.405.
[168] See R. Price, 'The senses of "virtu" in Machiavelli', *European studies review*, 3 (1973), pp.315–45.   [169] *Discorsi*, Bk 2, ch.2, p.282 (transl. Walker, 1970, p.278).

Rousseau was indebted to Machiavelli for all these ideas. Christianity has sapped men's courage[170] and men who do not love liberty fall easy prey to the first man driven by the lust for power who wishes to enslave them. The republic must have virtue as the ancients understood it, not the virtue of the Christian variety.[171] 'But I am mistaken in speaking of a Christian republic; the terms are mutually exclusive. Christianity preaches only servitude and dependence. Its spirit is so favourable to tyranny that it always profits by such a regime.'[172]

History contains many examples of men who gained their liberty through revolution or through chance circumstances. But these are rare events, says Rousseau, and are rather the exception than the rule. In general, anyone who seeks to correct the prejudice and vices of a people corrupted by their state of servitude is engaged on a 'perilous and vain' enterprise. If a people which has become decadent frees itself from the domination of a despot, it does not thereby regain its liberty since it no longer has the civic virtue necessary for true citizenship. It is quite possible that a barbarous race may provide for itself institutions which have the outward trappings of liberty, but it is almost impossible for a decadent society to become free: 'Free peoples, be mindful of this maxim: Liberty may be gained, but can never be recovered.'[173] This maxim very nearly copies Machiavelli word for word – 'A people accustomed to live under a Prince, should they by some Eventuality become free, will with difficulty maintain their freedom'[174] – and in another chapter of the *Discorsi*, 'A corrupt people,

---

[170] *De l'honneur et de la vertu*, *OC*, vol.3, p.506.

[171] For Rousseau, civic virtues are not opposed to 'human' virtues; the former appear to be, in fact, a necessary prerequisite for the latter. See on this issue the Dedication of the *Discourse on inequality*; on the relationship between the modern conception of virtue and the classical understanding of the term, see P. Emberley, 'Rousseau and the domestication of virtue', *Canadian journal of political science*, 18 (1984), pp.731–53; see also S. Ellemburg, *Rousseau's political philosophy. An interpretation from within*, Ithaca and London, 1976, especially pp.167–232.

[172] *Contrat social*, *OC*, vol.3, p.467 (transl. Cole, 1952, p.438).

[173] *Contrat social*, Bk 2, ch.8 (transl. Cole, 1952, p.402); see also n.2, p.1466, and the foreword to the *Projet de constitution pour la Corse*, *OC*, vol.3, pp.901–2, where Rousseau explains why the Corsican people is in a fortunate position to be able to establish a 'good government'. See also what he says in the *Considérations sur le gouvernement de Pologne*, *OC*, vol.3, p.974: 'Liberty is a heady potion, but difficult to digest; it requires strong stomachs to deal with it. I laugh at those decadent peoples who, allowing strong wine to go to their heads, dare to speak of liberty without having the slightest idea of what it is, while their hearts are full of all slavish vices, yet they imagine that to be free you need only to be a rebel.'

[174] *Discorsi*, Bk 1, ch.16 (transl. Walker, 1970, p.153).

having acquired liberty, can maintain it only with the greatest difficulty.'[175]

A people made soft by servitude is like an animal which in the natural state would be fierce and wild, but has spent its life in captivity with all its needs provided and then is suddenly abandoned to its fate in the forest. It will be totally incapable of avoiding capture. This is how it is with a people which has lost its moral fibre and is incapable of governing itself because it has learnt only to obey. This is why anyone who wants to follow such a people out of bondage must, as Machiavelli says, use 'extraordinary' methods and make himself master of the polity in order to 'poterne disporre a suo modo'.[176]

The exceptional methods of which Machiavelli speaks are violence, cruelty, injustice and deception. By these means the prince can be sure of attaining absolute power over his subjects, but at the same time – if the intention is to restore liberty to a decadent people – this same absolute power must be employed to re-assert the sovereignty of law. The restoration of the republican constitution can only be achieved by a man who has the well-being of the people at heart, but, if need be, this same man must be capable of employing deception and violence. It is therefore almost impossible to find a good man who is capable of using effective methods and who would subsequently be willing to use absolute power for the benefit of his fellow citizens:

But, to reconstitute political life in a state presupposes a good man, whereas to have recourse to violence in order to make oneself prince in a republic supposes a bad man. Hence very rarely will there be found a good man ready to use bad methods in order to make himself prince, though with a good end in view, nor yet a bad man who, having become a prince, is ready to do the right thing and to whose mind it will occur to use well that authority which he has acquired by bad means.[177]

By contrast, Rousseau never deals with the problems which arise when it becomes necessary to use exceptional methods, and the tragic dimension of politics, so vividly portrayed in the pages of Machiavelli, is completely absent from his work. In all the texts where he deals with 'true politics', the position he adopts is quite remote from that of Machiavelli. To a certain extent, it is possible to see Rousseau as espousing the traditional humanist conception of politics which Machiavelli had subjected to radical criticism. For example, in *On*

[175] *Discorsi*, Bk 1, ch.17 (transl. ibid., p.157).
[176] *Discorsi*, Bk 1, ch.18 (transl. ibid., p.163).
[177] *Discorsi*, Bk 1, ch.18 (transl. ibid., pp.163–4).

political economy, Rousseau notes that history shows that the sovereign who enjoys the greatest authority is the one who has learnt to endear himself to his people.

Even ambition is better served by duty than by usurpation: when the people is convinced that its rulers are labouring only for its happiness, its deference saves them the trouble of labouring to strengthen their power: and history shows us, in a thousand cases, that the authority of one who is beloved over those whom he loves is a hundred times more absolute than all the tyranny of usurpers.[178]

If the sovereign wishes to be strong and maintain his kingdom in being, he must, above all, be just and work for the good of his citizens. In the famous tenth chapter of the first book of the *Discorsi*, Machiavelli argues in the same vein: the just prince enjoys authority which is far more broadly based than that of any tyrant. But he adds that there are times when the prince must be able to make himself feared[179] and this is an aspect of Machiavelli's thought which is foreign to Rousseau.

Moreover, Machiavelli had emphasized on several occasions that, in order to be effective, political action requires the use of force as well as of prudence. Rousseau also writes that the skilled politician should never hesitate to use force:

But we ought not to confound negligence with moderation, or clemency with weakness. To be just, it is necessary to be severe; to permit vice, when one has the right and the power to suppress it, is to be oneself vicious.[180]

Nevertheless, for Rousseau, the supreme achievement of politics is not so much a question of finding the right balance between force and caution, but of working towards the elimination of force altogether. A statesman's skill is to be judged by his ability to govern in such a way that it seems that there is no need for a government at all. For Machiavelli the true prince must be able to hide his real purpose, but for Rousseau such dissembling, not to mention the 'mysteries of the

---

[178] *Economie politique, OC*, vol. 3, p. 254 (transl. Cole, 1952, p. 373). It is a recurring theme of republican political theory: 'And we recently discovered, if it was not known before, that no amount of power can withstand the hatred of the many. The death of this tyrant whose yoke the state endured under the constraint of armed force and whom it still obeys more humbly than ever, though he is dead, illustrates the deadly effects of popular hatred; and the same lesson is taught by the similar fate of all other despots, of whom practically no one has ever escaped such a death. For fear is but a poor safeguard of lasting power; while affection, on the other hand, may be trusted to keep it safe for ever' (Cicero, *De officiis*, Bk 2, 23–4).

[179] *Discorsi*, Bk 3, ch. 29; see also *Il principe*, ch. 17.

[180] *Economie politique, OC*, vol. 3, p. 254 (transl. Cole, 1952, p. 373).

cabinet', is no more than a ludicrous attempt to stem the corruption of social life. Policies founded on secrecy and dissimulation are themselves a manifestation of the corruption of the republic and can never be a remedy for these ills. To avoid the downfall of his kingdom, the prince must merely be courageous, moderate and, above all, just.

The difference between Machiavelli and Rousseau is not that the latter wrote that political skill was closely associated with a concern for justice, but that he stated that no prince had ever lost power because he was just: 'We find in history a thousand examples of pusillanimous or ambitious rulers, who were ruined by their slackness or their pride; not one who suffered for having been strictly just.'[181] Machiavelli would have found this a naive and reckless notion: a prince ready to follow Rousseau's advice, come what may, would soon be deposed. It is going too far to say that Rousseau does not understand the reality of politics. For him, 'true politics' is inseparably linked with the great 'legislators' who knew how to transform a mass into a people. In his works, politics is always described as a corrupt and corrupting activity or, alternatively, in the hypothetical case of a just republic, as a very simple activity which requires no particular talent. The notion, or the myth, of the great statesman who possesses an exceptional virtue and employs it to transform a corrupt city into a just and free one has no place in Rousseau's political vocabulary. A corrupt people has no hope of regaining its liberty: 'what it needs henceforth is a master, not a liberator'.

Civic virtue cannot hope to be born or survive amongst a people where some are very wealthy while others are wretched, and the sovereignty of law is not compatible with extremes of social inequality. The fact that there should be no marked inequalities of wealth is, for Rousseau, a logical consequence of his conception of liberty. To be free means not to be subject to another's will. But if poverty forces a man to obey someone else, then, because his freedom of action is limited by the latter's wealth, that man is no longer free, but a serf. Restricting the degree of inequality is necessary if certain citizens are not to be forced to submit to the will of another, for such an act is a violation of political liberty. Now, political liberty only allows for obedience to the general will and the law. If a poor man is forced to obey someone just because he is rich, this very act of submitting to the will of another makes it impossible for him to obey the general will. He cannot devote his energies to the pursuit of goals that

[181] Ibid.

he has freely chosen for himself and his freedom is therefore negated. The loss of political liberty therefore entails the loss of individual freedom.

When Rousseau proclaims the famous principle: 'No citizen shall ever be wealthy enough to buy another, and none poor enough to be forced to sell himself',[182] this is intended as a necessary condition for the maintenance of political liberty. What the poor man is in a position to sell to his rich neighbour is his obedience. But, as soon as he vows to obey, he has lost his political liberty, which consists precisely in obedience to the law and to the law alone. If there are men who are in the position of having to obey others, neither those who obey, nor those who command are acting in conformity with the law and if there are men who, by virtue of their wealth, are able to force others to obey them, by this very fact they are placing themselves above the law. This, according to Rousseau, is the essence of despotism and the corruption of legitimate government. The scourge of poverty reduces men to a state of servitude[183] and great wealth awakens lust for power. Therefore, the existence within society of too wide a gap between rich and poor is not compatible with a political order which is supposedly founded on the principle that the master–servant relationship is not acceptable. From the very beginning, political philosophers have, almost without exception, accepted as axiomatic that the presence of great wealth side by side with extreme poverty is a recipe for revolt. Rousseau has no doubts on this score.[184] However, every time he writes about the need to reduce inequality, he concentrates less on the dangers of revolt against the sovereign as such[185] than on the issue of the way in which the sovereignty of law and the general will may be undermined. Extremes of social inequality represent a threat to the well-being of the republic because this situation allows some men to buy or sell something which, in the republic, should be 'inaestimabilis'; that is liberty.[186]

---

[182] *Contrat social*, *OC*, vol.3, pp.391–2 (transl. Cole, 1952, p.405).
[183] 'The rich man has the law in his purse, and the poor man prefers bread to liberty', *Lettres écrites de la montagne*, *OC*, vol.3, p.890; Pufendorf had also stated that great wealth was capable of corrupting the moral equality of men: see *The law of nature and of nations* (1712), Bk 3, ch.2, s.9.
[184] *Economie politique*, *OC*, vol.3, pp.258–9; *Contrat social*, *OC*, vol.3, pp.391–2; *Lettres écrites de la montagne*, *OC*, vol.3, p.890; *Projet de constitution pour la Corse*, *OC*, vol.3, pp.924–6. [185] *Economie politique*, *OC*, vol.3, p.258.
[186] 'The battle of Pharsalia', says Rousseau in the *Parallèle entre Socrate et Caton*, 'did no more than to deliver to their Master peoples destined in their hearts to become slaves, for liberty is lost, not by being sold but from the very moment that a person contemplates setting a price upon it. This band of slaves had been waiting for someone to buy them for some time' (*OC*, vol.3, p.1897).

The rule of law is possible only when there are men who enjoy moderate prosperity. By contrast, laws 'are equally powerless against the treasures of the rich and the penury of the poor. The first mocks them, the second escapes them. The one breaks the meshes, the other passes through them.'[187] The sanctions which the sovereign authority has available to ensure that laws are obeyed are quite pointless when employed against those who have nothing to lose or against those who can call upon private resources which exceed those available to the community. If citizens are to respect the law, they must first hold it dear. There is no political authority strong enough to be able to make citizens respect a law which they do not cherish. Rousseau believes that citizens love their laws when they see in them, and the authority which lies behind them, the 'guarantees of communal liberty'.[188] But if 'powerful men' are able to dominate ordinary citizens, for this very reason the law is no longer the guarantee of liberty for all. Citizens are virtuous when they love their country. The love of one's country is born in citizens' hearts when they see their country and its laws as a 'common mother'[189] who protects everyone equally and guarantees to each one the tranquil enjoyment of what belongs to him. But it will be impossible for citizens to love their country when they see that some people derive much profit from the

---

[187] *Economie politique*, *OC*, vol.3, p.258 (transl. Cole, 1952, p.375). Rousseau closely follows Plutarch here. The passage which suggested to him the comparison between a spider's web and the law is to be found in the *Life of Solon* and is worth quoting: 'Solon, somewhat surprised at the readiness of the repartee, received him kindly, and kept him some time with him, being already engaged in public business and the compilation of his laws; which, when Anacharsis understood, he laughed at him for imagining the dishonesty and covetousness of his countrymen could be restrained by written laws, which were like spiders' webs, and would catch, it is true, the weak and poor, but easily be broken by the mighty and rich. To this Solon rejoined that men keep their promises when neither side can get anything by the breaking of them; and he would so fit his laws to the citizens, that all should understand it was more eligible to be just than to break the laws. But the event rather agreed with the conjecture of Anacharsis than Solon's hope' (transl. 'The Dryden translation', Great Books, Chicago, 1952, vol.14, p.66). Rousseau's meditation on the theme of what constitutes good government may be seen as the continuation of Solon's utopia. Rousseau also has as his aim the establishment of justice and the rule of law amongst men and he also seeks to demonstrate that it is more advantageous (in certain circumstances) to obey laws and respect justice than to go against them.   [188] Ibid., p.258.

[189] In his autobiographical writings Rousseau tells us that the desire to lead his life in a 'homeland' was always with him and that the idea of 'a better order of things' beyond this earthly life was associated with the notion of a homeland and a circle of friends (*Rousseau juge de Jean-Jacques*, *OC*, vol.1, p.827); in the *Considérations sur le gouvernement de Pologne*, Rousseau speaks of his homeland as 'the good mother', (*OC*, vol.3, p.962).

way society is structured, while the majority of citizens are weighed down with social responsibilities and have less protection than the wealthy and great.

For Rousseau, the principle of the sovereignty of law is closely linked to the idea that the social system must not always work in favour of the wealthy and powerful. The comparison he makes in *On political economy* between the different situations of the rich and the poor provides the most telling image of the violation of the principle that everyone should derive the same benefits from the social system:

Are not all the advantages of society for the rich and powerful? Are not all lucrative posts in their hands? Are not all privileges and exemptions reserved for them alone? Is not the public authority always on their side? . . . Men who are wealthy and highly esteemed can through these means alone be assured of impunity. Moreover, public resources are always being channelled for their protection and well-being. How different is the case of the poor man! The more humanity owes him, the more society denies him. Every door is shut against him, even when he has a right to its being opened: and if ever he obtains justice, it is with much greater difficulty than others obtain favours. If the militia is to be raised, or the highway to be mended, he is always given the preference; he always bears the burden which his richer neighbour has influence enough to get exempted from.

The man who is in need cannot count on the assistance of society to supply his fundamental needs. He is met on all sides with indifference and hostility. What is more he knows that he is never safe from the wrongs and injustices perpetrated by those who are more powerful than he is.[190]

A closer look at the picture painted by Rousseau reveals that it comprises a number of examples of violations of the fundamental law established by the social compact, the intention of which is that all should obey the same law and which will not allow anyone to place themselves above the law. The special exceptions, favours and preferential treatment he refers to are equally examples of the undermining of the principle of the sovereignty of law. Should any citizen be treated as a special case and be granted preferential treatment, then the law will have lost its universality, and the authority which has granted those favours is guilty of violating two of the governing principles of the social compact, namely, that the will of the sovereign

[190] *Economie politique*, *OC*, vol. 3, pp. 271–2.

power should be expressed through a code of law and that the sovereign has no right to discriminate between one citizen and another.

More than anyone else, it is in the ordinary citizen's interest to ensure that the law is sovereign and the state is founded on just principles. So long as the law retains its force and the general will is sovereign, the people will be protected from the depradations of the powerful and wealthy. The people, not the 'populace' nor the wealthy and powerful are the bastion of the republic. By contrast, the wealthy and those who have been appointed as magistrates often seek to place themselves above the law. They are attracted by the idea of wielding power over others and, as the law of the republic obliges them to treat their fellows as citizens and not slaves, they would be very happy if they could snap the bonds of law. Generally speaking, those who have attained positions of honour in society do not behave with moderation and they are not satisfied with being mere citizens, like all the others. Superiority means more to them than equality.

In a republic even the higher magistrates are subject to the law and are citizens, just like the others. In addition, citizens who have deserved well of their fatherland because of their civic virtue, are still subject to law; their reward is the honours they receive, but they are not granted privileges which place them above the law.[191] When the desire for supremacy is born in the heart of the great and powerful and grows out of all proportion, it will remain unsatisfied so long as they remain in a republic. When the law is sovereign the republic curbs the desire for supremacy. This is why those who long to achieve a position of unrivalled eminence seek to undermine the republic. The method they employ for this purpose is to weaken the sovereignty of law.

The people, defined as 'the middle order'[192], takes an entirely different attitude towards the law compared with those who hold power:

The Citizen only desires the law and that the law should be observed. Every individual knows very well that if exceptions to the laws are allowed they will not work in his favour. Thus everyone has reason to fear the practice of making special exceptions and this very fear is an indication that he loves the law. But with the ruling classes it is quite different: their social condition is based on privilege, and they seek such privileges everywhere. If they want to have laws, it is not in order to obey them, but to be the judges.[193]

[191] Ibid., p.249.
[192] *Lettres écrites de la montagne*, OC, vol.3, p.889.   [193] Ibid., pp.891–2.

Rousseau, once again, makes use of the notions of Machiavelli. Men are not attracted to the idea of 'vivere libero' for the same reasons: 'A small section of the populace desire to be free in order to obtain authority over others, but the vast bulk of those who demand liberty, desire but to live in security.'[194]

The people feels secure when it sees that no one is allowed to flout the law and that even kings themselves, for example the kings of France, cannot govern in a way which is contrary to law.[195] By contrast, those who have power and influence are driven by the desire to increase their power and wealth. Ambition drives them to bring about a change in 'vivere libero' and as they are powerful 'they can bring about changes with greater effect and greater speed'.[196] The people, on the other hand, cherishes 'vivere libero' and finds it in its interest for the law to be respected, for its greatest desire is to escape domination. The just republic ('republica bene ordinata'), therefore, is most secure when its people are free from corruption:

... and unquestionably if we ask what it is the nobility are after and what it is the common people are after, it will be seen that in the former there is a great desire to dominate and in the latter merely a desire not to be dominated. Consequently the latter will be more keen on liberty, since their hope of usurping dominion over others will be less than in the case of the upper class, so that if the populace is made the guardian of liberty, it is reasonable to suppose that they will take more care of it, and that, since it is impossible for them to usurp power, they will not permit others to do so.[197]

To return to Rousseau's account of the matter, if the republic is to preserve its integrity the people must be ready to carry out their civic duties, to love the common good and to extend its horizons beyond a petty parochialism: 'As soon as public service ceases to be the chief business of the citizens, and they would rather serve with their money than with their persons, the State is not far from its fall.'[198]

If the people does not take the trouble to attend the public assemblies, if it is unwilling to take up arms against all enemies, if it does not constantly keep watch over the activities of its magistrates,[199] the freedom of the polity will not last long. It will be crushed by a foreign

---

[194] *Discorsi*, Bk 2, ch.16, pp.175–6 (transl. Walker, 1970, p.156).
[195] Ibid. [196] *Discorsi*, Bk 1, ch.5 (transl. ibid., p.118).
[197] *Discorsi*, Bk 1, ch.5, p.139 (transl. ibid., p.116).
[198] *Contrat social*, *OC*, vol.3, p.428 (transl. Cole, 1952, p.421).
[199] 'Rest and liberty seem to me to be incompatible; one must choose' (*Considérations sur le gouvernement de Pologne*, *OC*, vol.3, p.955).

power, or destroyed from within by social factions pursuing their own narrow interests.

From the moment when the populace regards the duties it is required to perform for the good of the state as so many unpaid services from which they derive no benefit, the republic is close to ruin.[200] On the surface, the reasoning of the citizen who wants to avoid his public duties is quite logical. He may well think that others will make good his failure to do his share. He may also be of the opinion that even if the republic falls under the influence of a foreign power or a despot, he will be able to carry on devoting himself to his own private concerns, like the Greeks emprisoned in the Cyclop's cave, who lived waiting until their turn came to be devoured because each of them thought that someone else would be chosen as the monster's next victim.

When decadence has taken root, citizens think of the public good only if their own personal interests are at stake.[201] Thus, they are willing to sacrifice their greatest good – liberty – 'because of their mad desire for things of little worth'.[202] Believing they are acting in their own best interests, they refuse to carry out their civic duties and cause the downfall of the republic, since the wild ambitions of the governing elite now find no obstacle in their way and the foreign power is free to attack the polity when the majority of citizens is not ready to defend their liberty:

When the citizens are greedy, cowardly, and pusillanimous, and love ease more than liberty, they do not long hold out against the redoubled efforts of the government; and thus, as the resisting force incessantly grows, the sovereign authority ends by disappearing and most cities fall and perish before their time.[203]

Rousseau's attack on the institution of deputies or representatives is also fuelled by the fear that these institutions may sap civic virtues and make the loss of liberty more likely.[204]

When the republic falls into the hands of a despot, the citizens of the state, morally flawed as they are, would be hopelessly mistaken if they thought they could carry on quietly pursuing their own private interests: if the despot decides upon war as the means to satisfy his

---

[200] *Contrat social*, *OC*, vol.3, p.429.
[201] *Lettres écrites de la montagne*, *OC*, vol.3, p.881.
[202] *Considérations sur le gouvernement de Pologne*, *OC*, vol.3, p.956.
[203] *Contrat social*, Bk 3, ch.14 (transl. Cole, 1952, p.421).
[204] *Contrat social*, Bk 3, ch.15.

ambition, they must march away to battle; if the greed of the despot (or his supporters) can find satisfaction only through the imposition of ever-increasing taxation, then they will be forced to pay up; if one of the citizens is wronged or condemned unjustly, to whom can they turn to get justice? Then, and only then, perhaps, the citizens will understand that when political liberty is banished from the state, individuals, too, will lose their freedom, even if one takes the most usual definition of that word, that is, as representing the state where the individual is under no constraint to do what he does not want to.

For Rousseau, in the final analysis, real enjoyment of individual freedom does not depend on the natural rights that everyone has by virtue of being human, nor on the fundamental laws established by the social compact. Natural rights are without substance when there are men who heed only their own interests. In the same way there is no political law which can subdue men's passions, especially when the men in question have achieved status and power. The passions which tend to the destruction of the republic and of liberty must be met with other passions: the love of liberty and equality. A man 'without passions would certainly be a very poor citizen'[205], and if its citizens have no passions, then the republic cannot hope to preserve its integrity.

If citizens are to carry out their civic duties they must cherish the republic, for, as has already been stated, the calculation of self-interest alone would probably make them opt for what was to their immediate advantage and most likely to expand the sphere of their personal interests, and thus cause them to neglect the common good.

In the *Lettres de la montagne*, Rousseau strongly criticizes several cases of the abuse of power by the government in Geneva in its dealing with ordinary citizens; some of these cases were particularly serious (for example, an incident which took place in 1707, when a citizen was secretly tried in defiance of the law's provisions, found guilty and executed in prison by a firing squad), while others were minor incidents, such as the case of the bookseller, Bardin.[206] It is astonishing that the very writer who condemned so forcefully the abuse of state power against the individual should have been labelled the theoretician of totalitarianism and the advocate of the complete subordi-

---

[205] *Economie politique*, *OC*, vol.3, p.259; see also *Lettres écrites de la montagne*, *OC*, vol.3, p.704.   [206] *Lettres écrites de la montagne*, *OC*, vol.3, pp.882-7.

nation of the individual to the state. On this question Rousseau comes out clearly against the view of Helvetius who had stated that 'any action to promote the welfare of the community is legitimate and even virtuous'. Rousseau objected that 'the welfare of the community is as nothing if any of its members is deprived of his security.'[207]

Just as he has nothing but scorn for those states which do not respect the citizens' rights, so with equal zeal he holds up for particular approval, as examples of nobility and courage, those peoples which protect and respect the 'person' of each of their members. The peoples which Rousseau uses as examples are the ones whom he never tires of praising for their love of liberty and virtue. This is not surprising in that it is only among free men, like those of Sparta or Rome, 'where the dignity of man is realised'.[208] The Romans, in particular, 'distinguished themselves above all other peoples by the regard which their government paid to the individual and, by its scrupulous attention to the preservation of the inviolable rights of all the members of the State'.[209]

Far from the individual having no rights against the state, it is the opposite which is true: if a single one of the rights which each individual possesses, through his participation in the fundamental compact, is transgressed by sovereign, government or magistrate, all political obligations are cancelled:

The security of individuals is so intimately connected with the public confederation that, apart from the regard that must be paid to human weakness, that convention would in point of right be dissolved, if in the State a single citizen who might have been relieved were allowed to perish, or if one were wrongfully confined in prison, or if in one case an obviously unjust sentence were given. For the fundamental conventions being broken, it is impossible to conceive of any right or interest that could retain the people in the social union, unless they were restrained by force, which alone causes the dissolution of the state of civil society.[210]

While, for Hobbes, if an innocent person is punished then natural law has been violated,[211] for Rousseau, it is the fundamental laws of the republic which have been violated. The liberty and security of everyone is guaranteed so long as these laws remain sovereign. The integrity of the republic and the force of its laws can be retained only if

[207] *Notes sur 'De l'esprit' d'Helvétius, OC*, vol.4, p.1126.
[208] *Economie politique, OC*, vol.3, p.257 (transl. Cole, 1952, p.374).
[209] Ibid., p.257 (transl. ibid., p.374).
[210] Ibid., p.256 (transl. ibid., p.374).   [211] *Leviathan*, Part 2, ch.28.

the citizens' civil virtue remains unimpaired. Though civil virtue requires that certain services should be performed which are not in the immediate interest of the individual citizens, obedience to the commands of the republic alone can prevent the citizenry from becoming subject to one or more masters.

Republican order

The first two parts of this study have attempted to shed light on certain problems that Rousseau's political theory is intended to solve. These problems can be summarized under the heading of disorder. The third part of the work will concentrate on the antithesis between the republic and despotism, which represents the fundamental antithesis on which Rousseau builds his theory of the just society. For Rousseau, despotism is the worst form of disorder and it is therefore the one evil which must be avoided at all costs. By contrast, the just political order, the republic, is Rousseau's answer to the problem of disorder.

Certain of the fundamental characteristics of this political constitution have already been mentioned and also, as has been said, the antithesis between disorder and the just society coincides with the one between subjection and liberty. Where there is disorder there will be some who obey and others who command; in the republic no one has the right to impose his will on anyone else. It is now time to explain more fully why the republic is the solution to the problem of disorder. As has already been emphasized, disorder should be understood either as a state of generalized hostility in society, or as the result of individuals being allocated different status levels in a manner they hold to be unjust. According to Rousseau, the republic represents the best solution, as much to the problem of the harmony of human relations as to the problem of 'suum gradum'.

His theory of the just society is based on the premise of individualism and should be justified in individual terms (such a society is grounded in the fundamental compact which requires unanimous consent). But it still is necessary to see whether Rousseau's theory of political order is compatible with the individualist premises in which it is grounded. At the beginning of his investigations into what is essential if a government is to be legitimate, Rousseau had confronted this very problem, which he believed was soluble. But he was aware of the danger of being carried away by wishful thinking. One of the tasks of this final chapter is to see whether Rousseau was right to be cautious on this score.

Republican order is a quintessentially artificial one. It is a political order founded on the will of the sovereign authority. It is the general will which, through a code of law, institutes order and prescribes a rule for social relations: 'To provide a suitable rule to guide men's actions, it is first necessary to regulate carefully the different relations, which should exist amongst them.'[212]

Rousseau placed one of these observations at the beginning of his study of political institutions. In the *Lettres de la montagne*, written at a time when the *Social contract* was already completed and in print, he notes: 'The general will, therefore, constitutes order, the supreme rule, and this general and personified rule is what I call the Sovereign.'[213]

For Rousseau, the ground of political order is the legitimate sovereign and the laws through which he is empowered to act. This is not a spontaneous order, but one which is founded on the 'orders'. The natural history of society does not produce order, but conflict and injustice. As Rousseau sees it, order and society are two entities which, more often than not, are in conflict. Where society exists without political authority there is disorder; where there is natural order there is no society. Moreover, the fact that political authority exists is not, in itself, enough to ensure that there will be order in human affairs. The existence of a political authority guarantees that the relations between men will have some kind of regularity, but the pattern created may not be a desirable one; there must be a sovereign, but it is also essential that the sovereign should give the general will and the law the paramount place.

When Rousseau describes and praises the order of the universe, he uses the metaphor of the machine and its designer. The same metaphor appears in the *Social contract*. It is also to be found, and this is a significant point, in the chapter on the 'Legislator'. Just as God, the Great Designer has created the well-regulated and harmonious machine of the universe, so the legislator discovers which are the best and most suitable laws for all the different peoples and must be able to transform each individual, who is, himself, a perfect and separate en-

---

[212] *De l'état de nature*, *OC*, vol.3, p.480.
[213] *Lettres écrites de la montagne*, *OC*, vol.3, p.807; see also I. Fetscher, *Rousseaus politische Philosophie*, Neuwied and Berlin, 1968, ch.3.

tity, into a 'part of a greater whole'.[214] Rousseau specifically compares the legislator with the Deity. This analogy is possible not only because the great legislator[215] should, like God, possess superior intelligence and goodness. God and the legislator may be compared because one is the author of natural order and the other of political order.

The chapter on the legislator owes something to Machiavelli.[216] The fundamental difference between Machiavelli's 'prudente ordinatore' and Rousseau's great legislator is well-known. The former must possess power; what is more, he must gather all the power to himself ('debbe ingegnarsi di avere l'autorità solo'[217]). The latter does not have power, which remains within the gift of the sovereign.[218] Nevertheless, Rousseau's legislator like Machiavelli's, is an 'ordinatore'. The task of the former is to transform a multitude of men into a well-regulated society; the latter is responsible for instituting a 'republica bene ordinata'. The great legislator and the 'prudente ordinatore' are both working towards the same goal – the common good. This is why they have the great merit (though in their own particular fashion) of instituting the 'vivere civile e libero'.

Machiavelli's legislator is 'prudente'. Rousseau's must be 'wise'.[219]

[214] *Contrat social*, *OC*, vol.3, p.381 (transl. Cole, 1952, p.400).
[215] Rousseau is careful to distinguish between the 'legislator' and the 'makers of law'; see *Considérations sur le gouvernement de Pologne, OC*, vol.3, p.956.
[216] See in this connection the very pertinent observations of R. Derathé in his notes to the Pléiade edition of the *Contrat social*, vol.3, pp.1461–2; see also B. Gagnebin, 'Le rôle du Législateur dans les conceptions politiques de Rousseau', *Etudes sur le 'Contrat social'*, Paris, 1964, pp.277–90; see also P. Pasqualucci, 'Il mito rousseauiano del legislatore', *Rivista Internazionale di Filosofia del Diritto*, 55 (1970), pp.882–906.
[217] *Discorsi*, Bk 1, ch.9, p.153.
[218] 'For if he who holds command over men ought not to have command over the laws, he who has command over the laws ought not any more to have it over men', *Contrat social, OC*, vol.3, p.382 (transl. Cole, 1952, p.401); In Rousseau's institutional system the legislator is not part either of the magistrature or of the sovereign body. He is not part of the legislative power, which is the prerogative of the sovereign alone. He is not a magistrate since his function does not involve the task of seeing that the laws that others have created are respected. His institutional role is somewhat mysterious. It is possible to argue that the task of the legislator is to draw up the state constitution, even though certain passages (*Contrat social, OC*, vol.3, p.380) give the impression that the legislator's role goes beyond that of the constitution.
[219] *Contrat social, OC*, vol.3, p.384; for Montesquieu also the legislator must be prudent. His prudence consists in his ability to forestall the evil-doing which would cause him to render the legislature terrible (*Esprit des lois*, Bk 15, ch.15, p.342). It also consists in being careful to remain in accord with the spirit of the nation, provided that the latter is not completely contrary to the principles of government (*Esprit des lois*, Bk 19, ch.4, p.413). While Machiavelli is without doubt one of the main sources, amongst modern writers, of Rousseau's conception of the legislator, Montesquieu plays a similar role. For example, Rousseau is influenced by Montesquieu when he states that the good legislator should be capable of depriving men of their natural vigour; see *Esprit des lois*, Bk 27, single ch., p.170.

Immediately after the analogy between the legislator and God, Rousseau compares the legislator to the architect. The wisdom of the legislator is very similar to the skill of the architect, who 'surveys and tests the soil' before constructing the building. Like the 'prudente ordinatore', he must have a good knowledge of men and of different localities. If this were not so, the building would not survive the test of time, even if the legislator had provided what is, in the abstract, the best conceivable laws.

Republican order is founded on the sovereignty of the general will and on the wisdom of the legislator. It is an artificial order: it owes its inception to the artifice of the social compact and the art of the legislator, who, like a skilled engineer, is able to arrange all the parts of the machine so that they work in a harmonious way to achieve the purpose the machine was made for.

The republic may be considered as a rational response to the problem of disorder, since, in the first place, it guarantees that law is sovereign. As Rousseau writes in a famous passage in *Emile*, where men are reduced to a state of dependence, there is no order; in contrast, the republic allows for dependence only on the law and this is why it makes social order a reality. But the republic establishes order for other reasons as well.

As soon as men's interpersonal relations gain some element of permanency, as was pointed out in the second part of this study, men begin to compare themselves with others. They judge each other, using a mode of thought which has much in common with the price mechanism in economics. For each person the esteem and good opinion of other people become an important element in his personal identity. To be more highly esteemed and acclaimed than others, becomes everyone's main purpose in life. The dominant passion thus becomes the desire for distinction and preferment. As these are rewards enjoyed exclusively by their recipient and have to do with matters of opinion, as soon as men adopt these as their goal, they become mutual enemies. In a very schematic way, this may be compared with the mechanism which precipitates moral inequality and the ensuing social conflicts.

If we now consider what the consequence of the rule of law is, it is clear that the law acts in a way which is quite alien to the natural dynamic of society.[220] The natural history of society produces and re-produces moral inequalities (both social and political); the law and the general will in the first place provide for political and civil equality and seek to temper social inequality. Men strive for distinction and preferment; the law, on the other hand, will brook no special case.[221] So long as the republic embodies justice, everyone, whatever his or her physical or spiritual qualities, is as much a citizen as anyone else. Each person, by virtue of his status as a citizen, deserves the esteem and consideration of his fellow citizens and the magistrates, so long as he does not, through some crime, lose the title of citizen.[222]

The individual may have a greater or lesser degree of talent; he may be handsome or ugly, rich or poor. None of these things is of any importance, for he is first and foremost a citizen. Citizenship is not an exclusive right: one person cannot be more fully a citizen than another. The value of the title 'citizen' does not lie in the fact that one person has this title and others do not. In the republic instituted by the social compact, if *one* is a citizen *all* are. The compact provides every single person with a common identity. This common identity comes before all the other aspects of the personal identity of the individual. He may be strong or weak, rich or poor, be more or less intelligent, come from one class or another. In the republic all these qualities which go to make up the uniqueness of the individual recede into the background.

Finally, the essence of citizenship does not depend, as is the case with all other qualities which taken together form the personal ident-ity, on opinion. It is derived from the founding law. It is not just a moral quality, but a juridical title. Anyone who lives in a republic does not need to consult the opinion of other people to know that he is a citizen because what people think is simply not relevant to this fun-damental aspect of his personal identity. This fact is very important for the liberty which the citizens enjoy in the republic since in this re-spect they cannot be troubled by prejudice and the personal opinions of others.

---

[220] In connection with this, see the very pertinent remarks of J.N. Shklar, *Men and citizens; a study of Rousseau's social theory*, Cambridge, Mass., 1969, pp.185–97 ('The will against inequality').

[221] *Lettres écrites de la montagne*, *OC*, vol.3, p.843.

[222] See Rousseau's comments, recalling the memory of his father, in the Dedication to the *Discours sur l'inégalité*, *OC*, vol.3, p.118.

The republic is an order with degrees. On the foundation of equality under the law, a social structure is erected characterized by inequalities of status.

Rousseau has no hesitation in accepting Aristotle's principle which is that the state, unlike other forms of association, cannot take as its ruling principle any notion that its members may be regarded as identical. In the foreword to the *Discourse on inequality*, Rousseau uses the epithet 'ill-governed' to describe a state where the authority of the magistrates goes unrecognized and where the people itself claims to be, at one and the same time, legislator, prince and judge. He also adopts Montesquieu's argument that, taken to extremes, the spirit of equality is not compatible with the principle of democracy, and will, in fact, cause its downfall. In its extreme form, the spirit or equality will result in everyone wanting to be equal 'to those whom they had chosen to rule them'. Consequently, 'incapable of bearing the very power they have delegated, they want to manage everything themselves, to debate for the senate, to execute for the magistrate, and to decide for the judges.'[223]

The best political order is not a 'strict form of democracy', but one which has been 'modified with wisdom'[224] or an aristocracy, if that is defined as a regime in which the wisest rule.[225] In spite of their differences, both are legitimate (sovereignty remains with the people) and 'moderate' forms of government.[226] A just political order is compatible only with moderate or temperate governments. To use Montesquieu's phrase, the republic is imbued with the 'true spirit of equality' and not 'the extreme spirit of equality'.

The former does not imply that everybody should command, or that no one should be commanded, but that we obey or command our equals. It endeavours not to shake off the authority of a master, but that its masters should be none but its equals.[227]

---

[223] *Esprit des lois*, Bk 8, ch.2, p.149 (transl. Nugent, 1952, p.51).
[224] *Discours sur l'inégalité*, *OC*, vol.3, p.112.
[225] *Contrat social*, *OC*, vol.3, pp.406–8; *Lettres écrites de la montagne*, *OC*, vol.3, pp. 808–9.
[226] Montesquieu speaks of a 'well-regulated democracy' (*Esprit des lois*, Bk 8, ch.3) and he also notes (Bk 3, ch.4) that moderation is at the heart of aristocratic government. For Rousseau, also, good aristocratic government requires 'moderation from the rich and contentment in the poor'; *Contrat social*, *OC*, vol.3, p.407.
[227] See Montesquieu, *Esprit des lois*, Bk 8, ch.3. Extreme or strict equality is characteristic only of the natural state. The principle which is associated with civil society is that of distributive justice. Rousseau makes this point in the *Discours sur l'inégalité*: 'Distributive justice would oppose this rigorous equality of the state of nature, even were it practicable in civil society; as all the members of the State owe it their ser-

Society deprives men of their natural equality and 'they regain that equality only through the institution of law'.[228] In a democracy 'the only equality people have is as citizens', while in an extreme form of democracy 'everyone is equal, be they magistrate, senator, judge, father, husband or master'.

Rousseau adopts these principles of Montesquieu's and he makes equality as a citizen the foundation stone of any republic rooted in justice. At the same time, he echoes the main points which Montesquieu makes in criticism of the extreme manifestation of the spirit of equality. In fact, he notes that the republic is a political order for citizens who have equal rights but it is also a hierarchical order. Rousseau's theories do not envisage a political order which has an absolute equality (which would be despotism). The just political order should reduce inequality and status distinction by applying the principle of equality. It is now necessary to see what this moderate inequality (or moderate equality) would be like in practice and the nature of the criteria on which it is based.

In the *Nouvelle Héloise*, Saint-Preux spends a long time describing the house of Mme de Wolmar (Julie). In the first place he observes that the house is sensibly arranged without allowing the question of order to be an obsession:

What struck me most of all in that house was the feeling of being at ease, the liberty and gaiety accompanied by a sense of order and precision. The great drawback of houses which have been carefully planned is that they are wont to have a gloomy and claustrophobic atmosphere. The extreme punctiliousness of those who command always smacks of avarice, the whole atmosphere around them is one of inhibitedness; there is something rigorous about order which has a touch of servility about it, which is not easily borne. The servants carry out their task, but they do so in a disgruntled and fearful way.[229]

The Wolmars' unpretentious house is far more pleasant to look at and congenial to be in than great palaces where all is strife and discord and where 'everyone who lives there seeks their own fortune and happiness in other people's ruin and in a general state of disorder'.[230] In this unpretentious house, so tasteful in its arrangement,

a small number of gentle and peaceful people, united by mutual needs and reciprocated feelings of good will, all work together at their various tasks

---

vices in proportion to their talents and abilities, they ought, on their side, to be distinguished and favoured in proportion to the services they have actually rendered' (*OC*, vol.3, p.222; transl. Cole, 1952, p.360, n.1).
[228] Ibid.   [229] *La Nouvelle Héloise, OC*, vol.2, p.530.   [230] Ibid., p.546.

towards a common end: each one of them is quite content with his lot and, having no desire to change it becomes attached to it since he knows that it is his for life, and the only ambition he has is to perform his duty adequately. Those who command are so easy-going and those who obey do so with such enthusiasm that equals might share out the roles between them without being dissatisfied with what they have to do. Thus, no one hankers after someone else's job, and none of them dream of increasing their own fortune, save through increasing the wealth of the community; even the decision-makers only measure their happiness according to how happy the people around them are.[231]

The well-regulated house is very much like a just political order. In particular, the description of the Wolmars' home conveys a very good idea of the limited inequality to be found in the republic. Republican order, like the well-planned house, exhibits the workings of the hierarchical principle: the sovereign, the government, the magistrates, the people (defined here as the subjects and not the sovereign). As the sovereign is only the people gathered together in a sovereign body (to exercise legitimate power), there are actually only two levels within the hierarchy – the people and the magistrates. The latter, elected by the people, are entrusted with executive power and form the government.

The body of magistrates is made up of citizens, and magistrates and ordinary citizens are equal before the law. However, the preservation of republican order means that sovereign, magistrates and subjects must keep to their respective places and none of them is entitled to assume the role which belongs to another. As in the well-regulated house, everyone must be satisfied with his own 'gradus' and that is an important precondition if the republic is to remain in being:

If the Sovereign desires to govern, or the magistrate to give laws, or if the subjects refuse to obey, disorder takes the place of regularity, force and will no longer act together, and the State is dissolved and falls into despotism or anarchy.[232]

Magistrates should not receive special treatment,[233] and their reward for fulfilling their duties should not be a sum of money but their recompense should be the knowledge that they have the esteem and admiration of their fellow citizens.

[231] Ibid., pp.547–8. [232] *Contrat social, OC*, vol.3, p.397 (transl. Cole, 1952, p.407).
[233] *Economie politique, OC*, vol.3, p.249.

Magistrates in the republic have a higher status, which is theirs by virtue of their talent and moral worth,[234] and this status is made manifest by certain symbols which are the mark of the magistrate's special standing in the eyes of his fellow citizens.

Magistrates must exercise their power 'by virtue of their rank and through the instrument of law', and it is only on these grounds that the high status they enjoy can be reconciled with the principle of equality under the law which is so fundamental to the republic.[235] Very precise rules govern the allocation of public offices and symbols of status. Once again we find here a parallel between Rousseau's portrayal of the republic and Machiavelli's concept of 'vivere libero'. 'A state which enjoys freedom', he writes in the *Discourse*, 'assigns honours and rewards only for honest and determinate reasons, and, apart from this, rewards and honours no-one.'[236] In the Roman republic, wealth did not necessarily bring with it high social standing: 'poverty did not bar you from any office or from any honour, and that virtue was sought out no matter in whose house it dwelt'[237]

For Rousseau, also, it is one of the distinguishing traits of the just republic that social acclaim and the role of the magistrate should be granted only to the most virtuous and able citizens. By contrast, it is one of the most obvious signs of the corruption of the body politic when the most disreputable men receive public acclaim and the most dishonourable are heaped with praise.[238] When such men are appointed as magistrates, it is certain that they will take advantage of their position to advance their own interests. The method by which magistrates are chosen is, therefore, of the greatest importance for the preservation of political order.

Rousseau once again reveals himself as the loyal disciple of Montesquieu and Machiavelli when he says in the *Social contract* that it is the 'public voice' which must decide who are the citizens who most deserve to be given preferment. Under a monarchy 'those who rise to the top are most often merely petty blunderers, petty swindlers, and petty intriguers', whose petty talents cause them to get into the highest positions, while it is difficult to envisage 'a fool at the head of a

---

[234] *Contrat social*, *OC*, vol.3, p.399.
[235] See the eulogy given to the magistrates of Geneva, *Discours sur l'inégalité*, Dedication, *OC*, vol.3, p.117.
[236] *Discorsi*, Bk 1, ch.16 (transl. Walker, 1970, p.154).
[237] Ibid., Bk 3, ch.25 (transl. ibid., p.475). [238] *Economie politique*, *OC*, vol.3, p.253.

Republican government',[239] and this is a significant reason why Rousseau holds that a democratic government is to be preferred to a monarchy.

The magistrates of the republic, like those who wield authority in the Wolmar home, enjoy a degree of social superiority, which may be justified when one considers the function they perform and its usefulness to those who are subject to their authority. These magistrates are elected because of their moral worth and their talents, but as civil virtues essentially involve dedication to the pursuit of the common good, such a choice brings benefits also to those who have chosen the magistrates.

In the just republic, the superior standing enjoyed by the magistrates does not excite the envy of ordinary citizens. Their higher status is justified by their moral character and is in harmony with the common interest, and all those who aspire to the highest places in society only have to show themselves worthy of the honour.[240] In addition to this, the magistrates in the republic cannot count on receiv-

---

[239] *Contrat social*, Bk 3, ch.6, p.410 (transl. Cole, 1952, p.413). This passage drew criticism from Voltaire: 'We admit with regret that in republics, as in monarchies, intrigue makes it necessary to bring men to justice. Rome had its Verrès, its Milon, Clodius and Lépide, but we are forced to agree that no modern republic can boast of having produced ministers such as Oxenstiern, Sully, Colbert and the great men who were chosen by Elizabeth of England. Let us not defame either monarchies or republics', in *Idées républicaines par un membre d'un corps* (1762), in *Oeuvres complètes*, Paris, 1879, vol.24, p.422. It is interesting to compare what Rousseau writes in the chapter of the 3rd Book which deals with monarchy with chapter 34 of the 3rd Book of the *Discorsi*, the title of which is 'What kind of Reputation or Gossip or Opinion causes the Populace to begin to favour a Particular Citizen; and whether the Populace appoints to Offices with Greater Prudence than the Prince' 'Quale fama o voce o opinione fa che il popolo comincia a favorire uno cittadino; e se ei distribuisce i magistrati con maggiore prudenza che uno principe': transl. Walker, 1974, p.496. As regards Montesquieu, see *Esprit des lois*, Bk 2, ch.2. On the issue of the appropriate criteria for awarding honours, amongst Rousseau's sources, what Pufendorf has to say in Bk 8, ch.4 in the *Law of nature and nations* should not be forgotten. The attribution of honours and symbols of 'high esteem' is, for Pufendorf, the prerogative of the prince. But he adds that it is one of the characteristics of 'the most subtle policy that when the Prince assigns honours and status rewards he should also take into account services by which the individual has deserved well of the State'. Ibid., Bk 8, ch.23, para.23.

[240] 'The difference between good and bad men is determined by public esteem; the magistrate being strictly a judge of right alone; whereas the public is the truest judge of morals, and is of such integrity and penetration on this head that, although it may sometimes be deceived, it can never be corrupted. The rank of citizens ought, therefore, to be regulated, not according to their personal merit – for this would put it in the power of the magistrate to apply the law almost arbitrarily – but according to the actual services done to the State, which are capable of being more exactly estimated' (*Discours sur l'inégalité*, *OC*, vol.3, pp.222–3; transl. Cole, 1952, p.360, n.1).

ing any privileges or wealth which would place them in a very different position from other citizens. Thus, a hierarchy founded on justice will bring harmony to social life; by contrast, a hierarchy which lacks all justice arouses envy and spite. In the republican order the different levels within society – and this is as true of power as it is of wealth – must not be very far apart. The purpose of republican institutions is to prevent social inequality from becoming extreme and also to ensure that any status differences are ones which reflect different qualities of character and natural endowments, for any other form of inequality undermines the sovereignty of law.

The strength of law is certainly an indispensable means for the preservation of the moderate degrees of inequality which are essential to the republic. The sovereign can, and must, use the law as an instrument to prevent the accumulation of vast fortunes. But for Rousseau it is impossible to create laws 'which are proof against being misused by men driven only by their passions'.[241] If men are obsessed by an uncontrollable desire for wealth, the laws cannot long keep them in check. Sooner or later the republic's just constitution will be corrupted by the strength of that desire. For Rousseau, therefore, it is not a question of curbing desire, which seems to him to be a vain enterprise, but of directing it to other goals than wealth. This means that it is necessary to educate opinion and change men's ways of behaviour.

The problem of how men's customs and beliefs are to be changed reveals the fundamental theoretical link between the doctrine of political order and the theory of inequality.

In the course of his reflections on the problem of inequality, Rousseau had observed that men's deepest longing is to gain preferment. The desire to become rich and then to gain still more wealth can be explained as a consequence of the urge to gain preferment. Men do not seek great wealth simply because it allows them to acquire possessions, but rather because they wish to be admired and revered by others. The proof of this is that men do not limit themselves to the pursuit of the 'modest rewards' which are sufficient to ensure their well-being. It is the case that 'everyone wants to attain a level of wealth which will draw every eye like a magnet, but which also has the effect of increasing trouble and care and almost becomes as great a burden as poverty itself'. This is clearly so, adds Rousseau 'from the

---

[241] *Considérations sur le gouvernement de Pologne*, *OC*, vol.3, p.955.

foolish way the rich employ their wealth. They are not the ones who enjoy such lavish displays and they are put on only to attract the attention and the admiration of others.'[242]

Consequently, in a world in which the wealthy were not looked up to and wealth itself was not a source of moral or political distinction, it would no longer exercise the same fascination as it does now. Men would be satisfied to lead a life of moderation, which is the major source of the republic's strength. This probably was the guiding principle which directed Rousseau's thinking from the very beginning of his investigation into the nature of sound government. The idea that a society in which esteem and respect were meted out according to criteria other than wealth, birth, or the possession of talent without moral worth, came to him through the revelation of the nature of the ancient republics or, at least, through images in literature.

I admit that wealth always presents itself as the most obvious way, for, apart from the esteem it attracts, it also is the means to achieving life's commodities, but accompanied by all the ills which life in a self-centred way inflicts on custom, the State and on citizens. It is therefore necessary to arrange things in such a way that no respect would be gained from being rich, and that one would even lose esteem thereby.[243]

Rousseau has no intention of abandoning his fundamental hypothesis, which is that the unacknowledged and ultimate goal of men's actions is to achieve the admiration and esteem of their fellow men. He sets out to discover whether it is possible to encourage men to pursue the same goals by different means. The desire to be admired and made much of by others is an ineradicable trait of the character of any man who lives in society, and is foreign only to the experience of men who live in the isolation of the natural state; it is an inner driving force which cannot be eliminated so long as men live in society. Nevertheless, how it is that certain objects come to be seen as valuable and as signs of worldly success is a question which has to do with the operation of fashion, and that is something which can be modified: 'Right men's opinions, and their morality will purge itself. Men always love what is good or what they find good; it is in judging what is good that they go wrong. This judgement, therefore, is what must be regulated.'[244]

Currents of opinion which develop spontaneously within society

---

[242] *De l'honneur et de la vertu*, *OC*, vol.3, p.502.   [243] Ibid., p.503.
[244] *Contrat social*, *OC*, vol.3, p.458 ('De la censure') (transl. Cole, 1952, p.434).

are the exact opposite of the temperate judgements which are necessary for the health of the body politic. This brings us back to the antithesis between nature and artifice. Opinions which develop naturally as a product of social relationships must, in effect, be transformed artificially. The natural tendencies of society, which Rousseau has defined in the *Discourse on inequality*, are incompatible with the requirements of a just political order. It is, therefore, the same engineer who has constructed the political machine who must, through his art, modify social attitudes. To be able to transform men's tastes and values in this way is the greatest proof of the legislator's skill.[245]

The wise legislator can (and should) institute laws which convey 'the approval or disapproval of the public in the form of reward or punishment'. The solution to the problem 'of arousing the desire, and of making it easy, to attract the same degree of admiration through virtue as today may only be gained through wealth'[246] may be to create laws which apportion praise and blame. In Rousseau's view, laws should not only have a negative function, discouraging wrong-doing through the threat of punishment, but should also exercise a positive influence (urging men to do good by holding out the possibility of a reward):

This is the principle by which we must judge what the law can do, not only to make vice out clearly for what it is, but also to encourage virtue. I know that the highest reward of good actions is the pleasure of having done them, but men can come to know what this pleasure is like only by experiencing it, and they need more tangible rewards to get them into the habit of doing good. These rewards that provide their motivation must be carefully selected, for if they are not, far from bringing honour they will only excite hypocrisy and nourish avarice. The choice of rewards and how they are to be distributed are supreme examples of the legislator's art.[247]

Rousseau's project is to provide a theoretical definition of the most suitable ways in which men's views can be altered and to make them moderate and temperate, without forsaking the principle that the individual acts only in accord with what he judges to be his interest. He does not claim that men no longer strive to obtain great wealth

---

[245] *Projet de constitution pour la Corse*, *OC*, vol.3, p.937.
[246] *De l'honneur et de la vertu*, *OC*, vol.3, p.502; 'Arrange things in such a way that simplicity is cause for vanity and that a wealthy man is at a loss as to how his money can bring him renown' (*Projet de constitution pour la Corse*, *OC*, vol.3, p.936); see also *Considérations sur le gouvernement de Pologne*, *OC*, vol.3, p.962.
[247] *Des loix*, *OC*, vol.3, p.495.

because they have become altruistic, but rather because it is not in their interest to pursue wealth.[248] If the greatest good man can hope for in a society is the acclaim and esteem of others and if great wealth does not provide these rewards, it will not long be in their interest to become rich. By contrast, if virtue and moderation are more likely to receive the accolade of the public, men will behave in a moderate and virtuous manner out of self-interest.[249]

The idea of a just political order is associated in Rousseau's mind with a fairly precise image of social order. The problem of social order is connected with the definition of the rules which govern the way individuals are channelled to the various forms of employment available (or, to use a more precise term, the division of labour).

Treated systematically, social order is considered as a prime necessity if the republic's constitution is to be preserved. As far as Rousseau is concerned, the aim should be the moral good of the individuals, not political order. This does not mean that the state should regard it as part of its task to make men happy or virtuous. Instead, it should provide the conditions which make happiness possible and which encourage the individual to lead a moral life.[250] The purpose of a state rooted in justice is to give to all equality of opportunity. This is why the community has a duty to ensure that no one individual gains too much power. It also has the responsibility to see that each person has the opportunity to gain personal fulfilment irres-

---

[248] *De l'honneur et de la vertu, OC*, vol.3, p.503.

[249] Every time Rousseau goes into detail concerning the rewards that the law can provide in order to arouse the admiration of the populace, he never fails to mention symbolic rewards; see *Projet de constitution pour la Corse, OC*, vol.3, p.936; *Considérations sur le gouvernement de Pologne, OC*, vol.3, p.962.

[250] 'The government which can force Citizens to lead a happy life does not exist, the best government is the one which gives them the opportunity to be happy, if they act reasonably. And the populace as a whole will never enjoy this happiness.' *Du bonheur public, OC*, vol.3, p.513. As for communal happiness, Rousseau demonstrates a profound aversion for 'holist' conceptions: 'do not imagine that the State can be happy when all its members are suffering. This moral being that you call communal happiness is in itself a mere fantasy: if no single individual has a feeling of well-being, it is as nothing and the family cannot flourish where the children do not prosper', *Du bonheur public, OC*, vol.3, p.510. The happiness of the individual, in Rousseau's view, consists in the attainment of oneness with the moral self ('make man one and you will make him as happy as it is possible for him to be', ibid). In a society which forces him to live in permanent conflict with others, the individual has no chance of attaining such oneness. If he does not wish to be a victim of injustice, he himself must act unjustly. But to act unjustly and wickedly sets man against his true moral nature. A just society should above all else, allow men to acquire a moral oneness which, for Rousseau, is the ground of true happiness.

pective of the caprices of fortune. Which family one is born into is just a question of chance, and that is true of the degree of wealth, physical prowess and the qualities of body and mind one may inherit. As was mentioned above, in a republic which has a sound constitution these elements of chance should not be allowed to prevent someone having access to the good life, to command the esteem and respect of his fellows, and even to obtain official honours.

Rousseau adopts very similar principles with regard to the question of social order. What (from the normative point of view) is the more important is not the good of the 'whole' – in this case of the society – but of the individuals. In attempting to answer the question, what is the best political constitution, Rousseau was seeking, in effect, to define the political constitution most likely to promote happiness and virtue amongst its citizens. Grappling with the problem of social order, he asks himself which form of social order might best be suited to preserve the moral integrity of society and assist men to become, as far as possible, happy and virtuous. In this context, one of the most important passages is to be found in the fifth part of *La Nouvelle Héloise*, where Saint-Preux writes to Milord Edouard about a discussion he has had with Mme de Wolmar, whose deepest conviction is that it does not do to try and bring about change in men's social condition. Against this, St Preux objects that nature seems to have given everyone the talents which make him suited to a particular job. The kind of work in which people are engaged and their status (for this is the conception of social order defended by St Preux) should be evaluated according to the qualities and talents possessed by individuals. Everyone should fill the place to which he is most suited on the basis of his talents and capabilities. St Preux believes that men should not have to spend their lives in the social situation they were born into. By contrast, a far more equitable social order would be one which allowed everyone to gain employment in accordance with his ability. Moreover, if jobs and situations in society are allotted to the men who are most suited to them, society in general will be better off. Mme de Wolmar opposes St Preux's more dynamic vision of society with an image of social order which is more 'archaic' and which derives from a very different way of thinking about the good of individuals.

According to St Preux, each person should be given the place in the division of labour for which nature has intended him. This principle is justified as much on the grounds of the good of society in general as for the benefit of the individual citizen. It is for the good of the individual because he has the satisfaction of knowing that others have recognized his personal qualities and he can improve his social standing. Society derives benefit in that the various posts are filled by the people who are most fitted by nature for these posts.

According to Mme de Wolmar, on the other hand, the fundamental principle of the social order must be the preservation of good customs and civic virtue. This principle must shape the way society develops, and it is against this standard that society must be measured:

'Man', she said, 'is too noble a creature to be used as a mere instrument for others, and he should not be employed in ways that might work to their advantage without asking him what he considers it suitable for him himself to do; for men do not exist just to fill a social role, but roles exist for their benefit, and, to achieve this, it is not so much a question of asking what work a man is most suited for but what is the kind of work most suited to each man, to make him good and happy as far as is possible.'[251]

In an earlier version which was later changed, Rousseau had made it even clearer that he regarded individual happiness and civic virtue as having overriding importance as norms governing social order: 'For it is even better for society to lack cohesion and all the citizens to be happy and honest than for society to function smoothly and all the citizens to be wretched and evil-doers.'

Through Mme de Wolmar's words, Rousseau makes his view clear that the best social order is the one which attaches men most closely to the land and is least vulnerable to change. He also argues that the social order which encourages social mobility is not a desirable one. Experience had taught Rousseau that it is not the best who triumph in the struggle to obtain the most highly prized employment. In this pursuit, 'those who succeed and make their fortune nearly always do so by the dishonest methods which lead to this kind of success'; while those who fail, and this is the majority, are condemned to a life of misery.

Moreover, happiness does not come from change and the struggle to get on in society, but, and this is Rousseau's view, from stability of character and inner balance between desires and qualities.[252] The

---

[251] *La Nouvelle Héloise, OC*, vol.2, p.537.

[252] It is not without importance that, towards the end of his life, Rousseau should write: 'One of the things which pleases him most is to find himself in old age, having roughly the same social status as was his at birth, without having gone very far up or down in the world during his life. Fate has brought him back to where nature had originally set him. He congratulates himself everyday on this convergence between the two', *Rousseau juge de Jean-Jacques, OC*, vol.1, p.850. Rousseau is influenced by

principle to be adopted if society is to function harmoniously is to ensure that everyone is happy with his lot. This does not mean that men will be happy whatever the condition in which they live. The idea that every condition of life has the same proportion of happiness and sorrow is rejected unequivocally as a

maxim as gloomy in its implications as it is untenable; if everyone is equally happy why should I put myself out for anyone else. Let each person stay as he is: let the slave be maltreated, let the one who is sick continue to suffer, and let the rogue perish; they have nothing to gain by changing their situation.

The difference between the misfortunes of the rich and those suffered by the poor is that the rich are entirely to blame when things go wrong for them, but the sufferings of the poor are due to things outside their control and the grim logic of fate. The aim of making everyone happy in the situation in which they find themselves is not an invitation merely to accept their lot and resign themselves to the force of circumstance or the will of other men. What is really meant is that in the just society each person would find it possible to be happy whatever his lot might be as a result of the division of labour. If employment and honest labour provide those who work with the same degree of dignity and respect and almost the same economic rewards, everyone will be content with his situation: 'Men are lazy by nature, but enthusiasm for work is the first fruit of a well-regulated society and when people become slothful and lose hope, it is always because they have been abused by that same society.'[253]

The just social order grows out of the constitution of the state and the will of the sovereign. It rests with the government to see that work is held in respect. In an imperfect society it is often the most worthwhile jobs which carry with them the lowest social status, which generally makes the lot of those who do them an unenviable one, while it is quite the reverse when it comes to the kind of jobs which are rewarded with wealth and prestige. In such a situation the happiness of each person will depend on his ability to rise to levels of employment which are most highly regarded and best paid. Everyone's

Plutarch here: see *Oeuvres morales*, 1557, vol.1, ch.10: 'On the contentment or the repose of the spirit', pp.68–75 in ch.26; 'There is sufficient evil-doing to make man discontented', pp.137–8. Like his master, Plutarch, Rousseau does not accept the Stoic doctrine of virtue and happiness: it is not, as the Stoics would have it, 'that virtue alone can make a man happy. To complete human happiness it is necessary to add to virtue the necessities of life and good health: see Rousseau à François-Joseph de Conzie, comte de Charmettes, 17 Jan. 1742, *Correspondance complète*, 1965–84, ed. R.A. Leigh, vol.1, pp.137–8. [253] *Projet de constitution pour la Corse*, *OC*, vol.3, p.941.

possibility of success or failure will depend entirely on blind chance.

In a just society, on the other hand, it is not necessary for the individual to engage in pitiless rivalry with others if he wants to better himself: he will have nothing to gain either in terms of material rewards or of status. The guiding principle of the just society should be, therefore, that each person must be helped to achieve contentment whatever his situation:

It is not enough for the people to have bread and a basic living standard; they must also live in pleasant conditions so that they can carry out their duty in a more satisfactory way and not always be fretting to escape their trials and tribulations, and also so that public order should be more soundly based. Good social customs are far more dependent on people's being satisfied with their lives than one is inclined to think. Manipulation and the spirit of intrigue are born out of anxiety and discontent: everyone starts going wrong when someone else seeks to take his employment. You must love your work if you are to do it well. The State soup bowls are only good and solid when everyone is seated in his place, and individual energies are united and working for the public good, instead of being worn out in conflict as they are in any State where injustice reigns.[254]

In a well-regulated society the happiness of individuals does not depend on fate, chance or birth but, ultimately, on the individual himself. Finally, when virtue is prized and vice punished, the just political constitution re-establishes on earth the moral order perverted by man's unrestrained passions.

It would seem that, at least from the point of view of its internal coherence, the difficult task of elaborating a theory of political order, starting from the premise of individualism, has been carried out successfully. Men 'as they are', seeking only what is in their own interest and what will benefit them, have a reasonable chance of becoming good citizens. They are capable of understanding that the preservation of the republic and the sovereignty of law is of great benefit to them, because this means that they do not have to place all their trust in any other person and they are protected from all ills. Moreover, they have the opportunity to satisfy the desire they have to distinguish themselves: the greater their virtue, the more they are esteemed. The same reasons which cause them to be admired by their

---

[254] *Jean-Jacques Rousseau citoyen de Genève à Mr d'Alembert*, 3rd edn, Amsterdam, Michel Rey, 1762, p.214.

fellow citizens make them eligible for the highest public offices, such as the magistracy.

It is true that it is very difficult to recognize true merit. Moreover, those who use underhand methods to advance their position try to make sure that the really deserving go unrewarded.[255] Nevertheless, from the perspective adopted by Rousseau, it is not likely that the people will err in their choice of magistrates. The republic, it must be remembered, should be small, and, when 'all the citizens know each other and can closely observe each other's behaviour, those who resort to intrigue to get on have less chance of success'.[256]

As has already been stated, the republic is the form of political constitution in which law is sovereign. But Rousseau, himself, writes as follows:

Making man subordinate to law is a political problem which I think may be compared to the squaring of the circle in geometry. Solve this problem and the government established on the basis of this solution will be a good one and without flaws. But, until that day, be sure that, even though you may believe that you have made law supreme, it will be men who rule. The only just and sound constitution possible is that where law reigns in the hearts of the citizens. So long as the influence of law is excluded from this sphere, the law will never be universally obeyed.[257]

Should we see what Rousseau says here as an admission that the just republic is an ideal which can never be realized? If so, it would indicate that Rousseau's theoretical project had proved impossible. In my view, Rousseau's statement should be interpreted in a different way. Its precise meaning is that a just republic can be preserved only if its customs are admirable – good laws by themselves are not enough. Rousseau is quite clear about the difference between law and custom: 'the law operates only in an external way and its influence goes no further than men's actions; customs alone reach the inner man and direct men's wills.'[258]

It is probable that Rousseau had borrowed the idea that law and custom should not be confused from Montesquieu, who had developed this notion in the nineteenth book of the *Spirit of laws*. Rousseau also went to Montesquieu for the argument that laws could assist in the

[255] *La Nouvelle Héloise, OC*, vol.2, p.537.
[256] *Considérations sur le gouvernement de Pologne, OC*, vol.3, p.970; see also *Economie politique, OC*, vol.3, pp.254–5.
[257] *Considérations sur le gouvernement de Pologne, OC*, vol.3, p.955; see also the famous *Lettre* to Mirabeau of the 26 July 1767, *Correspondance complète*, ed. R.A. Leigh, vol.33, pp.238–42.   [258] *Des moeurs, OC*, vol.3, p.555.

creation of generally accepted modes of behaviour within a given society.[259] However, it seems to me that the main source of Rousseau's ideas on this question of the relation between law and custom was Machiavelli, who writes in the *Discourses*, 'If custom is corrupted, good legislation is of no avail' ('le leggi bene ordinate non giavono').[260] And he adds in the following chapter: 'Because, just as for the maintenance of good customs, laws are required, so if laws are to be observed, there is need of good customs' (Perché cosí come gli buoni costumi per mantenersi hánno bisogno delle leggi, cosí le leggi per osservarsi hanno bisogno de' buoni costumi'). 'Moroever, good laws give rise to sound education and sound education is the source of so many examples of virtue ('tanti esempli di virtú').[261]

Rousseau uses very similar terms to expound this idea. Like the 'ancient governments' the republic must be able to change generally accepted patterns of behaviour and this is something which could be achieved, even without having recourse to the 'force of law'.[262] Good laws and the rewards a citizen can hope to earn may be able to promote good customs. If the magistrates set a becoming example, this would be even more likely. It would be well within the bounds of possibility that citizens might respect the law and the magistrature and that, as a result, the order of the republic would be preserved.

The preservation of a stable political order does not only require that the citizens should obey the magistrates, attend the general meetings, pay their taxes and be prepared to fight courageously against any enemy. The preservation of the order of the republic cannot be achieved unless the men are sober, hard-working and temperate, and the women chaste, demure and devoted to the running of household affairs. Even their private lives should be open to public scrutiny. In the *Social contract*, Rousseau also suggests that a special office should be created within the magistrature with the appointment of a censor, whose task it would be to see that the general behaviour within society did not become too lax. In this context,

---

[259] *Esprit des lois*, Bk 20, ch.27.
[260] *Discorsi*, Bk 1, ch.17 (transl. Walker, 1970, p.159).
[261] Ibid., Bk 1, ch.18 (transl. ibid., p.160).
[262] *Economie politique*, *OC*, vol.3, pp.252–4; The text in which Rousseau explains in greatest detail his ideas on the most appropriate way to preserve good custom is the *Lettre à Mr d'Alembert*. In this text Rousseau notes several times that the best way of shaping public opinion, and thus customs also, cannot be through the application of 'rigid laws', that is to say by edicts and laws, nor 'by any kind of coercion'; see *Jean-Jacques Rousseau citoyen de Genève à Mr d'Alembert*, Amsterdam, 1762, pp.113–14. The censor, alone, may use the 'law' of public opinion (*Contrat social*, Bk 4, ch.7).

Rousseau takes as his model, in addition to Rome under the republic, the Geneva of Calvin. To fulfil his ambition that Geneva should be the 'New Jerusalem', Calvin had in fact set up a special tribunal, the Concistore, responsible for preserving high standards of behaviour.

According to Rousseau, a man cannot be free and also tolerate corrupted behaviour. Nevertheless, the best way to preserve high standards is not through having strict laws. The sanctions imposed by law are not the appropriate instrument for shaping custom. The legislator must seek to influence custom through laws which act as a channel for public disapproval or acclaim.

Rousseau's critics have frequently drawn attention to the repressive implications of his ideas for social mores and for the relationship between the private and the public spheres. Benjamin Constant, for example, noted that in the ancient republics each citizen's life was tightly controlled by the group, and any form of private life free from the interference of the society at large was out of the question. These same aspects of the ancient republics reappear in Rousseau's republic. It is for this reason that the latter is incompatible with the 'modern' conception of freedom.[263]

Constant's criticism is very much to the point and raises a very important issue. According to Rousseau, the purpose of the just society is to provide a space for individual freedom which, in the first instance, consists of the protection of the individual and the enjoyment of property rights. Yet, in working to preserve a just social order and freedom of the individual, he proposes to use means which are in contradiction with the goals that he desires to attain. Once any kind of public inspection and control of the citizen's private life and religious and moral beliefs is permitted, the private life ceases to exist.

This lack of consistency is particularly apparent in the chapters on censorship and on civil religion. Especially in the latter, it is difficult to reconcile what Rousseau has to say with what he had written on other occasions. In the *Lettre à Voltaire*, for example, he had denied that the state had the right to 'control men's inner conscience' in the context of religious belief and he adds that the activity of the state should not go beyond 'civil duties'.[264] In the chapter on civil religion, Rousseau writes that the sovereign has the right to call on his subjects

---

[263] B. Constant, *De l'esprit de conquête et de l'usurpation dans leurs rapports avec la civilisation européenne* (1814), in *Oeuvres de Benjamin Constant*, ed. A. Roulin, Paris, 1957, chs.6 and 7; see also by the same author Introduction to the *Mélanges de littérature et de politique*, Paris, 1829. [264] *Lettre à Voltaire*, *OC*, vol.4, p.1072.

to account for their beliefs in the measure that these beliefs have some bearing on the life of the community, but the citizen's beliefs are not, of themselves, any concern of the state's. What is important is the practical consequences of religious dogma for morality and social duties. The 'purely civil profession of faith' should contain articles (inserted by the sovereign) which should not be considered as 'religious dogma' but as 'sentiments of sociability', without which it is impossible to be a good citizen or a loyal subject.[265] But how is it possible to tell whether or not anyone is endowed with such feelings? And who is to pass judgement?

In the chapter on civil religion, Rousseau no longer speaks of encouraging men to become good citizens through the instrumentality of law (which deals on the level of actions and not beliefs) and the provision of good examples, or rewards for good deeds; instead he suggests that any citizen who states openly that he does not believe in the precepts of civil religion should be banished for his unsocial attitude and that anyone who professes to believe the civil religion and then behaves as if, in fact, he did not believe it, should be put to death. A civil court might well be able to prove that some positive law had been broken, but what court could show that a man 'had behaved' as if he did not believe in the dogma of the civil religion?[266]

Rousseau had written the first version of the chapter on civil religion on the reverse side of the folio on which he had sketched the outline for the chapter on the legislator. This is an interesting detail and the conclusion of the chapter on the legislator in the *Geneva manuscript* is a clear indication of the fundamental importance of the civil religion in Rousseau's political theory.

He says that 'every citizen is sufficiently persuaded of the benefits accruing from political union', but 'it is no less an advantage to be able to give the morality which binds all together an inner strength which

[265] *Contrat social*, Bk 4, ch.8 (transl. Cole, 1952, p.439).
[266] The dogmas are: 'The existence of a mighty, intelligent and beneficent Divinity, possessed of foresight and providence, the life to come, the happiness of the just, the punishment of the wicked, the sanctity of the social contract and the laws', *Contrat social*, Bk 4, ch.8 (transl. Cole, 1952, p.439). M. Launay seems to me to be incorrect when he argues that the final version of the chapter on civil religion 'expressly excludes any inquiry into opinions and matters of conscience', *Jean-Jacques Rousseau écrivain politique*, Cannes, 1971, pp.404–5; in this connection see R. Derathé, 'La Religion civile selon Rousseau', in *Annales de la Société Jean-Jacques Rousseau*, 35 (1959–62), pp.161–80; P.M. Masson, *La Religion de Jean-Jacques Rousseau*, Geneva, 1970 (reprint of the 1st edn, Paris, 1916), ch. 'The problem of civil religion'; B. Groethuysen, *J.-J. Rousseau*, Paris, 1949, pp.263–81.

can pervade the soul and is untroubled by life's weal or woe and un-affected by the deeds of men'. There is a great difference between someone who is loyal to the state because he has sworn allegiance, or because he thinks that this will be of some use, and someone else who is loyal to the state and respects its laws because he 'considers it to be a divine and indestructible institution'.[267]

In Rousseau's conception, civil religion should act to strengthen the law. Like the legislators of the ancient world, Rousseau thinks it necessary to call upon the assistance of religion to give the body politic a firmer basis than can be provided by the social contract and positive law alone. The principal source of this idea is Machiavelli, explicitly referred to in a note in the chapter of the *Social contract* devoted to the legislator. In this respect, a reading of the *Discourses* side by side with the *Social contract* is a fruitful exercise.[268]

Referring to Numa, Machiavelli observes: 'Nor, in fact, was there ever a legislator who, in introducing extraordinary laws to a people, did not have recourse to God.'[269] The reason for this is that there is no other way of getting untutored men to accept the laws. Since there are many things which are beneficial (like good laws) whose value is not properly appreciated by mankind, they must be convinced by other means: 'Hence wise men, in order to escape this difficulty have recourse to God. So Lycurgus did; so did Solon, and so have many others done.'[270]

Now let us consider the *Social contract*.

In all times [writes Rousseau] legislators have been forced to have recourse to divine intervention and credit the gods with their own wisdom in order that the people, submitting to the laws of the State as to those of nature, and recognising the same power in the formation of the city as in that of man, might obey freely and bear with docility the yoke of public happiness.

The reason why the great legislators of antiquity had to appeal to a divinity is the one given also by Machiavelli. It is a question of con-vincing men, who are blind to the social dimension and who are incap-able of understanding through reason the advantages of a just political constitution, that they should accept the 'sound maxims of politics' and just laws, in spite of the limitations that these impose on the individual: 'The legislator, therefore, being unable to appeal to

---

[267] *Manuscrit de Genève, OC*, vol.3, p.318.
[268] See on this subject A. McKenzie, 'Rousseau's debate with Machiavelli in the "Social contract" ', in *Journal of the history of ideas*, 43 (1982), pp.209–28.
[269] *Discorsi*, Bk 1, ch.11 (transl. Walker, 1970, p.141).   [270] Ibid.

either force or reason, must have recourse to an authority of a different order, capable of constraining without violence and persuading without convincing.'[271]

Rousseau adopts the conclusions that Machiavelli himself had drawn from his observations on the Romans with regard to the political importance of religion ('la Religione bene usata'). But the religion which is suited to the republic cannot be either Christianity ('I know nothing more contrary to the social spirit') nor the 'religion of the Priest', which gives men 'two codes of legislation, two rulers, and two countries, renders them subject to contradictory duties and makes it impossible for them to be faithful both to religion and to citizenship'. Finally, of course, it is out of the question to consider a restoration of the pagan religion – apart from anything else it was 'tyrannous and exclusive' and made the people 'bloodthirsty and intolerant'.[272] The idea of purely civil religion was conceived from the conviction that it is necessary for each citizen to have a religion other than Christianity or the religion of paganism. But, in suggesting a civil religion, Rousseau distances himself from Machiavelli, who had, in fact, gone no further than to advocate a far more cynical approach to the matter. 'The wise prince', he remarked, 'must take special care to preserve religious ceremonies' and especially 'to maintain incorrupt the ceremonies of their religion'[273] and above all 'should hold them in veneration'. Machiavelli was not saying that a new religion should be instituted but simply that the forms of ritual already in existence should be encouraged: 'The rulers of a republic or of a kingdom, therefore, should uphold the basic principles of the religion which they practise in, and, if this is done, it will be easy for them to keep their commonwealth religious, and in consequence good and united.'[274]

Rousseau, like Machiavelli, adopts the point of view of the politician and the legislator. What interests him here is not whether a religion is true or not, but the consequence a religion has for the unity of the body politic[275]; however, while Machiavelli thinks it enough for a people to have 'the fear of God' and to perform the rituals (including forms of superstition which encourage the fear of God), Rousseau also asks that a religion should be in conformity with reason and the

[271] *Contrat social*, Bk 2, ch.7 (transl. Cole, 1952, p.401).
[272] Ibid., Bk 4, ch.8 (transl. Cole, 1952, p.437).
[273] *Discorsi*, Bk 1, ch.12 (transl. Walker, 1970, p.142).
[274] Ibid., (transl. ibid., p.143).   [275] *Lettres de la montagne*, *OC*, vol.3, pp.703, 706.

Gospels, tolerant, free from superstition and with the simplest possible forms of liturgy'.[276] Only a religion like that described in the
Profession de foi du vicaire savoyard, giving cohesion by maxims which
prescribe social duties, is suitable for the republic. Like the republic,
such a religion does not exist, and it is necessary to bring it into
being.[277] In the chapter on the legislator and civil religion, Rousseau
attempts to translate the lesson of the *Discourses* into a different political theory based on the principles of the social contract. It seems to
him that a transformation of this kind is both necessary and possible:
necessary because the social contract by itself is not sufficient to
guarantee the survival and the unity of the republic; possible because
he sees no contradiction between the principle of the social contract
and civil religion. Rousseau may have believed that he had, in this
chapter, shown the best way to deal with the forces of decay which
constantly threaten the republic. There is reason to doubt whether
Rousseau's suggestion will work and also whether it is compatible
with the prime purpose of a just political order which is, in the last
analysis, liberty. But it is, above all, necessary to pose a more general
question concerning the compatibility of the two main sources of
Rousseau's political doctrine: the republican tradition and the school
of natural law. This is the issue that must now be addressed by focus-
ing on the forces of decay which threaten the republic.

The dissolution of the republic

Rousseau's ideas about social order and order within the state are
modelled on the practice of the ancient republics. He is well aware
that his conception of political order may appear to 'modern' eyes as a
utopia, yet he does not regard the republic as a mere fantasy: 'The
bounds of possibility, in moral matters, are less narrow than we
imagine: it is our weakness, our vices and our prejudices that confine
them. Base souls have no belief in great men; vile slaves smile in
mockery at the name of liberty.'[278]

The two main elements, essential to Rousseau's theory of political
order, are, on the one hand, the tradition of thinkers advocating some
form of social contract and, on the other, classical and modern
republican tradition. These are two different traditions which may be
combined in a political theory only with difficulty. The first is

[276] Ibid., pp.697–701.
[277] Ibid., p.701.   [278] *Contrat social*, *OC*, vol.3, p.425 (transl. Cole, 1952, p.420).

founded on the premise of a thoroughgoing individualism; the second makes civil virtue the foundation of political order; the former, whose mode of reasoning is normative and abstract, appeals to the calculative rationality of men; the latter emphasizes the importance of the passions, especially love of liberty and of the fatherland.

Rousseau's doctrine of political order owes much to each of these traditions and it is this weaving together of these two strands of thought within the theory that is responsible in large part for its originality in comparison with the rest of modern political philosophy. The tradition of the social contract and the republican tradition are, moreover, used in different theoretical contexts.

Rousseau makes use of the first of these traditions when he confronts the problem of how political authority is to be justified. In fact, when he explains that the only form of political constitution to which individuals motivated only by hopes of gaining some personal advantage could rationally give their consent is the republic, he is doing no more than developing the idea which lies at the heart of the theory of the social contract. When he criticizes Grotius or Hobbes, he does not reproach them for being contractualists, but for advocating a form of contractualism which lacks coherence.

From the republican tradition, Rousseau derives the fundamental traits of a just political order. It is from this same tradition that he borrows most of his observations concerning the necessary preconditions for the preservation of political order[279] founded on the

---

[279] Rousseau's commitment to republicanism is apparent in his first writings where he notes that he had learnt to love republican principles from his youth,

> But different lessons helped to shape my youth
> I was taught to do my duty without ignoble deeds
> To respect the Great, Magistrates, and Kings
> To value my fellow beings and obey the laws;
> But I also learnt that having from my birth
> The right to share in supreme power
> As small as I was, a weak and unknown Citizen
> I was, nevertheless, a member of the Sovereign Body
> That I had to make myself worthy of such a privilege
> By having a hero's heart, the virtue of a sage,
> That, in short, liberty, that dear present given by Heaven
> Is only a curse for evil hearts.
> We imbibed these maxims with our mother's milk
> So that one day we should be able to provide ourselves
> With the finest magistrates and the most equitable laws.

Epître à Monsieur Parisot (1742), *OC*, vol.2, p.1137; see also *Le Verger de Madame la Baronne de Warens*, ibid., pp.1124–9; *Epître à M. Bordes*, *OC*, vol.2, pp.1130–3; see on this subject M. Launay, 'Les Hésitations de l'esprit républicain dans les premiers textes de Rousseau (1728–1748)', in J. Viard (ed.), *L'Esprit républicain*, Paris, 1972, pp.133–41.

sovereignty of law. Finally, and this is perhaps where he is most greatly indebted, he takes his concept of liberty from the republican writers. If the tradition of natural-law theory seems to him to offer the most satisfying solution to the problem of the rational *justification* of legitimate government,[280] the republican tradition, with its insistence on the civic virtues and the need to exercise control over the emotions, provides him with most of his ideas concerning the *preservation* of the just political order.

All the measures which Rousseau holds to be prerequisite for the maintenance of social harmony within the republic – the limitation of its territory, the elimination of extreme economic inequalities, rewards for virtue, the tribunate, the election of magistrates by the people, periodical assemblies of all the people, the office of censor, civil religion[281] – these are the principal means through which the life of the republic can be prolonged.

We have already discussed some of the moral measures intended to reform social attitudes and direct men's emotions towards worthy ends. Territorial limits should be strictly adhered to because, amongst other reasons, this is necessary if civic virtue is to remain strong. In a small community the fact that people see each other every day strengthens social bonds and it is easier for people to realize what is for the common good. Moreover, in a small republic it is more difficult to avoid carrying out one's share of communal duties.

There is another reason which Rousseau advances for restricting territorial limits and this is that it is necessary to curb the 'desire for conquest' which is one of the chief threats to the liberty of the polity:[282]

This desire, occasioned often by a different species of ambition from that which it seems to proclaim, is not always what it appears to be, and has not so much, for its real motive, the apparent desire to aggrandise the Nation as a secret desire to increase the authority of the rulers at home, by increasing the

[280] For this reason I cannot agree with J.N. Shklar's comment that 'in spite of the title of his most celebrated book, the social contract itself plays an insignificant part in his political thought' (*Men and citizens*, Cambridge, Mass., 1969, p.177). On the contrary, the theoretical device of the original compact is of central importance to Rousseau's political doctrine. In effect it allows him to maintain that the only form of political constitution which can be justified rationally is the one in which the people is the holder of the sovereign power and in which the general will is supreme; the importance of the theory of the social contract in Rousseau's political doctrine has recently been emphasized by J.B. Noone, *Rousseau's 'Social contract'. A conceptual analysis*, London, 1980, p.4.
[281] *Economie politique, OC*, vol.3, p.254; *Discours sur l'inégalité*, Dedication, *OC*, vol.3, pp.111–12. [282] *Discours sur l'inégalité*, Dedication, *OC*, vol.3, p.113.

number of troops, and by the diversion which the objects of war occasion in the minds of the citizens.[283]

Rousseau is also firmly within the republican tradition when he advocates civil militia as guarantors of liberty. He shows that conquering races do not themselves long remain free: in subjecting others to alien rule, they bring nearer the day when they too will be enslaved by their leaders. A people which desires to remain free must be capable of defending itself against external enemies, but it should not go beyond that and try to take away the liberty of other peoples.

Periodic and regular assemblies of all the people, the election of magistrates by the people and the institution of courts represent the specifically constitutional means whereby political order is to be preserved. The election of magistrates has already been discussed and the constitutive assemblies will be referred to below.

With regard to the 'tribunate', it is important to realize that Rousseau attaches the greatest degree of significance to this specific form of magistrature: 'The tribunate, wisely tempered, is the strongest support a good constitution can have.[284]

The task of the tribunate is to maintain a balance between the various bodies which constitute the state: the sovereign, the government (the magistrates) and the people. Depending on circumstances, it should protect the prerogatives of the sovereign against the government, or support the government against the people, or temper the actions of the government and protect the laws.

However, Rousseau does not restrict himself to making suggestions of a constitutional nature or which are relevant to the task of forming a civic consciousness. In all his political writings, he places great emphasis on the relation between the political constitution and the economic structure of society. A society not characterized by 'extremes of wealth and poverty', to borrow a term from the current

---

[283] *Economie politique*, *OC*, vol.3, p.268 (transl. Cole, 1952, p.380). On this point Rousseau diverges from Machiavelli, who praised the constitution of Rome because it was apt, if necessary, to support territorial expansion. See *Discorsi*, Bk 1, ch.6: 'Wherefore, since it is impossible, so I hold, to adjust the balance so nicely as to keep things exactly to this middle course, one ought, in constituting a republic, to consider the possibility of its playing a more honourable role, and so to constitute it that, should necessity force it to expand, it may be able to retain possession of what it has acquired' (transl. Walker, 1970, p.226).

[284] *Contrat social*, *OC*, vol.3, p.454 (transl. Cole, 1952, p.432).

political vocabulary, is one of the fundamental preconditions to be fulfilled if the state is to live up to its claim to provide justice for all its citizens: 'What is most necessary, and perhaps most difficult in government, is rigid integrity in doing strict justice to all, and above all in protecting the poor against the tyranny of the rich.'[285]

The obstacle to achieving this is that property is one of a citizen's basic rights; a right which, in certain respects, is more important than freedom itself. Property, writes Rousseau in *On political economy*, 'is the cornerstone of civil society, and the rational guarantee that the citizens will be true to their word'.[286] This is why he never suggests that the state should resort to the expropriation of property in order to reduce social inequality, but only to political measures calculated to prevent the concentration of wealth in few hands:

It is one of the most important of a government's tasks to ensure that extreme inequalities of wealth do not arise; but this should be done not by depriving the rich of their fortunes, but by striking at the means by which such wealth is accumulated and rather than build hospices for the poor, the government should give the citizens confidence concerning the future.[287]

What Rousseau is primarily advocating in *On political economy* is the use of fiscal measures. According to Rousseau, the same compact which establishes property rights as the fundamental law obliges each individual, 'at least tacitly', to contribute to the public purse.[288] The amount of taxation to be paid by the individual to offset public expenditure must be decided by the general will. This implies that fiscal policy is the responsibility of the sovereign and should be regulated by laws and not by decrees. In order to achieve some kind of social equality, there should be heavy taxation on luxury goods and support for agriculture and industry. By employing a sound fiscal policy the republic will gradually be able to reduce differentials in wealth, 'thus bringing personal fortunes closer to the average which is the strength of the State'.[289]

The well-regulated state should therefore have as one of its aims a social policy, and that is one of the preconditions for the preservation

---

[285] *Economie politique*, *OC*, vol.3, p.258 (transl. Cole, 1952, p.375).
[286] Ibid., p.263 (transl. ibid., p.377).
[287] Ibid., p.258 (transl. ibid., p.375); see also *Contrat social*, *OC*, vol.3, p.292; *Projet de constitution pour la Corse*, *OC*, vol.3, pp.936–7.
[288] *Economie politique*, *OC*, vol.3, p.270.   [289] Ibid., p.277 (transl. ibid., p.384).

of its legality. Thanks to this policy of gradualism, the republic will be protected from the twofold threat posed by the growth of internal centres of power based on wealth, and the formation of a disloyal and fickle populace.

In his reflections on the most appropriate means to ensure the stability of the republic, Rousseau is clearly influenced by Aristotle's observation on the reasons which make a 'moderate republic' the best and most stable of constitutions.[290] The stability of a moderate republic, where government is in the hands of the middle classes is, in the first place, a consequence of the principle of rewarding people according to their merit. This principle of proportional equality is for Aristotle absolute justice, but it often happens that men, because they are equal in one respect (for example, before the law), will believe that they are equal in every other respect (for example, the extent to which they participate in the exercise of sovereign power). Alternatively, because they are unequal in one respect (for example in their personal fortune), they will think themselves unequal in every way. In the first instance, the republic's constitution will degenerate into a 'popular government', in the second, into an oligarchy.[291] But both are constitutions which are equally unstable and prone to dissension. By contrast, the political constitution which is founded on the principle of 'the avoidance of excess' has no cause to fear the revolutions which plague the 'flamboyant' democracies and the oligarchy, because it can count on a strong middle class composed of citizens who have neither too many nor too few possessions.[292] These men who enjoy a moderate prosperity are the linchpin of the republic, since they have learnt to heed the voice of reason and control their desires. These citizens are very different from those who are unwilling to submit to any authority at all (as is true of those who have great wealth) and also from those who are capable only of servile obedience (like those who suffer extreme poverty). This fact explains why the moderate middle classes are the true strength of a state of free men.[293]

In Rousseau's view, however, attempts to stave off the dissolution of the republic through constitutional means and through the inculcation of moral attitudes can no more succeed than can using the

---

[290] *Politics*, 1295e.30–35; 1302a.10–15.   [291] Ibid., 1302a.
[292] Ibid., 1295b–1295b.5.   [293] Ibid., 1295b.30–5.

economy as an instrument.[294] The dissolution of the republic can be delayed but not avoided altogether:

If Sparta and Rome perished, what State can hope to endure for ever? If we would set up a long-lived form of government, let us not even dream of making it eternal. If we are to succeed, we must not attempt the impossible, or flatter ourselves that we are endowing the work of man with a stability of which human conditions do not permit.[295]

What Rousseau means by the 'death of the body politic' is, as he explains in the preceding chapter, the degeneration of the republic into despotism. He defines this tendency as 'the natural and inevitable slippery slope which awaits even the most soundly based governments'.

The commentary which appears in the *Complete works* mentions Montesquieu as Rousseau's most probable source here and quotes the following passage from the *Spirit of laws*: 'As all human things have an end, the state we are speaking of will lose its liberty, will perish. Have not Rome, Sparta and Carthage perished?'[296] There can be some truth in this, but, because of the close similarity of ideas, I would suggest that the most direct source is to be found at the beginning of the third book of Machiavelli's *Discorsi*,

It is a well-established fact that the life of all mundane things is of finite duration. But things which complete the whole of the course appointed them by heaven are in general those whose bodies do not disintegrate, but maintain themselves in orderly fashion so that there is no change, or, if there is change, it tends rather to their conservation than to their destruction. Here I am concerned with composite bodies, such as are states and religious institutions,

[294] The theme of the dissolution of the state comes also in the treatises of the natural-law theorists; the chapter which deals with the dissolution of the state always comes at the end; see Grotius, *Du droit de la guerre et de la paix*, Bk 2, ch.9, s.5, and Pufendorf *The law of nature and of nations*, Bk 8, ch.12 ('Of changes and of the destruction of states'). For Hobbes, in his *De cive* and in *Leviathan*, the chapter which deals with the dissolution of the state comes after the analysis of the forms of government and before the chapters which set out the duties which those who hold power in the state must carry out to delay as long as possible the dissolution of the state, whether the causes are internal or external.

[295] *Contrat social, OC*, vol.3, p.424 (transl. Cole, 1952, p.419); in the *Jugement sur la Polysnodie, OC*, vol.3, p.639, Rousseau says: 'While it is true that the natural inclination is always towards corruption and consequently towards Despotism, it is difficult to see through what political resources the Prince could, even if he wished to, reverse this inclination in such a way that his work could not be undone by his successors and their ministers in the future.'

[296] *Esprit des lois*, Bk 11, ch.6 (transl. Nugent, 1952, p.74).

and in their regard I affirm that those changes make for their conservation which lead them back to their origins.[297]

The returning to their origins ('la riduzione inverso i principi') is precisely what Rousseau recommends as a means of postponing the threat of dissolution which constantly hangs over the republic. Moreover, he suggests that a specific institution should be established in order to reaffirm the fundamental principles of the republic. This institution is the periodic and regular assembly of all the people. The function of this constitutive assembly is to 're-establish good order' and maintain the social compact. But the social compact is nothing other than the constitutive principles of the republic and thus these assemblies act as a means of returning the republic to its principles.

Rousseau considers that the republic is dissolved (and this is not at all the same thing as a change in the form of government) when the formal link which unites every part of the body politic is broken or destroyed. When the republic is dissolved, the people no longer exist as such; it reverts to being an aggregate. This may be government by a tyrant but it is no longer possible to call it a people. The bond which unites individuals in a republic (which is an artificial moral body) is the citizens' duty to the sovereign who is common to them all, as well as the duty which the sovereign owes to each citizen to defend those rights enjoyed by all and to administer the laws impartially.[298] If the sovereign or the magistrate treats one citizen more severely than another, condemns the innocent or wrongs someone, then the citizens no longer have a duty to obey. If any citizens become so powerful that the magistrates fear them, the republic is dissolved since there is no longer equality under the law: magistrates would be in no position to enforce the law against those who have accumulated

[297] *Discorsi*, Bk 3, ch.1 (transl. Walker, 1970, p.385).

[298] Both the definition of the state as an 'Artificial Moral Body' and the definition of the dissolution of the form of the people as a destruction of the community of right and of law are borrowed, very probably, from Pufendorf, *The law of nature and of nations*, Bk 8, ch.12, s.7–9; see also Grotius, *Du Droit de la guerre et de la Paix*, Bk 2, ch.9, s.6: 'The *form* of the people is destroyed when it loses in whole or in part the common *rights* that it enjoyed as a people'; see also s.8 where Grotius speaks of the form of artificial bodies. Hobbes also deals with the dissolution of the state (*Leviathan*, Part 2, ch.29). For Hobbes the dissolution of the state consists in the sharing or the weakening of sovereign power. In a way that is quite consistent with his theory of the social compact, the dissolution of the state occurs as soon as the sovereign is no longer in a position to protect his loyal subjects ('there is no farther protection of Subjects in their loyalty'). The idea that the dissolution of the state might come as a result of the violation of any obligation that he might have towards his subjects is quite alien to Hobbes's conception, because the sovereign has no obligations of this kind.

so much power. The republic is also dissolved if its subjects refuse to obey the laws which they themselves, as members of the sovereign body, have created. Citizens who act thus have a certain amount of logic on their side, since they stand to gain more than would have been the case if they had obeyed the law. But such conduct would be condemned because those who adopt this attitude are quite happy for others to do their duty without applying the principle to themselves, and this is a violation of the rule that everyone should be treated fairly. Moreover, to act in this way is, in the long run, self-defeating, since if everyone does the same, sooner or later the republic will collapse and with the collapse of the Republic comes the loss of liberty.

In fact, each individual, as a man, may have a particular will contrary or dissimilar to the general will which he has as a citizen. His particular interest may speak to him quite differently from the common interest; his absolute and naturally independent existence may make him look upon what he owes to the common cause as a gratuitous contribution, the loss of which will do less harm to others than the payment of it is burdensome to himself; and, regarding the moral person which constitutes the State as a *persona ficta*, because not a man, he may wish to enjoy the rights of citizenship without being ready to fulfil the duties of a subject. The continuance of such an injustice could not but prove the undoing of the body politic.[299]

But can one expect citizens to be so clear-sighted and wise as to foresee the long-term effects of their conduct, apparently subject to such a degree to the vagaries of chance. Can one, therefore, expect them to become good citizens through a rational calculation of their interest?

Rousseau thinks not. Men do not act by first calculating rationally what it is in their interest to do, and it would be too much to hope that they should shape their actions in accordance with a rational assessment of what is in the public interest. The dynamic of men's actions lies in their passions and this means that men may become good citizens through the love of their community, not out of self-interest. This is not to say that to be a good citizen is contrary to the individual's interest, but that the reason why men do become good citizens is not due to a rational calculation of their interest, but because they are moved by an emotion – more precisely by love of their community.

What is of major importance for political theory is, therefore, the

---

[299] *Contrat social*, *OC*, vol.3, p.363 (transl. Cole, 1952, p.393).

set of institutions and social processes which cause men to hope that they are members of a community and to identify with it. The task of the great legislator must be to form a community, not an association. Once again the example comes from the ancients:

The same spirit guided all the ancient legislators in their institutions. They all sought to create bonds which might unite the citizens with their country and with each other, and they found them in specific customs, in religious ceremonies which, by their nature, were exclusive and national [see the end of the *Social contract*], in the games which used to bring the citizens together, in exercises which through their vigour and energy increased their pride and self-esteem, in epic drama which, by re-enacting the history of their ancestors, their sufferings, their virtuous deeds, their triumphs, awakened interest within them and enflamed their hearts with a strong desire to rival such heroics, and bound them closely to the country which, thus, became a constant theme in their lives.[300]

The games, festivals, national education and public ceremonies gave the people a common character and its own customs. Love for the fatherland sprang from an awareness of a common identity and from the desire to protect the community. In his reflections on the conditions which are necessary for the development of a community and the creation of civic consciousness, Rousseau adopts a remarkably different point of view from the one he had used in formulating the theory of the social contract. In the *Social contract*, he approached the problem of legitimacy of political authority from the point of view that the individual makes a choice based on a rational calculation of his long-term interest. In the texts where he analyses real or possible political communities, such as the *Lettre à Mr d'Alembert* or in the *Considérations sur le gouvernement de Pologne*, he no longer makes use of the concept of the rational calculation of self-interest but of such notions as 'customs', 'the character of a people', 'religion', 'the feeling of belonging', 'common patterns of behaviour', which refer to collective identity and to identification.

Rousseau's emphasis on the institutions and the collective practices which help to form a community are a sign of the limitations of the model built around the idea of rational choice: if one starts with the hypothesis of individuals whose every action is based on the calculation of their self-interest, it is impossible to explain how any community can exist, even less so to indicate ways in which it can be kept in being. The tension between these two models is very clear. The

---

[300] *Considérations sur le gouvernement de Pologne*, *OC*, vol.3, p.958.

Social contract begins from the rationalist perspective in vogue at the time, but finishes by envisaging civil religion as necessary to strengthen those communal bonds which, according to the premise initially adopted, were impossible. Rousseau's political theory of natural law, starts from premises derived from the theory of natural law, but as he continues he is forced to recognize the importance of dimensions of collective life embodied in customs, acknowledged as the authentic expression of the political community, but much neglected by the doctrines of natural law. To present the matter somewhat schematically, one could say that he starts from the theories of natural law to arrive at a position very close to Hegel's point of departure for his radical revision of the natural law doctrine of the state: *die Sitten*.[301]

Responsibility for the dissolution of the republic may lie with the magistrates, or the rich and powerful, or again it may be the people who are to blame (to mention only internal causes); but, whatever the cause, dissolution always involves law being subordinated to the will of men, or, to express the same idea in different terms, the subordinating of the public interest to the interests of individuals.

Rousseau makes it very clear that the dissolution of republican or legitimate order is the result of the undermining of two constitutive principles: namely, that law should be sovereign and that the individual will must be subordinate to the general will. By contrast, the republic would fall apart from the moment when 'public vices have a greater effect in enervating the laws than the laws in the repression of such vices'.[302] As soon as the defenders of the common good are reduced to impotence and fear prevents citizens from coming to its defence, there is the danger that tyranny may stifle the republic. Liberty is lost when the general will becomes ineffectual:

Convince everyone that the public interest has no point of contact with any individual interest and by that single act serfdom will have been instituted, for, when everyone's neck is bent beneath the yoke, where is communal liberty? If anyone who dares to speak out is crushed the moment he does so, who will he have to emulate him? and how will the general interest be represented when each person holds his peace?[303]

The dissolution of the republic opens the way for despotism and this may take the form of despotic rule by one man or a generalized

[301] See N. Bobbio, 'Hegel e il giusnaturalismo', in N. Bobbio *Studi hegeliani*, Turin, 1981, pp.3–33   [302] *Economie politique*, *OC*, vol.3, p.252 (transl. Cole, 1952, p.372).
[303] *Lettres écrites de la montagne*, *OC*, vol.3, p.893.

despotism. This latter is nothing other than a 'free-for-all',[304] which is what freedom degenerates into when citizens are not content to obey rules and have lost all respect for authority. These are the same ideas as Montesquieu had put forward, on the subject of the degeneration of the spirit of equality into an extreme form of egalitarianism:

When virtue is banished, ambition invades the minds of those who are disposed to receive it, and avarice possesses the whole community. The objects of their desires are changed; what they were fond of before has become indifferent; they were free while under the restraint of laws, but they would fain now to be free to act against law; and as each citizen is like a slave who has run away from his master, that which was a maxim of equity he calls rigour; that which was a rule of action he styles constraint; and to precaution he gives the name of fear . . . the strength of the republic is now only the power of a few, and the licence of many.[305]

The good order of the republic is threatened not only by extremes of inequality but also by an extreme egalitarianism, which is unwilling to acknowledge duties, distinctions or laws. The former leads to tyranny exercised by a single person or a small clique, the latter to a generalized tyranny – a state of disorder in which everyone gives orders and no one is willing to carry them out. Whichever form it takes, despotism is incapable of restoring the lost unity of the body politic; in Rousseau's view, in such a system, subjects owe no duty to the despot. They are an 'aggregate', not an organic whole. As it is only through the tyrant's monopoly of force that they have even a semblance of unity, 'as soon as the tyrant is removed from power, everything crumbles and is turned to dust, like an oak reduced to a pile of ashes when the fire which has consumed it dies out'.[306]

According to Rousseau's theory, the individual's inveterate pursuit of his own interests, his ambition and thirst for social acclaim are not in themselves traits impossible to reconcile with republican order. His theory of the social contract demonstrates that it is in everyone's best interest to live under a political constitution which allows everyone to enjoy their freedom without their conduct being governed by the will of others. Moreover, the fact that men have always been willing to make great sacrifices to preserve their freedom is evidence of the high value they place upon this idea. In addition, the

---

[304] *Discours sur l'inégalité*, Dedication, *OC*, vol.3, p.113; *Lettres écrites de la montagne, OC*, vol.3, pp.889–90.   [305] *Esprit des lois*, Bk 3, ch.3 (transl. Nugent, 1952, p.10).
[306] *Manuscrit de Genève, OC*, vol.3, p.303.

republic provides everyone with the same opportunity to distinguish himself and gain public esteem.

On the other hand, what Rousseau finds quite impossible to reconcile with republican order and with freedom is moral turpitude, a servile attitude, and an unbridled ambition akin to madness which drives men on in pursuit of they know not what. The reprobate who seeks to escape the duties imposed on him by just laws and avoid his social responsibilities is dazzled by the prospect of a quick gain and is oblivious of the fact that what he is doing is putting at risk something whose value is infinitely greater, namely liberty. The wealthy man who counts on his personal fortune winning prestige for him is, in fact, someone of little worth because he inwardly senses that he lacks the true nobility of character which comes from good deeds and a morally upright life and yet he still wants to attain superiority by other means. Similarly, those who try to obtain magistrature and other honours through flattery and intrigue must, by the nature of things, be hostile to the republic, because, as long as its order resists corruption, they can never hope for success.

It is not so much the individual but social factions and interest groups which threaten to overturn the just social order. Machiavelli had noted that it was not the enmity which existed between the various social orders which posed the greatest threat to the republic. The Roman republic was continually being swept by conflicts between plebeians and patricians, but these conflicts, far from being the cause of the dissolution of the republic, 'were the primary cause of Rome's retaining her freedom' ('furono prima causa del tenere libera Roma').[307]

Rousseau agrees with Machiavelli that the real danger threatening the well-being of the body politic is the divisions which take the form of 'sects and factions' ('dalle sette e da partigiani accompagnate'), but he sees this strife and civil unrest as a sign of the imminent dissolution of the body politic.[308] The wise legislator should not regard it as his responsibility to free the polity from any internal conflicts, which would manifestly be impossible. He should, rather, prevent them from growing into sects ('che non vi siano sette') and ensure that none of these social factions can increase its power to the point where it can

---

[307] *Discorsi*, Bk 1, ch.4 (transl. Walker, 1970, p.113).
[308] *Contrat social*, Bk 4, ch.2; see also *Contrat social*, Bk 3, ch.9: 'what makes the race truly prosperous is not so much peace as liberty'.

gain a monopoly.[309] Social factions are dangerous because the individuals who are members of these groups feel that their membership justifies the pursuit of preferment and privilege. The individual acting alone may find it distasteful to put himself before others, but the feeling of belonging to a group 'causes him to deem it a privilege to do his share, whatever be the cost, to achieve the goals which the group he belongs to has set itself'. It is very difficult for the individual alone to obtain preferment and privilege. This is far more likely to occur in the case of a group or of someone who has accumulated power and can count on the assistance of his henchmen.[310]

Because he knows how strong are the forces working to destroy the republic, Rousseau acknowledges that, between the premise of individualism on which he has built his theory and the ideal of social order, there exists a conflict which can never be resolved in any lasting way. The strong passions continually generated in men's hearts by their experience of life in society have all the force of a natural process. The task of good government is not to suppress these strong passions and frustrate all private interests, but to ensure they do not go beyond certain limits and to direct them towards a goal compatible with the common good and liberty. The republic is not a society created for angels or saints. A society made up of men without personal interests and lacking emotional drive 'will fall into a state of apathy'. If there is to be a political society it is inevitable that the company of angels must have its Lucifer and the band of apostles would not be complete without its Judas.[311]

An order of men who are cold and unfeeling, and with no appetite for what might benefit them, unmoved by any desire to improve their lot, would be the order of the graveyard. An order founded on the sovereignty of law has nothing in common with the extravagant order founded on fear, which Rousseau describes in the *Nouvelle Héloise*,[312] and which Montesquieu considers to be exemplified in Asiatic despotism.[313] Even if liberty is always conflict, it is nevertheless to be preferred to the unruffled calm of servitude: 'I prefer liberty with

---

[309] *Contrat social*, Bk 2, ch.4.
[310] *Jugement sur la Polysnodie, OC*, vol.3, pp.644–5.
[311] 'Rousseau à Usteri 18 juillet 1763', in *Correspondance de Jean-Jacques Rousseau avec Léonard Usteri*, ed. P. Usteri and L. Ritter, Geneva and Zurich, 1910, pp.73–8.
[312] *La Nouvelle Héloise, OC*, vol.2, pp.530–1.
[313] *Considérations sur les causes de la grandeur des Romains et de leur décadence, Oeuvres complètes*, Paris, 1950, vol.3, pp.414–15.

danger to peace with slavery' ('malo periculosam libertatem quam quietum servitium').[314]

The tension created because violent passions formed spontaneously in the depths of society must somehow co-exist with a political order which is, as in Hobbes, artificial, is of permanent duration. The republic must be seen as no more than a short-lived and unexpected victory over the forces of spontaneity at work within the life of society, forces whose final triumph is assured. The republic can never free itself from the threat of dissolution since it represents what is for the common good and men are more concerned for what is to their immediate advantage than they are for the common good. At the beginning of the modern era, Machiavelli had noted that even if the 'vivere libero' represents the common good – which consists in 'the possibility of enjoying what one has, freely and without incurring suspicion, for instance, the assurance that one's wife and children will be respected, the absence of fear for oneself – that common advantage which results from a self-governing state 'is not recognised by anybody so long as it is possessed'.[315]

Rousseau uses very similar language about justice and the social harmony guaranteed by the sovereignty of law. The sound political constitution enhances the life of every citizen, but even while they are enjoying this blessing, men are incapable of appreciating its true worth: 'justice, like good health, is a blessing which you enjoy without realising it, which arouses no great enthusiasm and which one does not truly appreciate until it is lost'.[316]

The survival and the very existence of the republic is at risk as much from internal as from external enemies, and the problem of relations between states is as important as relations between the different parts of the social body. Within each civil state, men are subject to laws, but relations between states have more in common with the natural liberty enjoyed by men before the institution of civil society.[317] In instituting civil societies men have accomplished only a part of their task, since the persistence of the natural state in international relations puts in doubt the continued existence of every state. In a situation in which every state is perfectly independent of every other, each of them is forced to consider its own position in relation to all the

---

[314] *Contrat social*, Bk 3, ch.4 (transl. Cole, 1952, p.411, n.2). See also on this point Spinoza, *Tractatus politicus*, ch.6, 11.3–10. *Political works* ed. A.G. Wernham, Oxford, 1958.   [315] *Discorsi*, Bk 1, ch.16 (transl. Walker, 1970), p.154).

[316] *Considérations sur le gouvernement de Pologne*, *OC*, vol.3, p.955.

[317] *L'Etat de guerre*, *OC*, vol.3, p.610.

others.[318] Just as men need others to compare themselves with if they are to find their own identity, so each state is forced to compare itself with others in order to gain self-knowledge.[319] The security and preservation of each state requires that they all become more powerful than their neighbours and, once started, this process knows no end.

States bound together by a shared hostility have a mutual inclination to destroy their rival or reduce its power 'by all means available to them'. The permanence of the state of warfare underlines the need to be prepared to resist others for the well-being of the citizenry.[320] Moreover, war, or even the very threat of war, is the best ally of despotism.[321] The money and men raised from a people of slaves are used to dominate another such people and war is the best excuse to impose taxes and maintain great armies 'to keep the people in their place'.[322]

So long as relations between states are ones of rivalry and independence, in this respect comparable to the situation of men in the natural state, it will be very difficult for a sound political constitution to survive for long in the internal life of these states. If a republican constitution is to be brought into being and preserved, it will, therefore, be necessary for an international juridical order to be created and for all states to recognize a superior authority. In Rousseau's view, such a project, which had been worked out by l'Abbé de Saint-Pierre, was by no means absurd.[323] If sovereign governments were guided by reason, and capable of acting in accordance with their true interests, they would not delay its realization. On this subject Rousseau repeats the ideas he had put forward concerning the institution of the republic, but now seen as relevant to 'la paix perpétuelle':

Far from imagining men as they should be – good, generous, unselfish, and cherishing the common good out of sheer humanity – we have assumed them to be as they are – unjust, greedy and placing their selfish interest before everything else. The only assumption made on their behalf is that they have sufficient sense to see what is to their advantage and enough courage to achieve their own happiness.[324]

[318] Ibid., p.605.   [319] Ibid.
[320] *Extrait du projet de paix perpétuelle, OC*, vol.3, p.564.
[321] *Jugement sur le projet de paix perpétuelle, OC*, vol.3, p.593.   [322] Ibid., p.593.
[323] *Extrait du projet de paix perpétuelle, OC*, vol.3, pp.588–9.   [324] Ibid., p.589.

But the essential problem is that men in general are not reasonable, and, more to the point, those who wield power are no different. They would stand to gain everything if strife could be banished for good, but they prefer the vicissitudes of chance to the acceptance of the rule and protection of law. Wisdom beckons the prince in the direction of a federation of states, but ambition causes them to choose instead complete independence, 'like a demented captain who, in order to display his worthless store of knowledge and the extent of his command over his sailors, would prefer to sail through rocky straits during a storm, rather than to secure his vessel with the anchors'.[325]

The prince knows that to engage in warfare entails risks, but the illusion that things will turn out to his advantage, if he does, entices him to defy fortune and refuse to submit to a higher authority. If individuals reasoned in the same way as their political masters, the social contract would be no more than a pious hope. Everyone would think it preferable to live in a state of natural independence rather than submit to a common law. For men to give their consent to a republican constitution, it is not necessary that they should be good; it does not matter whether they are self-centred, providing they are guided by reason and not blinded by their passions.

This is why the republican constitution is, to quote Kant, 'the most difficult to establish and even more so to preserve'.[326] Yet, for Kant, the problem of creating and keeping in existence a republican constitution should be soluble, 'even by a nation of devils (so long as they possess understanding)'.[327] According to Kant, nature assists reason to solve the problem of the just social order. It has given man an in-built bias in favour of himself, but in interacting with others this selfishness is rendered less acute and this makes possible the creation of a political constitution that is in accordance with the principle of right. Once again it seems to be nature which shows the way in which states can be made to conform with the principle of right and thus secure peace both at home and abroad.[328] For Kant, as for Rousseau, the sovereignty of law must be extended to embrace the sphere of international relations if men are to develop their moral potential. But if, on the other hand, the present state of anarchy, which charac-

---

[325] *Jugement sur le projet de paix perpétuelle, OC,* vol.3, p.592.
[326] Kant, *Zum ewigen Frieden. Ein philosophischer Entwurf,* (1795), *Immanuel Kants Werke,* Hildesheim, 1973, vol.6, p.452 (transl. H. Reiss, 1970, p.112).
[327] Ibid.   [328] Ibid., pp.453–4 (transl. Nisbet, 1970, pp.113–14).

terizes the relations of states with each other, persists, then men's
situation will be parlous:

Man to man, [says Rousseau] we live in the civil state subject to the law; but on
the level of international relations each State enjoys natural liberty: which,
ultimately, makes our situation worse than if these distinctions were
unknown. For, living both in the social order and in the natural state, we have
all the disadvantages of each without the security of either.[329]

Man can only hope to escape the ill effects of his divided state if an
order based on international law, similar to that envisaged by l'Abbé
de Saint-Pierre, is established. But, for Rousseau, such an idea is mere
fantasy, even more difficult to realize than a republican constitution.
Men are not sufficiently rational for this and there are too many
passions and special interests ranged against it. If these obstacles are
ever to be overcome it will be necessary to use 'a degree of force which
humanity may well shrink from'.[330]

Kant ranges himself alongside Rousseau to stress that it is necessary
for international relations to be governed by law. In the *Idea for a
universal history with a cosmopolitan purpose* (Seventh Proposition), he
states that the idea of a federation of nation states ruled by a superior
authority appears unrealistic, even to l'Abbé de Saint-Pierre and
Rousseau, but this does not alter the fact that the setting up of a supra-
national political constitution would 'force States to make exactly the
same decision (however difficult it may be for them) as that which
man was forced to make, equally unwillingly, in his savage state – the
decision to renounce his brutish freedom and seek calm and security
within a law-governed constitution'.[331]

Although Kant approaches the problem of how to get an effective
system of international law in the same way as Rousseau, his solution
is quite different, appealing to the internal workings of nature and the
obligations created by moral law. In his doctrine of perpetual peace,
Kant distances himself from Rousseau, not only because of his confidence in the inner workings of nature, but even more with his appeal
to the moral law. While, for Kant, the duty to work for enduring
peace is derived from the moral law,[332] for Rousseau international

---

[329] *L'Etat du guerre*, *OC*, vol.3, p.610.
[330] *Jugement sur le projet de paix perpétuelle*, *OC*, vol.3, p.600.
[331] I. Kant, *Idee zu einer allgemeinen Geschichte in weltbürgerlicher Absicht* (1784), *Immanuel
Kants Werke*, Hildesheim, 1973, vol.4, pp.158–69 (transl. H. Reiss, 1970, pp.
47–8).
[332] Kant, *Zum ewigen Frieden* (1795), 1973, p.453 (transl. Nisbet, 1970, p.113).

relations – even more than interpersonal relations – are the arena for violent and passionate conflict and it is quite hopeless to seek to impose order here by appealing to a moral law.[333]

But there is also another difference which is, perhaps, of still greater importance with regard to the problem being discussed here: Kant's moral law is grounded in the incomparable worth of the human race and is not at all the same as the 'virtue' of the ancients to which Rousseau refers in his political theory. The former appeals to the moral perfection inherent in the ideal of humanity,[334] the latter, to the qualities of courage and love of the fatherland. Republican virtue flourishes when society is under threat from some alien force, whether it be a tyrant, a foreign power, or the passions at work within each man, which constantly threaten to enslave him.[335] The horizons of republican virtue are bounded by the fatherland and the body of citizens. It teaches men to struggle against tyrants and enemies of the fatherland, but it does not preach the virtues of humanity. Cato's ideal may very well be adequate as the ground of political theory for the state and within the state, but it is incapable of sustaining a system of international relations rooted in law. Though he was aware that the creating of an international political order was a necessary prerequisite for the preservation of any just political constitution, Rousseau leaves this problem to be grappled with by the political philosophers of our own time.

[333] See on this issue V. Goldschmidt, *Anthropologie et politique. Les principes du système de Rousseau*, Paris, 1974, pp.629–32.
[334] Kant, *Die Religion innerhalb der Grenzen der blossen Vernunft* (1794), *Immanuel Kants Werke*, Hildesheim, 1973, vol.6, p.201.
[335] Ibid., pp.197–200.

Bibliography

Primary sources: works by Jean-Jacques Rousseau

Les Confessions de Jean-Jacques-Rousseau (1764–70), in Jean-Jacques Rousseau, *Oeuvres complètes*, ed. B. Gagnebin and M. Raymond, Bibliothèque de la Pléiade, Paris, 1959–69, vol. 1; transl. J. M. Cohen, *The confessions of Jean-Jacques Rousseau*, Harmondsworth, 1953.

Considérations sur le gouvernement de Pologne, in *Oeuvres complètes*, vol. 3, transl. G. D. H. Cole, Chicago, 1952.

Du Contrat social ou essai sur la forme de la république, (première version), in *Oeuvres complètes*, vol. 3; transl. J. R. Masters, *On the 'Social contract' with 'Geneva Manuscript' and 'Political Economy'*, New York, 1978.

Du Contrat social, ou Principes de droit politique (1760–2), in *Oeuvres complètes*, vol. 3.

Correspondance complète de Jean-Jacques Rousseau, ed. R. A. Leigh, 44 vols., Geneva and Oxford, 1965–85.

Correspondance générale de Jean-Jacques Rousseau, ed. T. Dufour, 20 vols., Paris, 1924–34.

Correspondance de Jean-Jacques Rousseau avec Léonard Usteri, ed. P. Usteri and L. Ritter, Geneva and Zurich, 1910.

Dictionnaire de musique, in *Oeuvres de Jean-Jacques Rousseau*, ed. Werdet and Lequien, Paris, 1827, vols. 14 and 15.

Discours sur l'économie politique, in *Oeuvres complètes*, vol. 3.

Discours sur l'origine et les fondements de l'inégalité parmi les hommes, in *Oeuvres complètes*, vol. 3; transl. G. D. H. Cole, *A discourse on the origin of inequality*, Chicago, 1952.

Discours sur les richesses, ed. F. Bovet, Paris, 1853.

Discours sur les sciences et les arts, in *Oeuvres complètes*, vol. 3; transl. Roger D. and J. R. Masters, *The first and second discourses*, New York 1964.

Dissertation sur la musique moderne, in *Oeuvres de Jean-Jacques Rousseau*, ed. Werdet and Lequien, Paris 1827, vol. 13.

Emile ou De l'éducation, in *Oeuvres complètes*, vol. 2, transl. B. Foxley, *Emile*, Everyman, London, 1974.

Epître à M. Bordes, in *Oeuvres complètes*, vol. 2.

Epître à Monsieur Parisot, in *Oeuvres complètes*, vol. 2.

Essai sur l'origine des langues, in *Oeuvres de Jean-Jacques Rousseau*, ed. Werdet and Lequien, Paris, 1827, vol. 13; transl. J. H. Moran and A. Gode, *On the origin of language: two essays by Jean-Jacques Rousseau and Johan Gottfried Herder*, New York, 1966.

L'Etat de guerre, in *Oeuvres complètes*, vol. 3.

Extrait du projet de paix perpétuelle de M. l'Abbé de Saint-Pierre, in *Oeuvres complètes*, vol. 3.

Fragments politiques, in *Oeuvres complètes*, vol. 3.

Fragment sur la liberté, in *Oeuvres complètes*, vol. 3.

Institutions de chimie, ed. M. Gauhier, *Annales de la société Jean-Jacques Rousseau*, 12, (1918–19) and 13 (1920–21).

Jean-Jacques Rousseau citoyen de Genève à Mr d'Alembert, 3rd edn, Amsterdam, Michel Rey, 1762; transl. A. Bloom, *Politics and the arts: letters to M. d'Alembert on the theatre*, Ithaca, 1960.

Jugement sur la Polysnodie, in *Oeuvres complètes*, vol. 3.

Jugement sur le projet de paix perpétuelle, in *Oeuvres complètes*, vol. 3.

Julie ou la Nouvelle Héloise, in *Oeuvres complètes*, vol. 2; transl. J.H. McDowell, *Julie or the New Eloise*, University Park, Penn., 1968.

Lettre à Christophe de Beaumont, in *Oeuvres complètes*, vol. 4.

Lettre de J.-J. Rousseau à M. de Voltaire (Le 18 Aout, 1756), in *Oeuvres complètes*, vol. 4, pp. 1059–77.

Lettres écrites de la montagne, in *Oeuvres complètes*, vol. 3.

Lettres philosophiques, ed. H. Gouhier, Paris, 1974.

Narcisse ou l'Amant de lui-même, in *Oeuvres complètes*, vol. 2.

Notes sur 'De l'esprit' d'Helvétius, in *Oeuvres complètes*, vol. 4, p. 1123.

Oeuvres et correspondance inédites de J.-J. Rousseau, ed. M. G. Streckeisen-Moultou, Paris, 1861.

Parallèle de Socrate et de Platon, in *Oeuvres complètes*, vol. 3.

Political writings, ed. C. E. Vaughan, 2 vols. Oxford, 1962.

Polysnodie de l'Abbé de Saint-Pierre, in *Oeuvres complètes*, vol. 3.

Préface de Narcisse, in *Oeuvres complètes*, vol. 2.

Profession de foi du vicaire savoyard. Edition critique d'après les manuscrits de Genève, avec une introduction et un commentaire historique par P. M. Masson, Freibourg and Paris, 1914.

Projet de constitution pour la Corse, in *Oeuvres complètes*, vol. 3.

Que l'état de guerre naît de l'état social, in *Oeuvres complètes*, vol. 3.

Les Rêveries du promeneur solitaire, in *Oeuvres complètes*, vol. 1; transl. J. G. Fletcher, *The reveries of a solitary*, New York, 1971.

Rousseau juge de Jean-Jacques, in *Oeuvres complètes*, vol. 1.

Traduction du premier livre de l'histoire de Tacite, in *Oeuvres de Jean-Jacques Rousseau*, Paris, 1827, vol. 12.

Le Verger de Madame de Warens, in *Oeuvres complètes*, vol. 2.

Secondary sources

Alatri, P., 'Introduction to Jean-Jacques Rousseau', *Scritti politici*, Turin, 1979.

Aldridge, A. O., 'The state of nature: an undiscovered country in the history of ideas', *Studies on Voltaire and the eighteenth century*, 98 (1972), pp. 7–26.

Allen, G. O., ' "La volonté de tous" and "la volonté générale": a distinction and its significance', *Ethics*, 72 (1961).

Althusius Joannes, *Politica Methodice Digesta*, with an introduction by C. J. Friedrich, Cambridge, Mass., 1932 (reprint of the 1614 edition); transl. by F. S. Careny, *The politics of Johannes Althusius*, London, 1965.

Andrivet, P., 'Jean-Jacques Rousseau: quelques aperçus de son discours politique sur l'antiquité romaine', *Studies on Voltaire and the Eighteenth century*, 151 (1976), pp. 131–48.

Antonelli, M., ed., *Rousseau negli scritti di B. Groetuysen, M. Blanchot, J. Starobinsky, C. Levy-Strauss*, Milan, 1977.

Argenson, Marquis d', *Considérations sur le gouvernement ancien et présent de la France*, Amsterdam, Michel Rey, 1764.

Aristotle, *The Politics*, transl. M. Rackam, London, 1932.
The Nichomachean ethics, transl. M. Rackam, London, 1932.

Arrow, K. J., *Social choice and individual values*, New Haven and London, 1963.

Augustine, St *The City of God against the pagans*, transl. G. E. McCracken and W. M. Green *et al.*, 7 vols., London, 1957–72.

Avineri, S., *Hegel's theory of the modern state*, Cambridge, 1972.

Babbit, I., *Rousseau and romanticism*, Boston and New York, 1935.

Baczko, B., *Rousseau. Solitude et communauté*, Paris, 1974.
'Rousseau and social marginality', *Daedalus*, 107, no. 3, pp. 27–40.

Barker, E., ed., *Social contract. Essays by Locke, Hume and Rousseau*, Oxford, 1971.

Barnard, F. M., 'National culture and political legitimacy: Herder and Rousseau', *Journal of the history of ideas*, 44 (1983), pp. 231–54.

Barry, B. M., 'Preferences and the common good', *Ethics*, 73 (1962), pp. 141–2.

Barth, H., 'Volonté générale et volonté particulière chez J.-J. Rousseau', in *Rousseau et la philosophie politique*, special number of *Annales de philosophie politique*, 5 (1965), pp. 35–50.

Bastide, P., 'Rousseau et la théorie des formes du gouvernement', in *Etudes sur le 'Contrat social' de Jean-Jacques Rousseau*, Paris, 1964, pp. 315–28.

Bayle, P., *Dictionnaire historique et critique*, 3 vols., 2nd edn, Rotterdam, Reiner Leers, 1702.

Benichou, P., 'Réflexions sur l'idée de nature chez Jean-Jacques Rousseau', *Annales de la Société Jean-Jacques Rousseau*, 39 (1972–77), pp. 22–45.

Bensussan, D., *L'Unité chez J.-J. Rousseau: une quête de l'impossible*, Paris, 1977.

Bentham, J., *A fragment on government and an introduction to the principles of morals and legislation*, Oxford, 1948.

Berlin, I., *Four essays on liberty*, London, 1969.

Besse, G., 'Le Sage et le citoyen selon Jean-Jacques Rousseau', *Revue de métaphysique et de morale*', 78 (1973), pp. 18–31.

Bobbio, N., *Il futuro della democrazia*, Turin, 1984.

Da Hobbes a Marx, Naples, 1965.

'Il modello giusnaturalistico', in N. Bobbio and M. Bovero, *Società e stato nella filosofia politica moderna*, Milan, 1979.

Studi hegeliani, Turin, 1981.

'Sulla nozione di giustizia' *Teoria politica*, 1 (1985), pp. 7–19.

Bodin, Jean, *Les Six Livres de la République*, second reprint of the Paris edn, 1583, Scientia Verlag, Aalen, 1977; transl. *The six books of Commonwealth*, ed. Kenneth D. Merae, Cambridge, Mass., 1962.

Boileau-Despréaux, Nicolas, *Satires*, Paris, Les Belles Lettres, 1952.

Bonnant, G., 'Les impressions genevoises au XVII siècle de l'édition dite de la 'Testina' des oeuvres de Machiavel', *Annali della scuola statale superiore per archivisti e bibliotecari dell'Università di Roma*, 5 (1965), pp. 83–9.

Borghero, C., 'Sparta tra storia e utopia: il significato e la funzione del mito di Sparta nel pensiero di Jean-Jacques Rousseau', in G. Solinas (ed.), *Saggi sull'illuminismo*, Cagliari, 1973, pp. 253–318.

Bosanquet, B., 'Les Idées politiques de Rousseau', *Revue de métaphysique et de morale*, 20 (1912), pp. 321–40.

Bovero, M., 'Politica e artificio. Sulla logica del modello giusnaturalistico', *Materiali filosofici*, 6, (1981), pp. 71–95.

Società e stato nella filosofia politica moderna, Milan, 1979.

Brandt, R., 'Droit et intérêt dans le "Contrat social" ', *Annales de la Société Jean-Jacques Rousseau*, 39 (1972–7), pp. 113–21.

Bréhier, L., 'Lectures malebranchistes de Jean-Jacques Rousseau', *Revue internationale de philosophie*, 1 (1938), pp. 98–120.

La Bruyère, *Les Caractères ou les moeurs de ce siècle*, Paris, 1964 (1st edn, Paris, 1688).

Burgelin, P., 'Hors des ténèbres de la nature', in *Rousseau et la philosophie politique*, Paris, 1965, pp. 21–34.

'L'Idée de place dans l' "Emile", *Revue de littérature comparée*, 40 (1961), pp. 529–37.

'*Kant lecteur de Rousseau*', in *Jean-Jacques Rousseau et son oeuvre, problèmes et recherches*', Commémoration et colloque de Paris, Paris, 1964, pp. 303–17.

La Philosophie de l'existence de Jean-Jacques Rousseau, Paris, 1952.

Burlamaqui, Jean-Jacques, *Principes du droit politique*, s.l., n.d. (Geneva, Barillot and Son, 1751).

Cameron, D., *The social thought of Rousseau and Burke. A comparative study*, London, 1973.

Casini, P., *L'antichità e la ricerca della patria ideale*, in Istituto della Enciclopedia Italiana, *Rousseau secondo Jean-Jacques*, Geneva and Rome, 1979, pp. 87–95.

Rousseau, Rome and Milan, 1968.

'Rousseau e Diderot', *Rivista critica di storia della filosofia*, 19, no. 3 (1964), pp. 243–70.

'Rousseau, il popolo sovrano e la repubblica di Ginevra', in A. Santucci (ed.),

Lezioni sull'illuminismo, Bologna, 1974, pp. 39–47.

Cassirer, E., *Die Philosophie der Aufklärung*, Tubingen, 1932.

Das Problem Jean-Jacques Rousseau, Darmstadt, 1970.

'L'Unité dans l'oeuvre de Jean-Jacques Rousseau', *Bulletin de la Société française de philologie*, 1932, reprinted in *Pensée de Rousseau*, Paris, 1984.

Chapman, R., *Rousseau totalitarian or liberal?*, New York, 1968.

Charron, Pierre, *De la sagesse*, in *Toutes les oeuvres de Pierre Charron*, Paris, 1635.

Charvet, J., 'Rousseau and the ideal of community', *History of political thought*, 1 (1980), pp. 69–80.

The social problem in the philosophy of Rousseau, Cambridge, 1974.

Chinard, G., 'L'Influence des récits de voyage sur la philosophie de J.-J. Rousseau', *Publications of the Modern Language Association of America*, 28 (1911).

Choulguine, A., 'Les Origines de l'esprit national moderne et J.-J. Rousseau', *Annales de la Société Jean-Jacques Rousseau*, 26 (1937), pp. 9–28.

Cicero, M. T., *De officiis*, in Ciceronis, Marci Tullii, *Opera quae extent omnia*, Studio atque industria Jani Guglielmii et Jani Grutari, additis eorum notis integris nunc demo recognita ab Jacobo Grenovio, Laudanum, 1690; transl. J. Higginbotham, *Cicero on moral obligation*, London, 1967.

De re publica. De legibus; transl. Clinton Walker Keynes, London and Cambridge, Mass., 1970.

Philippics; transl. Walter C. A. Ker, London, 1969.

Pro Cluentio Avito, in *Opera quae extent omnia*, Laudanum 1690, Pars quarta, vol. 2; transl. W. Peterson, London, 1895.

Cobban, A., *Rousseau and the modern state*, London, 1934.

Cohler, A. M., *Rousseau and nationalism*, New York and London, 1970.

Constant, Benjamin, *De l'esprit de conquête et de l'usurpation dans leurs rapports avec la civilisation européenne*, Oeuvres de Benjamin Constant, ed. A. Roulin, Paris, La Pléiade, 1957.

Mélanges de littérature et de politique, Paris, Pinchou et Didier, 1829.

Principes de politique, in *Oeuvres*, 1957.

Cotta, S., 'Come si pone il problema della politica in Rousseau', *Ethica*, 12 (1973), pp. 3–21.

'Filosofia e politica nell'opera di Rousseau', *De homine*, 3 (1964), pp. 293–4.

Cousin, J., 'Rousseau interprète des institutions romaines dans le "Contrat Social" ', in *Etudes sur le 'Contrat social' de Jean-Jacques Rousseau*, Paris, 1964, pp. 13–24.

Cranston, M., *Jean-Jacques. The early life and works of Jean-Jacques Rousseau, 1712-1752*, London, 1983.

'The mask of politics', in *The mask of politics and other essays*, London, 1973, pp. 1–25.

'Rousseau's "Social contract" ', *The mask of politics*, London, 1973.

'Violence et force chez Thomas Hobbes', *Cadmos*, 12 (1980).

Cranston, M., and Peters, R. S., eds. *Hobbes and Rousseau: A collection of critical essays*, Garden City, NY, 1972.

Crifo, G., 'Di alcuni aspetti della libertà in Roma', *Archivio giuridico Filippo Serafini*, 23 (1958), pp. 1–72.

Colletti, L., 'Rousseau critico della società civile', in L. Colletti, *Ideologia e società*, Bari, 1968.

Crocker, L. G., 'The priority of justice or law', *Yale French studies*, 28 (1962), pp. 34–42.

'Rousseau et la voie au totalitarisme', in Institut International de Philosophie Politique, *Rousseau et la philosophie politique*, Paris, 1965, pp. 99–136.

Rousseau's 'Social contract'. An interpretative essay, Cleveland, 1968.

Cucchi, P., 'Rousseau lecteur de Machiavelli', in M. Launay, ed., *Jean-Jacques Rousseau et son temps*, Paris, 1969, pp. 17–35.

Cumberland, Richard, *Traité philosophique des lois naturelles, où l'on recherche et l'on établit, par la nature des choses, la forme de ces lois, leurs principaux chefs, leur ordre, leur publication et leur obligation: on y refute aussi les eléments de la morale et de la politique de Th. Hobbes*, transl. of the Latin by Monsieur Barbeyrac, Leyden, T. Haak, 1749.

Dahrendorf, R., *Essays on the theory of society*, London, 1968.

Philosophy, politics and society, New York, 1962.

Davy, G., *Thomas Hobbes et Jean-Jacques Rousseau*, Oxford, 1953.

De Beer, G., *Rousseau and his world*, London, 1972.

De Jouvenel, B., 'Rousseau évolutioniste pessimiste', in Institut International de Philosophie Politique, *Rousseau et la philosophie politique*, Paris, 1965, pp. 1–19.

Delaruelle, L., 'Recherches sur les sources du "Discours sur l'inégalité" ', *Revue d'histoire littéraire de la France*, 19 (1912), pp. 245.

Delbos, V., 'Rousseau et Kant', *Revue de métaphysique et de morale*, 20 (1912), pp. 429–39.

Della Volpe, G., *Rousseau e Marx*, Rome, 1964.

Del Vecchio, G., *Su la teoria del contratto sociale*, Bologna, 1906.

Derathé, R., 'L'Homme selon Rousseau', in *Etudes sur le 'Contrat social'*, reprinted in *Pensée de Rousseau*, Paris, 1984, pp. 109–204.

'Montesquieu et Jean-Jacques Rousseau', *Revue internationale de philosophie*, 33 (1955), nos. 3–4, pp. 366–86.

'La Place et l'importance de la notion d'égalité dans la doctrine politique de J.-J. Rousseau', in R. A. Leigh (ed.) *Rousseau after two hundred years*, Cambridge, 1982, pp. 55–63.

'Les Rapports de l'exécutif et du législatif chez J.-J. Rousseau', in *Rousseau et la philosophie politique*, Paris, 1965, pp. 153–69.

Le Rationalisme de Jean-Jacques Rousseau, Paris, 1948.

'Les Réfutations du "Contrat social" au XVIII siècle', *Annales de la Société Jean-Jacques Rousseau*, 32 (1950–2), pp. 7–54.

'Les Réfutations du "Contrat social" en France dans la première moitié du dix-neuvième siècle', in S. Harvey, M. Hobson, D. Kelley, and S. Taylor, (eds.), *Reappraisals of Rousseau*, Manchester, 1980, pp. 90–110.

'La Religion civile selon Rousseau', *Annales de la Société Jean-Jacques Rousseau*, 35, (1959–62), pp. 161–80.

'Rousseau et le problème de la monarchie', in *Le Contrat social*, (May–June 1962), 6, no. 3, pp. 164–8.

Rousseau et la science politique de son temps, Paris, 1970.

Deregibus, A., *Il problema della morale in J.-J. Rousseau e la validità dell'interpretazione kantiana*, Turin, 1956.

Diaz, F., *Filosofia e politica nel Settecento francese*, Turin, 1962.

Diderot, *Droit naturel* in *Encyclopédie. Ou Dictionnaire raisonné des sciences, des arts, des métiers*, D. Diderot and P. le Ronde d'Alembert (eds), Neufchastel, 1751–80, vol. 5.

Duclos, *Considérations sur les moeurs de ce siècle*, 7th edn, Paris, 1780.

Duguit, L., *Souveraineté et liberté*, Paris, 1922.

Dunn, J., *The political thought of John Locke*, Cambridge, 1969.

Durkheim, E., 'Le "Contrat social" de Rousseau', *Revue de métaphysique et de morale*, 25 (1918), pp. 1–23 and 129–61.

Ehrard, J., *L'Idée de nature en France dans la première moitié du XVIII siècle*, 2 vols., Paris, 1963.

Einaudi, M., *The early Rousseau*, Ithaca, 1967.

Eisenmann, C., *La Cité de Rousseau*, in *Etudes sur le 'Contrat social'*, reprinted in *Pensée de Rousseau*, Paris, 1984, pp. 95–106.

Ellemburg, S., 'Rousseau and Kant: principles of political right', in R. A. Leigh (ed.) *Rousseau after two hundred years*, Cambridge, 1982, pp. 3–22.

Rousseau's political philosophy. An interpretation from within, Ithaca and London, 1976.

Elster, J., *Sour grapes. Studies in the subversion of rationality*, Cambridge, 1983.

Emberley, P., 'Rousseau and the domestication of virtue', *Canadian journal of political science*, 18 (1984), pp. 731–53.

Escherny, F. d', *De l'égalité, ou principes généraux sur les institutions civiles, politiques et religieuses, précédés de l'éloge de J.-J. Rousseau en forme d'introduction*, Basle, 1796.

Fabre, J., 'Examen du "Contrat social" de J.-J. Rousseau avec des remarques pour servir d'antidote à quelques principes, publiés d'après le manuscrit original', *Annales de la Société Jean-Jacques Rousseau*, 22 (1933), pp. 7–153.

'Réalité et utopie dans la pensée politique de Rousseau', *Annales de la Société Jean-Jacques Rousseau*, 35 (1959–62), pp. 181–221.

Fabry, A. S., *Etudes autour de la 'Nouvelle Héloise'*, Sherbrooke, 1977.

Faguet, E., *Dix-huitième siècle*, Paris, 1890.

Favre, P., 'Unanimité et majorité dans le "Contrat social" de Jean-Jacques Rousseau', *Revue du droit public et de la science politique en France et à l'étranger*, 92 (1976), pp. 111–86.

Fayette, Denise Leduc, *Rousseau et le mythe de l'antiquité*, Paris, 1974.

Featherstone, J., 'Rousseau and modernity', *Daedalus*, 107 (1978), pp. 167–92.

Felice, D., 'Jean-Jacques Rousseau in Italia: bibliografia (1850–1982)', in *Studi settecenteschi*, 3–4 (1982–3), pp. 319–98.

Fetscher, I., *Rousseaus politische Philosophie zur Geschichte des demokratischen Freiheitsbegriffs*, Neuwied am Rhein and Berlin, 1968.

Fleuret, C., *Rousseau et Montaigne*, Paris, 1980.

Fralin, R., *Rousseau and representation*, New York, 1978.

Friedrich, C. J., 'Law and dictatorship in the "Contrat social"', in *Rousseau et la philosophie politique*, Paris, 1965, pp. 77–97.

Gagnebin, B., 'Le Rôle du législateur dans les conceptions politiques de J.-J. Rousseau', in *Etudes sur le 'Contrat social'*, Paris, 1964, pp. 277–90.

Garin, E., Introduzione a Jean-Jacques Rousseau, *Scritti politici*, Bari, 1971, pp. 7–61.

Gaudemet, J., 'Utilitas publica', *Revue historique de droit français et étranger*, 29 (1951), pp. 465–99.

Gildin, H., *Rousseau's 'Social contract'. The design of the argument*, Chicago and London, 1983.

Goldschmidt, V., *Anthropologie et politique. Les principes du système de Rousseau*, Paris, 1974.

'Individu et communauté chez Rousseau', *Revue de théologie et de politique*, 114 (1982), reprinted in *Pensée de Rousseau*, Paris, 1984, 147–61.

'Les Renversements du concept d'égalité des anciens aux modernes', in *L'Egalité*, vol. 4, Travaux du Centre de philosophie du droit de l'Université Libre de Bruxelles, Brussels, 1966.

Gouhier, H., *Les Méditations métaphysiques de Jean-Jacques Rousseau*, Paris, 1970.

Rousseau et Voltaire. Portraits dans deux miroirs, Paris, 1983.

Griffin-Collard, E., 'L'Egalité: condition de l'harmonie sociale pour J.-J. Rousseau', in H. Buch, P. Foriers, C. Perelman (eds.), *L'Egalité*, Brussels, 1971, pp. 258–71.

Grimsley, R., *Jean-Jacques Rousseau. A study in self-awareness*, Cardiff, 1969.

The philosophy of Rousseau, Oxford, 1973.

Groethuysen, B., *J.-J. Rousseau*, Paris, 1949.

Grotius, Hugues, *Du Droit de la guerre et de la paix*, 'new transl.' by Jean Barbeyrac, Amsterdam, P. de Coup, 1724, 2 vols.; in one transl. anon. *The rights of war and peace*, London, 1738.

Guillemin, H., 'L'homme selon Rousseau', *Annales de la Société Jean-Jacques Rousseau*, 30 (1943–5), pp. 7–26.

'Rousseau républicain', *Gazette de Lausanne*, 23–24 June 1962, Literary Supplement.

Guinle, J. P., 'Le Législateur de Rousseau et les heros hégéliens', *Revue philosophique de la France*, 18 (1978), pp. 305–16.

Gunn, J. A., *Politics and the public interest in the seventeenth century*, London, 1969.

Gusdorf, G., *Dieu, la nature, l'homme au siècle des lumières*, Paris, 1972.

Halbwachs, V., Introduction to the *Contrat social*, Paris, 1943.

Havens, G. R., *Voltaire's marginalia on the pages of Rousseau*, New York, 1966.

Hayek, F. A., *The constitution of liberty*, Chicago, 1960.

Law, legislation and liberty. A new statement of the liberal principles of justice and political economy, London, 1973.

Haymann, F., *J.-J. Rousseaus Sozialphilosophie*, Leipzig, 1898.

'La Loi naturelle dans la philosophie politique de J.-J. Rousseau', *Annales de la Société Jean-Jacques Rousseau*, 30 (1943–5), pp. 65–109.

Hegel, G. W. F., *Phaenomenologie des Geistes*, in *Werke*, Frankfurt am Main, 1969, vol. 3.

Vorlesungen über Rechtsphilosophie, 1818–31, K. H. Ilting (eds.), Stuttgart, 1973; transl. T. M. Knox, *Hegel's 'Philosophy of right'*, Oxford, 1967.

Vorlesungen über die Philosophie der Geschichte, Stuttgart, 1975, transl. J. Sibree, *The philosophy of history*, New York, 1956.

Helvétius, *De l'esprit*, in *Oeuvres complètes*, Georg Olms Verlag, Hildesheim, 1969, vols. 1–2.

Hendel, C. W., *J.-J. Rousseau moralist*, 2 vols., London and New York, 1934.

Herrman, L., 'Rousseau traducteur de Sénèque', *Annales de la Société Jean-Jacques Rosseau*, 13 (1920–1), pp. 215–24.

Hill Green, T., *Lectures on the principle of political obligation*, London, 1907.

Hirschman, A., *The Passions and the interests. Political arguments for capitalism before its triumph*, Princeton, 1977.

Hobbes, Thomas, *Philosophical rudiments concerning government and society*, *The English works of Thomas Hobbes*, W. Molesworth ed., London, 1966, vol. 2.

Leviathan or the Matter, form, and power of a commonwealth ecclesiastical and civil, ibid., vol. 3.

Hoffmann P., 'La Liberté de l'âme heureuse selon Rousseau', *Revue de métaphysique et de morale*, 91, no. 2 (1986), pp. 160–80.

Hoffman S., *Rousseau, la guerre et la paix*, in Institut International de Philosophie Politique, *Rousseau et la philosophie politique*, Paris, 1965, pp. 195–240.

d'Hont J., ed., *Hegel et le siècle des lumières*, Paris, 1974.

Howells, R. J., 'The metaphysic of nature: basic values and their application in the social philosophy of Rousseau', *Studies on Voltaire and the eighteenth century*, 60 (1968), pp. 109–200.

Hubert, R., *Rousseau et l'Encyclopédie. Essai sur la formation des idées politiques de Rousseau (1742–1746)*, Paris, 1928.

Hume, David, *Enquiries concerning human understanding and concerning the principles of morals*, Oxford, 1985.

Janet, P., *Histoire de la science politique dans ses rapports avec la morale*, 2 vols., Paris, 1887.

Jellinek, G., *Die rechtliche Natur der Staatenverträge*, Vienna 1880.

Kant, I., *Anthropologie in pragmatischer Hinsicht*, (1800), *Immanuel Kants Werke*, Hildesheim, 1973, vol. 8, pp. 1–228.

Idee zu einer allgemeinen Geschichte in weltbürgerlicher Absicht (1784) *Immanuel Kants Werke*, Hildesheim, 1973, vol. 4, pp. 148–66; transl. in *Kant's political writings*, ed. H. Reiss, Cambridge, 1971.

Die Metaphysik der Sitten (1797), *Immanuel Kants Werke*, Hildesheim, 1973, vol. 7, pp. 1–310.

Mutmasslicher Anfang der Menschengeschichte (1786), *Immanuel Kants Werke*, Hildesheim, 1973, vol. 4, pp. 325–42, transl. L. W. Beck and R. E. Anchor, *On history*, Indianapolis and New York, 1963, pp. 53–68.

Die Religion innerhalb der Grenzen der blossen Vernunft, (1794) *Immanuel Kants*

Werke, Hildesheim, 1973, vol. 6, pp., 139–353.

Uber den Gemeinspruch: Das mag in der Theorie richtig sein, taugt aber nicht für die Praxis (1793), *Immanuel Kants Werke*, Hildesheim, 1973, vol. 6, pp. 335–98; transl. in *Kant's political writings*, ed. H. Reiss, Cambridge, 1971.

Zum ewigen Frieden. Ein philosophischer Entwurf (1795), *Immanuel Kants Werke*, Hildesheim, 1973, vol. 6, pp. 425–74; transl. in *Kant's political writings*, ed. H. Reiss, Cambridge, 1971.

Keohane, N. O., *Philosophy and the state in France. From the Renaissance to the enlightenment*, Princeton, 1980.

Lafrance, G., 'Jean-Jacques Rousseau et l'idéal républicain', in *Philosophie de la Cité*, Montreal and Paris, 1974, pp. 161–81.

Lamy, Bernard, *Entretiens sur les science. Première lettre de Théodore à Eugène*, Lyon, 1706.

Landucci, S., *I filosofi e i selvaggi*, Bari, 1972.

Launay, M., 'Les Hésitations de l'esprit républicain dans les premiers textes de Rousseau (1728–1748)', in *L'Esprit républicain*, Colloque d'Orléans, 4–5 Sept. 1970, J. Viard (ed.), Paris, 1972, pp. 133–41.

Jean-Jacques Rousseau écrivain politique, Cannes, 1971.

Le Vocabulaire politique de Jean-Jacques Rousseau, Geneva and Paris, 1977.

Launay, M., and Proschvitz, G. von, *Index du 'Contrat social' (texte de 1762) et 'Manuscript de Genève'. Collection des index et des concordances de J.-J. Rousseau*, Geneva and Paris, 1977.

Leduc Fayette, D., *J.-J. Rousseau et le mythe de l'antiquité*, Paris, 1974.

Leigh, R. A., 'Jean-Jacques Rousseau and the myth of antiquity in the eighteenth century', in R. R. Bolgar (ed.), *Classical influences on western thought 1650–1870*, Cambridge, 1979, pp. 155–68.

'Liberté et autorité dans le "Contrat social" ', in *Jean-Jacques Rousseau et son oeuvre. Problèmes et recherches*, Commémoration et colloque de Paris (1962), Paris, 1964, pp. 249–64.

Leigh, R. A., ed., *Rousseau after two hundred years: Proceedings of the Cambridge Bicentennial Colloquium*, Cambridge, 1982.

Léon, P. L., 'L'Evolution de l'idée de souveraineté avant Rousseau', in *Archives*, 7 (1937), pp. 152–85.

'L'Idée de volonté générale chez Rousseau et ses antécédents historiques', in *Archives*, 6 (1936), pp. 158–200.

'La Notion de souveraineté dans la doctrine de J.-J. Rousseau', in *Archives*, 8 (1938), pp. 231–69.

'Le Problème du contrat social chez Rousseau', in *Archives*, 5 (1935), pp. 157–201.

'Rousseau et les fondements de l'état moderne' in *Archives de philosophie du droit et de sociologie juridique*, 4 (1934), pp. 197–238.

Levine, A., *The politics of autonomy. A Kantian reading of Rousseau's 'Social contract'*, Amherst, 1976.

Levy, Y., 'Machiavel et Rousseau', *Le Contrat social*, 6 (1962), pp. 169–74.

Livy, Titus, *From the founding of the city*; transl. B. O. Foster and F. G. Moore *et al.*, London, 1966–76.

Locke, John, *Two treatises of government*, P. Laslett (ed.), Cambridge, 1970.

Lough, J., 'The "Encyclopédie" and the "Contrat social" ' in S. Harvey, M. Hobson, D. Kelley, and S. Taylor, (eds.), *Reappraisals of Rousseau: studies in honour of R. A. Leigh*, Manchester, 1980.

Lovejoy, A. O., *The great chain of being*, Harvard, 14th edn., 1978.

'The supposed primitivism of Rousseau's "Discourse on inequality" ', in *Essays in the history of ideas*, Westport, Connecticut, 1978, pp. 14–37.

Lowith, K., 'Human rights in Rousseau, Hegel and Marx', in AA.VV., *Les Fondements des droits de l'homme*, Florence, 1966.

Luporini, L., *L'ottimismo di Jean-Jacques Rousseau*, Florence, 1982.

'Rousseau di fronte all'utopia', in *Atti e memorie dell'Accademia toscana di scienza e lettere 'La Colombaria'*, 4–5 (1980), pp. 133–74.

McAdam, J. I., 'The "Discourse on inequality" and the "Social contract" ', *Philosophy*, 47 (1972), pp. 308–21.

Machiavelli, Niccolò, *The discourses*, transl. J. Leslie, S. J. Walker, and Bernard Crick, Harmondsworth, 1970.

The prince, transl. G. Bull, Harmondsworth, 1961.

McKenzie, A., 'Rousseau's debate with Machiavelli in the "Social contract"', *Journal of the history of ideas*, 43 (1982), pp. 209–28.

McManners, 'The "Social contract" and Rousseau's revolt against society', in M. Cranston and R. Peters (eds.), *Hobbes and Rousseau, a collection of critical essays*, Garden City, NY, 1972, pp. 291–317.

Magri, T., *Saggio su Thomas Hobbes. Gli elementi della politica*, Milan, 1982.

Maihofer, W., 'Hegels Prinzip des modernen Staates', in I. Fetscher (ed.), *Hegel in der Sicht der Neueren Forschung*, Darmstadt, 1973.

Mandeville, Bernard de, *The fable of the bees, or Private vices, publik benefits*, London, 1714.

Manuel, F. E., and Manuel, F. P., 'The *monde idéal* of Jean-Jacques Rousseau', in F. E. Manuel, and F. P. Manuel, *Utopian thought in the western world*, Oxford, 1979, pp. 436–72.

Masson, P. M., *La Religion de Jean-Jacques Rousseau*, Paris, 1916; Geneva, 1970.

Masters, R. D., *The political philosophy of Rousseau*, Princeton, NJ, 1968.

'The structure of Rousseau's political thought', in M. Cranston and R. Peters (eds.), *Hobbes and Rousseau, a collection of critical essays*, Garden City, NY, 1972, pp. 401–36.

Matteucci, N., *Jacques Mallet Du-Pan*, Naples, 1957.

Mauzi, R., *L'Idée du bonheur au XVIII siècle*, Paris, 1961.

Meek, R., *Social science and the ignoble savage*, Cambridge, 1976.

Mely, B., *Jean-Jacques Rousseau. Un intellectuel en rupture*, Paris, 1985.

Millar, John, *Observations concerning the distinction of ranks in society*, London, 1771.

Miller, J., *Rousseau: dreamer of democracy*, New Haven and London, 1984.

Mondolfo, R., 'Rousseau nella formazione della coscienza moderna', *Rivista pedagogica*, 6 (1913), pp. 433–78.

Montaigne, *Essais*, ed. J. Plattard, Paris, 1946–8.

Montesquieu, *L'Esprit des Lois, Oeuvres complètes*, 3 vols., ed. A. Masson, Paris, 1950; transl. T. Nugent, revised by J. V. Prichard, Chicago, 1952.

Lettres Persannes, Oeuvres complètes (1950), vol. 1.

Considérations sur les causes de la grandeur des Romains et de leur décadence, Oeuvres complètes (1950), vol. 1, transl. by D. Lowenthal, New York, 1965.

Morel, J., 'Jean-Jacques Rousseau lit Plutarque', *Revue d'histoire moderne*, 2 (April–May 1926), pp. 81–102.

'Recherches sur les sources du Discours de J.-J. Rousseau sur l'origine et les fondements de l'inégalité parmi les hommes', *Annales de la Société Jean-Jacques Rousseau*, 5 (1909), pp. 119–98.

Mura, V., *La teoria democratica del potere. Saggio su Rousseau*, Pisa, 1979.

Namer, G., *Rousseau sociologue de la connaissance: de la creativité au machiavelisme*, Paris, 1978.

Le Système social de Rousseau: de l'inégalité économique à l'inégalité politique, Paris, 1979.

Naudin, P., 'Un Remède à la violence des rapports sociaux: la république du Contrat', in J. Viard (ed.), *L'Esprit républicain*, Paris, 1972.

Nisbet, A. R., 'Rousseau and the general will', in R. Nisbet, *The social philosophers: community and conflict in western thought*, London, 1974, pp. 145–58.

Social change and history. Aspects of the western theory of development, Oxford, 1969.

Noone, J. B., *Rousseau's 'Social contract'. A conceptual analysis*, London, 1980.

O'Mara, P., 'Jean-Jacques and Geneva', *The historian*, 20 (1958), pp. 127–52.

Pasqualucci, P., 'Il mito rousseauiano del legislatore', *Rivista internazionale di filosofia del diritto*, 55 (1970), pp. 882–906.

Rousseau e Kant, 2 vols., Milan, 1974–6.

'Il soggetto e la legge secondo Jean-Jacques Rousseau', *Rivista internazionale di filosofia del diritto*, 60 (1983), pp. 382–406.

Pasquino, P., 'Teoria della giustizia e dottrina dello stato in Thomas Hobbes', *Materiali filosofici*, 6 (1981), pp. 161–78.

Payot, R., *Jean-Jacques Rousseau ou la gnose tronquée*, Grenoble, 1968.

Pelczynski, Z. A., *The state and civil society in Hegel's political philosophy*, Cambridge, 1984.

Perkins, M. L., 'Liberty and the concept of legitimacy in the "Discours sur l'inégalité"' *Studies on Voltaire and the eighteenth century*, 89 (1972), pp. 1293–304.

Jean-Jacques Rousseau on the individual and society, Lexington, 1974.

Pezzillo, L., 'Aporie della filosofia politica di Rousseau: legislatore e religione civile', *Critica storica*, 4 (1978), pp. 78–126.

Philonenko, A., *Jean-Jacques Rousseau et la pensée du malheur*, 3 vols., Paris, 1984.

Pichois, C., 'Deux interprétations romantiques de Machiavel: de Rousseau à Macaulay', in *Hommage au Doyen Etienne Gros*, Gap, 1959, pp. 211–18.

Pintard, R., 'L'Influence de la pensée politique de la renaissance italienne sur la pensée française', *Revue des études italiennes*, 2–3 (April–September 1936).

Pire, G., 'Du bon Plutarque au citoyen de Genève', *Revue de littérature comparée*, 38 (1958), pp. 510–47.

Pitkin, H., 'Obligation and consent', in Laslett, Runcimann, Skinner (eds.),

Philosophy, politics and society, 4th series, Oxford, 1972, pp. 45–85.

Plamenatz, J., *Man and society*, London 1963, vol. 1, pp. 364–442.

' "Ce qui ne signifie autre chose sinon qu'on le forcera d'être libre" ', in Institut International de Philosophie Politique, *Rousseau et la philosophie politique*, Paris, 1965, pp. 137–52.

Plato, *Gorgias*, transl. W. R. M. Lamb, London, 1975.

Laws, transl. R. G. Bury, 2 vols., London, 1952.

The statesman, transl. H. N. Fowler, London, 1975.

Republic, transl. P. Shorey, 2 vols., London, 1978.

Plutarch, *Les Oeuvres morales et meslées*, transl. J. Amyot, De l'imprimerie de F. Estiene, Geneva, 1582; transl. F. C. Babbitt, *Plutarch's 'Moralia'*, London and Cambridge, Mass., 1927–61, vols. 1–4.

The parallel lives, transl. 'The Dryden translation', Great Books, Chicago, 1952, vol. 14, p. 66.

Pocock, J. G. A., *The Machiavellian moment. Florentine political thought and the Atlantic republican tradition*, Princeton, 1975.

Polin, R., *La Politique de la solitude*, Paris, 1971.

'Le Sens de l'égalité et de l'inégalité chez Jean-Jacques Rousseau', in *Etudes sur le 'Contrat social' de Jean-Jacques Rousseau*, Paris, 1964, pp. 143–64.

Pope, A., *Essai sur l'homme*, French transl. in Diderot, *Oeuvres complètes*, vol. 1, Paris, 1970.

Postigliola, A., 'De Malebranche à Rousseau: les apories de la volonté générale et la revanche du "raisonneur violent" ', *Annales de la Société Jean-Jacques Rousseau*, 39 (1972–7), pp. 123–38.

'Roma in Rousseau. L'esercizio della sovranità nel IV libro del "Contratto sociale" ', *Studi filosofici*, 4 (1980), pp. 153–77.

Price, R., 'The sense of "virtù" in Machiavelli', *European studies review*, 3 (1973), pp. 315–45.

Pufendorf, Samuel, le Baron de, *Les Devoirs de l'homme et du citoyen tels qu'ils lui sont prescrits par la loi naturelle*, transl. by Jean Barbeyrac, Amsterdam, H. Schelte, 1707; transl. A. Tooke, *The whole duty of man according to the law of nature*, London, 1716.

Le Droit de la nature et des gens, ou système général des principes les plus importants de la morale, de la jurisprudence et de la politique, transl. Jean Barbeyrac, Amsterdam, 1712.

Reale, M., 'Le convenzioni che fondano la società politica; autorità e libertà nel primo libro del "Contratto sociale" ', *Quaderni della rivista trimestrale*, 59–60 (1979), pp. 25–77.

'Rousseau: dal "Discorso sull'ineguaglianza" al "Contrat social". La "società genérale" e il "difetto di natura" ', *Quaderni della rivista trimestrale*, 55–6 (1978), pp. 203–44.

'Volontà generale, volontà di tutti e verifica della legge di maggioranza', *Quaderni della rivista trimestrale*, 64–6 (1981), pp. 91–120.

Riley, P. W. J., *Will and political legitimacy: a critical exposition of social contract theory in Hobbes, Locke, Rousseau, Kant and Hegel*, London and Cambridge, Mass., 1982.

Robinet, A., 'Lexicographie philosophique de l' "ordre de la nature" dans la

"Profession de foi du vicaire savoyard" ', *Revue internationale de philosophie*, 32 (1978), pp. 238–59.

Roggerone, G., *Saint Pierre e Rousseau*, Milan, 1985.

Rommen, H. A., *The natural law. A study in legal and social history and philosophy*, New York, 1979.

Rossi, P., *I filosofi e le macchine (1400–1700)*, Milan, 1971.

Introduzione to Rousseau, *Opere*, Florence, 1972, pp. ix–xlii.

Rosso, C., *Mythe de l'égalité et rayonnement des lumières*, Pisa, 1980.

Salien, J. M., 'Dialectique de la raison et des passions dans la pensée de J.-J. Rousseau', *International studies on philosophy*, 12 (1980), pp. 55–60.

Schinz, A., *La Pensée de Jean-Jacques Rousseau*, Paris, 1929.

Schlanger, J. E., *Les Métaphores de l'organisme*, Paris, 1971.

Schwartz, B. I., 'A Rousseau strain in the contemporary world', *Daedalus*, 107 (1978), pp. 193–206.

Shackleton, R., 'Montesquieu and Machiavelli: a reappraisal', *Comparative literature studies*, 1, no. 1 (1964), pp. 1–13.

Shaftesbury, Adam, *The moralists*, in *Characteristics of man, manners, opinions, times*, Basle, 1790.

An inquiry concerning virtue and merit, in *Characteristics of man, manners, opinions, times*, Basle, 1790.

Philosophie morale, Amsterdam, 1745.

Shklar, J. N., 'Jean-Jacques Rousseau and equality', *Daedalus*, (1978), pp. 13–26.

Men and citizens; a study of Rousseau's social theory, Cambridge, Mass., 1969.

'Rousseau's images of authority', in M. Cranstan and R. S. Peters (eds.), *Hobbes and Rousseau. A collection of critical essays*, Garden City, New York, pp. 333–65.

Skinner, Q., *The foundations of modern political thought*, 2 vols., Cambridge, 1978.

'The idea of negative liberty: philosophical and historical perspectives', in R. Rorty, J. B. Schneewind, and Q. Skinner, (eds.), *Philosophy in history*, Cambridge, 1984, pp. 193–221.

Smith, Adam, *The theory of moral sentiments*, ed. D. D. Raphael and A. L. Macfie, Oxford, 1976.

Solari, G., *La formazione storica e filosofica dello stato moderno*, Naples, 1934.

Spink, J. S., *Jean-Jacques Rousseau et Genève*, Paris, 1934.

Spinoza, Benedictus de, *Tractatus theologicus-politicus*, in *Political works*, ed. A. G. Wernham, Oxford, 1958.

Tractatus politicus, in *Political works*, ed., A. G. Wernham, Oxford 1958.

Stammler, R., *Theorie des Anarchismus*, Berlin, 1894.

Starobinsky, J., 'The accuser and the accused', *Daedalus* (1978), pp. 41–58.

'Du "Discours sur l'inégalité" au "Contrat social" ', in *Etudes sur le "Contrat social"*, Paris, 1964, pp. 97–109.

Jean-Jacques Rousseau. La transparence et l'obstacle, Paris 1971.

'Rousseau et Buffon', in *Jean-Jacques Rousseau et son oeuvre*, Paris 1964.

Stelling-Michaud, S., 'Rousseau et l'injustice sociale', in *Jean-Jacques Rousseau*, Publication de l'Université ouvrière et de la faculté des lettres de Genève, Neuchâtel, 1962, pp. 171–86.

Stephen, R., *Sur les pas de Jean-Jacques*, Grenoble, 1929.

Strauss, L., *Natural right and history*, Chicago, 1953.

'L'Intention de Rousseau', *Social research*, 14 (1947), reprinted in *Pensée de Rousseau*, Paris, 1985, pp. 67–94.

Talmon, J. L., *Les Origines de la démocratie totalitaire*, Paris, 1952.

Terrasse, J., *Jean-Jacques Rousseau et la quête de l'âge d'or*, Brussels, 1970.

Thomas, L., 'Sénèque et Rousseau', Académie Royal de Belgique, *Bulletin de la classe des lettres et des sciences morales et politiques et de la classe des beaux arts* (1900), pp. 391–421.

Tillyard, E. M. W., *The Elizabethan world picture*, London, 1956.

Todorov, T., *Frêle bonheur. Essai sur Rousseau*, Paris, 1985.

Trousson, R., 'Jean-Jacques Rousseau et son oeuvre dans la presse périodique allemande de 1750 à 1800', *Dix-huitieme siècle*, 1 (1969), pp. 283–310; 2 (1970), pp. 227–64.

Tuck, R., *Natural rights theories. Their origins and developments*, Cambridge, 1979.

Valentini, F., 'Problemi della democrazia rousseauiana', in *Studi su Jean-Jacques Rousseau, Studi filosofici*, vol. 1, pp. 89–99.

Vaughan, C. E., *Studies in the history of political philosophy before and after Rousseau*, Manchester, 1939.

Veca, S., 'Politica', in *Enciclopedia*, Einaudi, vol. 10, Turin, 1980, pp. 855–70.
Questioni di giustizia, Parma, 1985.
La società giusta, Milan, 1982.

Venturi, F., *Utopia and reform in the Enlightenment*, Cambridge, 1971.

Vernes, P. M., 'Nicolas Machiavel chez Jean-Jacques Rousseau: des leçons aux rois aux leçons aux peuples', in *Actes du colloque franco-italien de philosophie*, Paris, 1977, pp. 77–89.
La Ville, la fête, la démocratie: Rousseau et les illusions de la communauté, Paris, 1978.

Vernier, P., *Spinoza et la pensée française avant la révolution*, 2 vols., Paris, 1954.

Viano, C. A., *John Locke. Dal razionalismo all'illuminismo*, Turin, 1960.

Viroli, M., 'The concept of "ordre" and the language of classical republicanism in Jean-Jacques Rousseau', in A. Pagden (ed.), *The languages of political theory in early-modern Europe*, Cambridge, 1987, pp. 159–78.

Voisine, J., 'Deux contrats sociaux: Hume et Rousseau', in R. A. Leigh (ed.), *Rousseau after two hundred years*, Cambridge, 1982, pp. 37–54.

Voltaire, *Idées républicaines par un membre d'un corps*, in *Oeuvres complètes*, Paris, 1879, vol. 24, pp. 413–32.

Vossler, O., *Rousseaus Freiheitslehre*, Gottingen, 1963.

Wahl, J., 'La Bipolarité de Rousseau', *Annales de la Société Jean-Jacques Rousseau*, 33 (1953–5), pp. 49–55.

Waldmann, T., 'Rousseau on the general will and the legislator', *Political studies*, 8 (1960), pp. 221–34.

Weil, E., 'Rousseau et sa politique', *Critique*, 7 (1952), reprinted in *Pensée de Rousseau*, Paris, 1984, pp. 9–39.

Willey, B., *The eighteenth century background. Studies in the idea of nature in the thought of the period*, London, 1946.

Winch, P., 'Man and society in Hobbes and Rousseau', in M. Cranston and R. Peters (eds.), *Hobbes and Rousseau. A collection of essays*, Garden City, NY, 1972.

Wokler, R., 'The "Discours sur les sciences et les arts" and its offsprings: Rousseau in reply to his critics', in S. Harvey, M. Hobson, D. Kelley and S. Taylor (eds.), *Reappraisals of Rousseau: studies in honour of R. A. Leigh*, Manchester, 1980.

'Perfectible apes in decadent culture: Rousseau's anthropology revised', *Daedalus*, 107 (1978), pp. 107–34.

'Rousseau's perfectibilian libertarianism', in A. Ryan, (ed.), *The idea of freedom. Essays in honour of Isaiah Berlin*, Oxford, 1976, pp. 233–52.

Index

Althusius, Joannes, 164 n.135
Aristotle, 6, 99, 153, 160 n.120, 161 n.122, 165–6, 192, 216
artifice, *see* nature–artifice

Barbeyrac, Jean, 66 n.27, 99–100
Boileau-Despreaux, Nicolas, 61
Bruyère, 77, 91

Calvin, John, 207
Charron, Pierre, 59–60, 64–5, 98–9
Christianity, 174–5
Cicero, Marcus Tullius, 54, 98, 154, 160–1, 177 n.178
cognition, 18–21, 23
Constant, Benjamin, 8–11

despotism, 115–16, 163, 166–7, 173, 184, 187, 193, 207, 218
Diderot, 58 n.14, 123 n.26, 124, 168 n.146
dualism, 20
Duclos, 76–7, 93–4
Durkheim, Emile, 3

egotism, *see* self-love–egotism
equality–inequality, 4–5, 47, 54, 58, 64–88, 95–6, 115, 178, 191–3, 197, 215

general will, 3, 126, 135, 149–51, 157, 166, 188, 191
Geneva, 12, 185, 207
Grotius, Hugues, 99–101, 212, 217 n.294

Hegel, G.W.F., 6–9, 131, 221
Helvétius, 18–19, 186
Hobbes, Thomas, 1, 17, 23, 25, 46–8, 65–6, 78–84, 91, 112, 116–17, 121–3, 131, 133, 143 n.79, 153, 156, 165–8, 186, 218 n.208, 225

inequality, *see* equality–inequality

Kant, Immanuel, 2, 10–11, 96 n.85, 227–9

Lamy, Bernard, 29–30
law, 129, 132–3, 148, 155, 160–1, 165,

173, 180–2, 190–1, 197, 209
legislator, 188–90, 199
liberty, 11, 148–57, 159, 173
Locke, John, 17, 116 n.12, 134, 137, 164, 173 n.161

Machiavelli, Niccolò, 11–12, 14, 108 n.3, 115, 120–1, 168–72, 174–8, 183, 189, 195, 206, 209–10, 214 n.283, 217–18, 223
Marx, Karl, 5, 73 n.38
metaphysics, 16–18, 23
Montaigne, 57 n.12, 92–3
Montesquieu, 120, 166, 174, 192–3, 195, 205, 217, 222, 224

natural law, 124, 127, 132–46, 213, 217 n.294, 221
nature, 103, 111–12, 134, 138
nature–artifice, 2–3, 20, 22, 25–6, 32–6, 39 n.60, 41–2, 44–51, 64–72, 82–6, 188

order, 16–17, 22–4, 27–35, 38–9, 43–6, 53–7, 59, 63, 87–96, 102–3, 107–9, 113–18, 148, 159–60, 188, 200, 202, 222–3

Plato, 30 n.43, 123, 154
Plutarch, 158, 180 n.187, 117 n.14, 217 n.294
Pope, A., 57 n.12, 58
Pufendorf, Samuel, 56, 66–9, 80–3, 88–9, 91–2

republic, 161 n.123, 163, 168–9, 171–3, 182–4, 187–8, 190, 196, 205, 211, 216–19, 221–2, 224–5
republican tradition, 5, 12, 174, 177 n.178, 211–12, 214
Rousseau, Jean-Jacques,
    Les confessions, 109 n.4
    Considérations sur le gouvernement de Pologne, 133, 205, 220
    Du Contrat social (Social contract), 1, 8, 37, 39–40, 42, 110–12, 118–19, 121–3, 125, 129, 137, 139, 142, 144–6, 149, 156, 162–3, 168, 184, 188, 194–5, 206, 208–9, 219
    Discours sur l'économie politique (Discourse